ALIENS IN MEDIEVAL LAW
The Origins of Modern Citizenship

This original re-interpretation of the legal status of foreigners in medieval England boldly rejects the canonical view which has for centuries dominated the imagination of historians and laymen alike. Keechang Kim proposes a radically new understanding of the genesis of the modern legal regime and the important distinction between citizens and non-citizens. Making full use of medieval and early modern sources, Kim offers a compelling argument that the late medieval changes in legal treatment of foreigners are vital to an understanding of the shift of focus from *status* to the *State*, and that the historical foundation of the modern State system should be sought in this shift of outlook. The book contains a re-evaluation of the legal aspects of feudalism, examining, in particular, how the feudal legal arguments were transformed by the political theology of the Middle Ages to become the basis of the modern legal outlook. This innovative study will interest academics, lawyers, and students of legal history, immigration and minority issues.

KEECHANG KIM is the David Li Fellow in Law and College Lecturer at Selwyn College, Cambridge.

CAMBRIDGE STUDIES
IN ENGLISH LEGAL HISTORY

Edited by

J. H. BAKER
Downing Professor of the Laws of England
Fellow of St Catharine's College, Cambridge

Recent series titles include

Roman canon law in Reformation England
R. H. HELMHOLZ

Law, politics and the Church of England
The career of Stephen Lushington 1782–1873
S. M. WADDAMS

The early history of the law of bills and notes
A study of the origins of Anglo-American commercial law
JAMES STEVEN ROGERS

The law of evidence in Victorian England
CHRISTOPHER ALLEN

A history of the county court, 1846–1971
PATRICK POLDEN

John Scott, Lord Eldon, 1751–1838
The duty of loyalty
ROSE MELIKAN

Literary copyright reform in early Victorian England
The framing of the 1842 Copyright Act
CATHERINE SEVILLE

ALIENS IN
MEDIEVAL LAW

THE ORIGINS OF MODERN CITIZENSHIP

KEECHANG KIM

CAMBRIDGE
UNIVERSITY PRESS

CAMBRIDGE UNIVERSITY PRESS
Cambridge, New York, Melbourne, Madrid, Cape Town, Singapore,
São Paulo, Delhi, Dubai, Tokyo, Mexico City

Cambridge University Press
The Edinburgh Building, Cambridge CB2 8RU, UK

Published in the United States of America by Cambridge University Press, New York

www.cambridge.org
Information on this title: www.cambridge.org/9780521174077

First published 2000
First paperback edition 2010

A catalogue record for this publication is available from the British Library

ISBN 978-0-521-80085-3 Hardback
ISBN 978-0-521-17407-7 Paperback

TO PETER G. STEIN, MY TEACHER

CONTENTS

PREFACE

On what ground do we maintain a legal distinction between citizens and non-citizens? Some would regard this as a futile attempt to doubt the obvious. 'How could you *not* draw a distinction between citizens and non-citizens?' they would reply. When a concept or a categorical division has been widely and frequently used for a long period, one is tempted to think that the concept or the categorical division is somehow 'branded' in the very nature of human beings. Each and everyone would then be born with it. The division between citizens and non-citizens is perhaps one such categorical division. Even those who would firmly reject the legal distinction and discrimination based on all other criteria will have no difficulty in accepting the legal discrimination based on nationality. When a division becomes so persuasive, it becomes inescapable as well. Our imagination falls prey to this categorical division in the sense that any alternative arrangements one could possibly imagine would simply look 'unnatural' and absurd.

The present work is an attempt to study the *historical origin* of this categorical division often regarded by many as wholly natural and inescapable. Why, is there anything more to be said about the beginning of the legal distinction between citizens and aliens (non-citizens)? Do we not already know that feudalism in medieval Europe was an antithesis of the State structure? Is it not obvious that in the fragmented political and legal environment of medieval Europe, the personal legal division requiring a clear concept of the State (citizen vs. non-citizen) was unimportant and un(der)-developed? Is it not equally natural and inevitable that as feudalism gave way and the State structure was put in place, the legal distinction between citizens and non-citizens acquired greater prominence?

There is an alternative thesis which is also familiar and which can be resorted to when one senses that the above-mentioned feudal fragmentation thesis is not going to work well. This applies to the situation in post-Conquest England, which was undoubtedly a unified kingdom with a relatively strong central government. According to this thesis – masterfully presented by Professor Maitland – it was inevitable that when foreigners from Normandy became the rulers of the English, the legal distinction between foreigners and non-foreigners had to lose significance. But when the Norman kings were driven out of their Continental homeland and had to settle permanently in England, they gradually identified themselves as English. When this happened, it was inevitable that the legal distinction between foreigners and non-foreigners became important again.

It all sounds like we are dealing here with an inevitable and inescapable categorical division which is ever ready to resurface and reclaim its preordained place in our minds. As soon as the dark clouds of feudalism and Norman Conquest were cleared away from the horizon, the legal division between citizens and non-citizens would shine again in all its splendour. If this type of explanation has enjoyed such a widespread acceptance until today, it only shows how much we are the products of our own time. In other words, what has so far been written about the beginning of the legal distinction between citizens and non-citizens is the clearest testimony of how completely we have come to believe in the inevitableness of this categorical division.

No one will doubt the historical importance of the rise of the modern State structure and the ascendance of the rhetoric of national identity. However, very little has been written about the rise of the legal regime which purports to divide human beings into the categories of nationals and non-nationals. Without exception, the beginning of the law of alien and subject (citizen) status has been summarily dealt with as nothing more than a by-product of the rise of the modern State structure. This book aims to offer a different perspective. It will be suggested that the rise of the law of alien status in the later Middle Ages cannot be treated as a mere reflection or an inevitable by-product of political or other non-legal changes of the time. It was, I shall argue, a crucial turning point in the history of Europe which ultimately led to the rise of the modern State structure. It was, as it were, the cause rather than the effect of the birth of the modern State.

What holds together all political and legal arguments which 'we' moderners would regard as characteristic of the modern era is, after all, our own outlook – how we perceive ourselves, how we define our position in society, and how we understand the purpose of our existence in this universe. By looking at some of the mundane legal texts which closely record how medieval lawyers coped with various problem situations involving foreigners, we may perhaps have a glimpse of the important shift of outlook which took place towards the end of the Middle Ages and which ultimately determined the way we now perceive ourselves, others and the rest of our universe.

Coming down onto a more practical level, one can hardly overstate the significance of the State boundary in today's law and politics. At the same time, many of us are increasingly aware of the difficulties raised by the present regime. As far as the question of the State boundary is concerned, we are living in an era of uncertainty. It is going to be increasingly difficult to be complacent about the existing arrangements. It is against this backdrop that the present work is undertaken. If no history can be written without an agenda (explicit or implicit), the need or the desire to explore the future of the nation State structure forms the underlying agenda of this study of aliens in medieval law.

Among those to whom my thanks are due, I wish to mention Professors P. G. Stein, J. H. Baker and A. W. B. Simpson in particular. My debt to these teachers is too great for words. If there is anything worthwhile in this book, it should be to their credit. The rest, of course, is mine.

It is also my pleasant duty to acknowledge the debt I owe to the following: the Posco Scholarship Foundation, Pohang, South Korea – for their generous grant which enabled me to do the research from which this book is written; the University of Chicago Law School, Chicago, USA – for allowing me to use their excellent research facilities and the Regenstein Library of the University of Chicago; the President and Fellows of Queens' College, Cambridge, United Kingdom – for offering me a Research Fellowship and travel grants which allowed me to look at some of the manuscript sources; Frank Cass, Publishers, London, United Kingdom – for allowing me to reproduce a substantial part of my article '*Calvin's Case* (1608) and the Law of Alien Status' published in 17 *Journal of Legal History*, No. 2 (1996), 155–71.

TABLE OF STATUTES

INTRODUCTION

FUNDAMENTAL CHANGE – FROM BRACTON TO BLACKSTONE

In the section where writs dealing with the question of personal status are explained, the author of the late twelfth-century English law tract known as *Glanvill* (*c.* 1187) goes into a long discussion about the division between the free and the unfree status.[1] The detailed treatment is viewed by an influential editor of this work as 'some lengthy observations . . . which are outside the limited purpose of a commentary on writs'.[2] But, if anything, such an elaborate treatment shows the great importance the author attached to the division which he might have regarded as fundamental to the law of personal status.

What *Glanvill* failed to spell out with the crispness of a categorical declaration was succinctly expressed a few decades later by an able hand known by the name of Bracton. Students and practitioners of the common law in the thirteenth and fourteenth centuries must have admired the penetrating insight and clarity of expression of this celebrated author when they were reading the following passage from his *De legibus et consuetudinibus Angliae* (*c.* 1220–50):

The primary division in the law of personal status is simply that all men are either free or unfree (*serui*).[3]

---

[1] *The treatise on the laws and customs of the realm of England commonly called Glanvill*, ed. G. D. G. Hall, reprinted with a guide to further reading by M. T. Clanchy (Oxford, 1993) lib. 5. Glanvill refers to the unfree persons as *natiui* or *aliqui in uilenagio*.

[2] Ibid., p. xxiii.

[3] *Bracton on the laws and customs of England*, trans. Samuel Thorne, 4 vols. (Cambridge, Mass., 1968–77) II, p. 29 ('Est autem prima divisio personarum haec et brevissima, quod omnes homines aut liberi sunt aut serui').

The author of *Fleta* (*c.* 1290) was no doubt deeply impressed by the cardinal importance of this division. Accordingly, its very first chapter was devoted to introducing this principle.[4] *Britton* (*c.* 1292) largely followed the example of *Glanvill* in so far as the law of personal status is concerned. In the chapter dealing with the condition of villeins, the author revealed his outlook which was wholly based on the division between the free status (*fraunchise*) and the unfree status (*servage*).[5] However, *Britton* did not go as far as the *Mirror of justices* (*c.* 1290) whose author argued that the unfree status was ordained from time immemorial by divine law, accepted by human law and confirmed by the Canon law.[6] In France also, this basic principle of the law of personal status seems to have been upheld with equal respect during the same period. *Li livres de jostice et de plet*, which was written in the latter half of the thirteenth century, contains the following passage:

The good division of the law of persons is that all men are either free or servile (*serf*).[7]

Of course, the passages quoted above, as well as the principle expressed therein, came from Justinian's *Corpus Iuris* and medieval scholars' glosses and commentaries of this sixth-century compilation of the Roman law. The compilers of Justinian's *Digest* indicated that the principle was expounded by Gaius, who taught law in the second century. Thanks to the discovery of an almost complete fifth-century manuscript of Gaius' *Institutes* in the library of the Cathedral of Verona in 1816, we have his original phrase which is virtually identical to the above-quoted passage of Bracton.[8] For the late medieval readers of *Bracton* and *Britton* who accepted the principle of Gaius as a succinct and cogent statement of the law of personal status, the lapse of a millennium does not seem to have brought about much change.

This is not to say that the law of personal status remained

---

[4] *Fleta*, vol. II, 72 Selden Society (1955) lib. 1, c. 1.
[5] *Britton*, ed. Francis M. Nichols, 2 vols. (Oxford, 1865) I, pp. 194–210.
[6] *The mirror of justices*, 7 Selden Society (1893) p. 77.
[7] *Li livres de jostice et de plet*, ed. Pierre N. Rapetti (Paris, 1850) p. 54 ('La bone devise de droit des persones, des gens, est tele que tot homes ou il sont franc ou serf').
[8] *The Institutes of Gaius*, ed. E. Seckel and B. Kuebler, trans. W. M. Gordon and O. F. Robinson (Ithaca, N.Y., 1988) 1, 9 ('Et quidem summa diuisio de iure personarum haec est, quod omnes homines aut liberi sunt aut serui'). The passage found its way into Justinian's *Digest* (1. 5. 3) and *Institutes* (1. 3. pr).

unchanged in all its details. Nothing can be further from the truth. Behind its seemingly timeless façade, the terse statement of Bracton conceals the vast political, economic and social changes that transformed Europe from Antiquity to the Middle Ages. Just one example should be sufficient to demonstrate this point. As shown in the passage quoted above, the author of *Li livres de jostice et de plet* did not hesitate to translate 'serui' into 'serf'. By doing so, the French author plainly revealed one of such changes which had been left less explicit by the Latin language in which Bracton's work was written. That is, slavery, as an economic institution, was no longer viable in late medieval England and northern France. In other words, the 'serui' in *Bracton* and *Fleta* were not the same 'serui' to whom Gaius referred.[9]

What I would like to point out, however, is that the basic framework of viewing and analysing interpersonal legal relationships remained unchanged throughout this long period. Precisely who belonged to the category of *liberi*? What exactly were the legal capacities and disabilities of those classified as *serui*? How easy or how difficult was it to move from one category to another, and what were the procedures for doing so? Answers to these questions will vary widely depending on the numerous changes, big or small, which took place constantly since Gaius wrote his *Institutes*. Already by the sixth century, the compilers of Justinian's *Institutes* were noting the legislative reforms introduced in regard to the category of *libertini* (freed men).[10] But, from Gaius' time all the

---

[9] However, slavery persisted in Spain, Portugal, southern France and the Italian cities throughout the Middle Ages. See Iris Origo, 'The domestic enemy: the eastern slaves in Tuscany in the fourteenth and fifteenth centuries', 30 *Speculum* (1955) 321–66; William D. Phillips, Jr, *Slavery from Roman times to the early transatlantic trade* (Minneapolis, 1985) pp. 88–113. One can therefore argue that Azzo of Bologna, for example, might have understood 'serui' quite differently from his admirers in northern Europe such as Bracton. For an explanation that slavery gave way to various forms of servitude in medieval France and that, by the eleventh century, 'servus' came to mean a serf, see Charles Verlinden, *L'Esclavage dans L'Europe médiévale*, 2 vols. (Bruges, 1955) I, pp. 729–47; Marc Bloch, 'Liberté et servitude personnelle au moyen âge, particulièrement en France: contribution à une étude des classes' in his *Mélanges historiques*, 2 vols. (Paris, 1963) I, pp. 286–355 (English translation in *Slavery and serfdom in the Middle Ages: selected essays*, trans. W. Beer (Berkeley, 1975)).

[10] *Inst.* 1. 5. 2. Compare it with Gaius, *Institutes*, 1. 12–47. The reforms concerned the categories of *latini Iuniani* and *peregrini dediticii* which were abolished by successive legislative measures including the famous *Constitutio Antoniniana* of 212. Emperor Caracalla's *Constitutio* of 212 is commonly depicted as a general

way down to the era of *Glanvill*, *Bracton* and *Britton*, the primary tool for analysing legal relationships among human beings was the *varying amount* of privileges and franchises a person was allowed to enjoy.

The close connection between *Bracton* and medieval Roman law was noted by Carl Güterbock in the nineteenth century. F. W. Maitland and H. Kantorowicz took up this issue again and demonstrated exactly how much this thirteenth-century English law tract was influenced by Azzo of Bologna's *Summa* to Justinian's *Code* and *Institutes*.[11] However, what these authors did not bring out adequately is that it was the essential similarity of outlook on personal legal status which allowed Bracton to borrow what he did from Justinian's *Corpus Iuris* and Azzo's *Summa*. The important issue about the work of Bracton is not to prove or disprove the so-called civil law 'influences' or the English 'originality'. We must stress the firm and undeniable *continuity* of legal reasoning that had been maintained for over a thousand years.

Our argument will become clearer when we look at how the basic framework of legal reasoning changed since Bracton. Some 500 years after him, we encounter the following statement of Blackstone:

The first and most obvious division of the people is into aliens and natural-born subjects.[12]

Of course, Blackstone was summing up, as Gaius probably did in the second century, several centuries of legal development that went on before him. In *Calvin's case* (1608), for instance, Francis Bacon argued that 'there be but two conditions by birth, either alien or natural born'. The then Chief Justice Sir Edward Coke also stressed that 'Every man is either *alienigena*, an alien born, or

---

naturalisation legislation. But I doubt whether the modern legal concept of alien status may be used in analysing the legal status of *latini Iuniani* and *peregrini dediticii*. See below pp. 11–12, 189–96.

[11] Carl Güterbock, *Henricus de Bracton und sein Verhältniss zum Römischen Rechte* (Berlin, 1862); *Select passages from the works of Bracton and Azo*, 8 Selden Society (1894); H. Kantorowicz, *Bractonian problems* (Glasgow, 1941); H. G. Richardson, 'Azo, Drogheda, and Bracton', 59 *English Historical Review* (1944) 22–47.

[12] William Blackstone, *Commentaries on the laws of England*, 4 vols. (Oxford, 1765–69) I, p. 354.

subditus, a subject born.'[13] Bacon and Coke were also riding on the shoulders of their predecessors.

The change was certainly observable in *De laudibus legum Anglie* (*c.* 1468–70) where John Fortescue expressed some degree of uneasiness about servitude. He wrote:'Hard and unjust (*crudelis*), we must say, is the law which increases servitude and diminishes freedom, for which human nature always craves; for servitude was introduced by man on account of his own sin and folly, whereas freedom is instilled into human nature by God.'[14] Unfree status was already viewed as contrary to nature by Roman jurists of the Classical period.[15] Nonetheless, it was wholeheartedly accepted as provided by *ius gentium*. But Fortescue was raising moral doubts not only against the unfree status as such, but also against the law which institutionalised it (*'crudelis'* . . . *lex*). Such an attack certainly explains the disapproval and eventual demise of the legal approach which relies on the division between the free and the unfree status. Undoubtedly, legal reasoning was to move along the path leading to the notion of equality. But Fortescue's work indicates that lawyers would not have to deal with an equality which was boundless. In his work, men were viewed as 'bundled up' in units. Each such unit was portrayed as a mystic body, of which the king was the head. He wrote: 'Just as from the embryo grows out a physical body controlled by one head, so from the people is formed the kingdom, which is a mystic body governed by one man as the head.'[16] Then he went on to explain that the law (*lex*) was responsible for the internal cohesion and unity of the mystic body of kingdom:

The law, by which a group of men is made into a people, resembles the nerves and sinews of a physical body, for just as the physical body is held

---

[13] See below, p. 186.

[14] Our translation is based on Sir John Fortescue, *De laudibus legum Anglie*, ed. and trans. S. B. Chrimes (Cambridge, 1942) pp. 104–5 ('Crudelis etiam necessario judicabitur lex, quae servitutem augmentat, et minuit libertatem; nam pro ea Natura semper implorat humana. Quia ab homine, et pro vicio, introducta est servitus; sed libertas a Deo hominis est indita nature').

[15] See Florentinus' famous definition of slavery: 'Slavery is an institution of *ius gentium* whereby one is against nature subjugated to the ownership of another (*servitus est constitutio juris gentium, qua quis dominio alieno contra naturam subjicitur*).' *D.* 1. 5. 4. Justinian's *Institutes* repeats this definition. *Inst.* 1. 3. 2.

[16] *De laudibus legum Anglie*, ed. and trans. Chrimes, p. 30 ('sicut ex embrione corpus surgit phisicum, uno capite regulatum, sic ex populo erumpit regnum, quod corpus extat misticum uno homine ut capite gubernatum').

together by the nerves and sinews, so this mystic body [of people] is
bound together and united into one by the law, which is derived from the
word '*ligando*'.[17]

As I shall argue in this book, the moral and legal structure of the
kingdom envisaged by Fortescue lies at the core of the new
approach to the personal legal status.

An unequivocal statement of the new approach can also be
found in Thomas Littleton's *Tenures* (*c.* 1450–60). In explaining
the tenure in villenage, Littleton enumerates six categories of
persons who are debarred from bringing real or personal actions.[18]
It does not surprise us to see that villeins are included in the list.
What is surprising is the way in which Littleton explains such
legal disability. In *Old tenures*, we find the following statement:
'Note that a villein can have three types of actions against his lord,
i.e., the appeal of *mort d'ancestor*, the appeal of rape done to his
wife, and the appeal of maim.'[19] The same rule is repeated by
Littleton. But he says it in a completely different manner: 'Note
that a villein is able and free to sue all manners of actions against
any person except against his lord of whom he is a villein. Even
then, certain actions can be brought by a villein against his lord
[then follow the three types of actions explained in *Old tenures*].'[20]
Legal disability used to be the rule. Littleton now depicts it as an
exception. Of course, it would be wrong to imagine that the era of
legal inequality was over by the fifteenth century. But what is
evident is that the contemporary lawyers such as Fortescue and

---

[17] Ibid. ('Lex vero, sub qua cetus hominum populus efficitur, nervorum corporis
phisici tenet racionem, quia sicut per nervos compago corporis solidatur, sic per
legem, quae a *ligando* dicitur, corpus hujusmodi misticum ligatur et servatur in
unum').

[18] Edward Coke, *The first part of the Institutes of the laws of England; or a
commentary upon Littleton* (Coke on Littleton), 18th edn, 2 vols. (London,
1823), I, 127b–135b (§§ 196–201).

[19] The compilation of *Old tenures* is often ascribed to the reign of Edward III. The
text was printed in the early sixteenth century by several law printers. The
quotation which I translated is from the following passage: 'nota que villeyn
poet aver trois accions envers son seignour, scilicz, Appele de mort son aunc.,
Appele de rape fait a sa feme, et Appele de mayhayme.'

[20] Coke on Littleton, 123b (§ 189). T. Littleton, *Tenures*, printed by R. Pynson
(London, *c.* 1510) fo. xiv (r): 'Nota chescun villein est able et franke de suer
toutes maners des accions envers chescun person, forspris envers son seignour a
que il est villeyn. Et uncore certaines accions il poet aver envers son seignour
. . .'

Littleton were already treating the legal regime of inequality as if it was an embarrassing exception to their legal ideals.

Littleton's explanation merits a closer examination. As a class of persons who are debarred from bringing lawsuits, aliens are listed together with the villeins, those who are outlawed, those who are judged to be out of the king's protection, those who are excommunicated, and the religious who are deemed to be dead in secular law. Littleton explains that a person cannot bring lawsuits while under outlawry because the person is 'outside the law (*hors de la ley*)' to demand legal remedies during the period. Those judged to be out of the king's protection are also debarred from bringing lawsuits because 'the law and the king's writs be the things, by which a man is protected and helpen, and so, during the time that a man in such case is out of the king's protection, he is out of helpe and protection by the king's law, or by the king's writ'.[21] Obviously, the legal structure of the kingdom envisaged by Fortescue is deeply embedded in the mind of Littleton. The kingdom is viewed as a network of law branching out from the king. Aliens are portrayed as persons born out of this network (*hors de la liegance nostre seignor le roy*), hence out of the protection.

Littleton's explanation is conceived entirely in terms of the abstract notions of the king's law and the king's protection. It is a clear departure from concrete privileges and itemised franchises (*libertates*) which defined a person's legal condition in the Middle Ages. Littleton's notion of the king's law and protection could easily be understood to permeate evenly throughout the realm, thereby homogenising the legal conditions of the king's subjects. When Edward Coke argued in *Calvin's case* that 'the protection and government of the king is general over all his dominions and kingdoms', he was pursuing a conclusion whose direction was already set by Littleton.[22] For over a thousand years since Gaius, lawyers engaged in an analysis of personal legal relationships had been habitually asking the question, 'How free are you?' Littleton left no doubt that the long reign of Gaius' *summa diuisio perso-*

---

[21] Coke on Littleton, 129b (§ 199). Littleton, *Tenures*, fo. xiv (r): 'le ley et les briefes le roy sont les choses par queux homme est protecte et aide et issint durant le temps q home en tiel cas est hors de protec . . .'

[22] See below, p. 179.

narum was over. The new question to be asked persistently is 'Are you in, or are you out?'

The French Revolution dealt a fatal blow to the regime of legal inequality. All forms of inequality known to law were to be abolished in the name of liberty, equality and fraternity. But the enchantment of the revolutionaries went on even after the *summa diuisio* of Gaius was dismantled. Imbued with revolutionary zeal, the *Assemblée nationale* abolished the division based on nationality as well. In 1790, the so-called *droit d'aubaine*, which by then referred to various legal disabilities of aliens in France, was unconditionally abolished 'with regard to all the peoples of the world'.[23] However, their aspiration for boundless equality proved to be a short-lived episode without any durable impact. The reform was quickly undone by Napoleon.[24]

The latest restatement of the legal approach expounded by Fortescue and Littleton can be found in an article which is commonly inserted in various international conventions on human rights drafted in the twentieth century. For example, Article 2 of the Universal Declaration of Human Rights (1948) provides: 'Everyone is entitled to all the rights and freedoms set forth in the Declaration, without distinction of any kind, such as race, colour, sex, language, religion, political or other opinion, national or social origin, property, birth or other status.'[25] National origin, of course, does not mean nationality. The absence of nationality in this long list of criteria which *cannot* justify legal discrimination must not go unnoticed. Indeed, Article 16 of the Council of Europe Convention for the Protection of Human Rights and Fundamental Freedoms expressly provides that 'Nothing in Articles 10, 11, and 14 [Non-discrimination] shall be regarded as preventing the High Contracting Parties from imposing restrictions on the political activity of aliens.' All kinds of discrimination *except* the ones based on nationality are condemned. In fact, the

---

[23] 'Que la France libre doit ouvrir son sein à tout les peuples de la terre en les invitant à jouir . . . des droits sacrés et inviolables de l'humanité . . .' (Law of 6 August 1790). Philippe Sagnac, *La Législation civile de la Révolution française, 1789–1804: essai d'histoire sociale* (Paris, 1898) p. 252. For a searching analysis of the vicissitudes of the political argument behind this legislation, see Sophie Wahnich, *L'Impossible citoyen, l'étranger dans le discours de la Révolution française* (Paris, 1997).

[24] Paul Viollet, *Précis de l'histoire du droit civil français* (Paris, 1905) p. 414.

[25] Paul Sieghart, *The international law of human rights* (Oxford, 1983) p. 263.

new approach is so deeply ingrained in our minds that often we do not even use the word 'discrimination' to describe the differential legal treatment based on nationality. This is where we stand and it is not very far from where Littleton or Fortescue stood. Somewhere between Bracton and Littleton, therefore, there must have been a change of legal outlook. I believe it was not a minor change.

THE BEGINNING

This book examines the beginning of the law of alien status in medieval England because, in my view, it shows how the focus of European legal analysis shifted from *status* to the *State*. I have argued that just as Bracton represented an era where legal reasoning was based on the division between the free and the unfree status, so Sir John Fortescue and Thomas Littleton represent the new age where the legal relationship among human beings is conceptualised with constant reference to the allegiance to a political unit (a kingdom or a State). Precisely when and in what context clear indications of this change began to appear in England constitutes the main question which I propose to answer.

The assumption that meaningful historical inquiries can be made into the beginning of the law of alien status should not require lengthy justification as it is no longer seriously argued that systematic legal discrimination against aliens has existed from time immemorial.[26] Nevertheless, certain aspects of the assumption require clarification.

1. The 'beginning' presupposes a lack until the moment of beginning. But the lack of the law of alien status may not be explained by an absence of foreigners. No society has ever lacked the actual or potential presence of foreigners by means of which the group identity of its members can be formed and sharpened.

2. Nor does the lack of the law of alien status indicate the absence of the *psychological* category of foreigner. The division between 'we' and 'they' lies at the very core of human perception of the self. The words 'we' and 'they' themselves are the most

---

[26] This, however, seems to have been the prevalent opinion in the sixteenth and seventeenth centuries. See below, chs. 7 and 8.

eloquent evidence of such a cognitive mechanism which can never be transcended as long as human beings use language to define and express their perception. No doubt, *extranei, alienigenae, alienes, advenae* had been in common use ever since the Antiquity.[27] But the existence of such vocabulary should not be treated as evidence of a legal system based on the notion of alien status. As we shall see, the legal condition of foreign merchants (*mercatores alienigenae*) in medieval England was not so much determined by their foreign provenance as by their status as merchant free-men. Even though the perception of foreignness was expressed by the epithet *alienigena*, no definite set of privileges or disabilities was attributed to the quality of foreign provenance *per se*. I shall also argue that the legal condition of the foreign clergy in medieval England was not greatly affected by their foreign provenance either. The fact that they were not English was again clearly noted and expressed, but it did not have any immediate legal consequence until the moment which we consider as the starting point of the law of alien status. There is no historical beginning or end to human perception of the division between the self and the other. But the legal system based on a systematic discrimination against aliens is a historical phenomenon. Although its end is yet to be witnessed, its beginning was clearly observable in the course of European legal development.

3. Perception of the self and the other takes place at various levels. In many cases, such psychological perception is translated into a legal category. For instance, 'we' may refer to the burgesses of a particular town. Of course, it was a legal category whose membership was linked to the enjoyment of clearly defined privileges and franchises. 'We' may be the *omnes fideles* of the king. Its existence as a legal category throughout the Middle Ages is evidenced by countless writs and letters patent which were directed to *omnibus fidelibus suis*. Also, 'we' may refer to those who were under the jurisdiction of a particular bishop or parson as opposed to those coming from another

---

[27] *Thesaurus Linguae Latinae*, vol. I (Leipzig, 1903) and *Mittellateinisches Wörterbuch*, vol. I, fasc. 3 (Munich, 1960) list the recorded occurrences of the word *alienigena* from various Classical (up to AD 600) and medieval (up to the thirteenth century) sources. Of course, topographical names also express the perception of the self and the other.

bishopric or parish.[28] Of course, this list is not exhaustive. Our assumption about the beginning of the law of alien status must not be regarded as denying the existence of *any* of these legal categories during the period lying before the beginning. Existence of a concept does not determine its use or usefulness for legal reasoning. For instance, the concept of equality was always in existence. But whether and how it will be used in resolving disputes over distribution of resources will depend entirely on the particular approach adopted by members of the legal profession of a given time. Similarly, the existence of the legal concept of *fidelis* or *alienigena* should not, and need not, be denied in order to explain the contemporaneous lack of the law of alien status. The beginning of the law of alien status must not be confused with the emergence of an identifiable unit of government which makes use of the concept of *fideles* and *alienigenae*. Our aim is to explain rather the end, than the beginning, of a medieval state by examining the rise of the law of alien status, which I consider as the distinctive feature of the modern State. In short, our assumption about the 'beginning' *presupposes* the existence of the categories and the vocabulary of *fideles* and *alienigenae* rather than denying them.

4. The quest for the beginning of the law of alien status, then, is not a matter of locating the first occurrence of the term 'alien' in legal discourse. Nor do I believe that there is any ground to suppose a medieval 'revival' of the ancient legal rules for the treatment of foreigners.[29] Any attempt to isolate the term alien (or its equivalent) from the rest of the legal vocabulary and to trace its beginning or revival is bound to end up in a sterile exercise of antiquarianism. Meanings are not something that can be ascertained apart from the network of semantic

---

[28] Regarding the concepts of *incola, advena, vagus* and *peregrinus* in the medieval Canon law, see W. Onclin, 'Le statut des étrangers dans la doctrine canonique médiévale' in *L'Etranger*, part 2 (Brussels, 1958) pp. 37–64.

[29] For ancient Greek and Roman legal rules for the treatment of foreigners, see Raoul Lonis, *La Cité dans le monde grec: structure, fonctionnement, contradiction* (Paris: 1994) pp. 71–80; François Jacques and John Scheid, *Rome et l'intégration de l'empire, 44 av. J. C. – 260 ap. J. C.*, vol. I, *Les Structures de l'empire Romain* (Paris: 1990) ch. 6; Claude Nicolet, *Le Métier de citoyen dans la Rome républicaine*, 2nd edn (Paris: 1976) pp. 31–70; D Whitehead, *The ideology of the Athenian Metic* (Cambridge, 1977); R. Lonis (ed.), *L'Etranger dans le monde grec*, 2 vols. (Nancy, 1988, 1992).

relationships in which terms are put to use. Although the term 'alien' or its equivalent has always been in use, the *way* it is incorporated and used in legal argument is not always the same. To explain the *changing ways* of using alien and other related legal terms, therefore, is what I propose to do in this book. In my view, the beginning must be sought in the changing priority among various layers of *divisiones personarum*, with which lawyers express their perception of the self and the other. For Roman jurists, for example, the division between foreigners and non-foreigners was not as significant as the division between free-men and slaves, which was their *summa divisio personarum*. But today's lawyers would easily accept that the division between subjects and aliens is the most important *divisio personarum* which supersedes all other possible *divisiones personarum* one can envisage (divisions based on sex, age, lineage, family status, certain physical or cultural features, wealth, etc.). This shift of priority is what we understand as the beginning of the law of alien status. Thus understood, the history of the beginning of the law of alien status cannot, and must not, be a story of the 'fall' from the original, pristine innocence – where men were supposedly ignorant of the division between 'we' and 'they' – into the sinful knowledge of the vertiginous division separating 'us' from 'them'. My goal is rather mundane. I simply aim to examine how certain component-parts of the legal vocabulary have been re-shuffled and re-aligned in the fourteenth century, and how some of them have, as a result, acquired new relevance and new eloquence.

So far, legal historians have generally accepted the following remarks of Professor Maitland as a plausible explanation of the beginning of the English law of alien status:

[F]eudalism is opposed to tribalism and even to nationalism: we become a lord's subjects by doing homage to him, and this done, the nationality . . . and the place of our birth are insignificant. In England, however, a yet mightier force than feudalism came into play. A foreigner . . . conquered England, became king of the English, endowed his followers with English lands. For a long time after this there could be little law against aliens, there could hardly be such thing as English nationality . . . It is, we believe, in the loss of Normandy that our law of aliens finds its starting point.[30]

---

[30] F. Pollock and F. W. Maitland, *The history of English law before the time of Edward I*, 2nd edn, reissued with an introduction by S. F. C. Milsom, 2 vols.

The allusion to feudalism needs careful interpretation. Whether feudalism was actually against the establishment of a central government is still highly debatable. In an article summarising the most recent historical studies on feudalism in France, Professor Giordanengo argues: 'No one believes any more . . . that the very existence of the inter-personal [feudal] relationships would neces- sarily lead to the destruction of public authority or that its establishment would at least be hampered by those relationships, and the old expression 'feudal anarchy' makes one smile.'[31] He stresses that the oath of fidelity to the political ruler, as distinct from the feudal rite of homage, was a widespread practice vigor- ously maintained all over France throughout the Middle Ages.[32] This is a strong warning against the tendency to conceptualise the interpersonal legal relationships existing in a feudal monarchy by means exclusively or mainly of the tenurial relationship of homage. All medieval English law tracts also contain passages which suggest the unstinted importance of the relationship of fidelity between the king and his subjects, as distinct from the personal feudal relationship between the king and his tenants. *Glanvill*, for instance, stated that the rite of homage to mesne lords must be accompanied by a proviso saving the fidelity to the king (*salua fide debita domino regi et heredibus suis*).[33] In short, the importance of homage in feudal society did not necessarily weaken the bond between the king and his subjects (*fideles*). Professor

---

(Cambridge, 1968) I, pp. 460–1. Also ibid., I, p. 91 ('a King of the English who was but duke of the Normans was interested in obliterating a distinction which stood in his way if he was to be king of England'). Holdsworth quotes most of Maitland's explanation and repeats his view. W. S. Holdsworth, *A history of English law*, vol. IX (London, 1926) pp. 72–4. F. M. Powicke, *The loss of Normandy, 1189–1204* (Manchester, 1913) pp. 422ff. is responsible for the wide propagation of this view among other historians. See the bibliographical note at p. 228 below for a list of works dealing with the history of the law of alien status. All of them are based on an acceptance of Maitland's explanation.

[31] Gérard Giordanengo, 'Etat et droit féodal en France (XIIe.–XIVe siècles)' in *L'Etat moderne: Le droit, l'espace et les formes de l'état*, ed. N. Coulet and J.-P. Genet (Paris, 1990) pp. 64–5. For similar conclusions, see Jean Barbey, *Etre roi: le roi et son gouvernement en France de Clovis à Louis XVI* (Paris, 1992) pp. 111–12; Eric Bournazel and Jean-Pierre Poly, *La mutation féodale*, 1st edn (Paris, 1980) p. 276; Jacques Le Goff (ed.), *L'Etat et les pouvoirs, histoire de la France*, vol. II (Paris, 1989) p. 101.

[32] Giordanengo, 'Etat et droit féodal', p. 64.

[33] *Glanvill*, lib. 9, c. 1. *Bracton* and *Britton* also agree on this point. For a detailed discussion, see Keechang Kim, 'Etre fidèle au roi: XIIe–XIVe siècles', 293 *Revue Historique* (1995) 225–50.

Maitland's carefully worded suggestion that under feudalism, nationality was 'insignificant' for resolution of disputes involving foreigners, should not be construed as suggesting the absence or general unimportance of the concept of *fidelis* in the feudal monarchy of England.

The reference to the Norman Conquest may require some reconsideration. As far as medieval lawyers were concerned, the Conquest did not entail the process of 'nation building'. The legal relationship between Englishmen and the new kings from Normandy posed no new problem because Norman kings claimed to be the legitimate successors to the king of the English (*rex Anglorum*). The Normans remaining in Normandy did not automatically become English simply because their duke acquired the kingship over Englishmen. Their legal status remained the same as before. They were no different from other Frenchmen who were ruled by territorial princes of medieval France.[34]

However, those who came over from the Continent and settled down in England were identified as *Franci*, and were included among the *omnes fideles* of the king of the English. Many writs and charters issued in post-Conquest England were directed to *omnibus fidelibus suis, Francigenis et Angligenis*.[35] It is wrong to imagine that here the *Franci* or the *Francigenae* referred to Frenchmen in general. Writs and charters had clearly defined geographical and personal limits within which they were effective. The king of the English during that period had no claim over Frenchmen in general. Only the new settlers in England were referred to by the term *Franci*. To this extent, the scope of the king's *fideles* underwent a slight change as a result of the Conquest. But this does not mean that the distinction between peoples became any more difficult or insignificant. Rather, the Conquest actually sharpened the distinction as evidenced by the appearance of the legal rules dealing with their interrelationships.[36] For

---

[34] As subjects of the duke, Normans would eventually be subject to the French king's territorial claim over his kingdom. See Paul Jeulin, 'L'Hommage de la Bretagne . . .', 41 *Annales de Bretagne* (1934) 380–473.

[35] *Royal writs in England from the Conquest to Glanvill*, 77 Selden Society, (1958–9) Appendix, *passim*; *Cartulary of the Abbey of Ramsey*, Rolls series, 3 vols., ed. W. H. Hart and A. L. Ponsonby (1884–93) *passim*.

[36] George Garnett, '"Franci et Angli": the legal distinctions between peoples after the Conquest' in *Anglo-Norman studies*, ed. R. Allen Brown, vol. VIII (Woodbridge, 1986) p. 118.

Englishmen of the time, the Normans were only one of various groups of foreigners they came in contact with, peacefully or militarily. Foreign merchants, foreign monks and foreign clerics kept coming to England throughout the Middle Ages not only from Normandy but from all over the Continent. For the Norman rulers who came to England, on the other hand, the legal concept of *fidelis* was crucially important for the administration of the newly acquired territory. There is no ground to assume that inclusion of *Franci* in the *omnes fideles* of the king of the English made the concept of *fidelis* insignificant or unsuitable for legal purposes. We reject the suggestion that the psychological perception of ethnic identities or the legal concept of *fidelis* was blurred by the Norman Conquest or sharpened by the loss of Normandy.[37]

Maitland was not the first to attribute the beginning of the English law of alien status to the loss of Normandy. He was repeating a view which had been regarded as axiomatic since the latter half of the seventeenth century.[38] However, such a view is responsible for some unfortunate results. First, the development of the English law of alien status is portrayed as a uniquely English phenomenon which had nothing to do with the European legal development. Second, the beginning of the law of alien status is described as a strictly juridical process explainable wholly in terms of precedents and their judicial interpretation. It is high time that we discarded this view and examined the history of the English law of alien status from a fresh perspective.

THE EUROPEAN PERSPECTIVE

Conjectures surrounding the consequences of the Norman Conquest and the loss of Normandy have prevented the history of the English law of alien status from being studied on the broader

---

[37] The differential legal treatment between ethnic groups in post-Conquest England, which is observable in the institution of murder fine and Englishry, had little to do with the question of alien status. The king's *fideles* comprised men and women of widely different legal status. The disparity of legal status between *Franci* and *Angli* was just *one* of many examples of legal inequality which existed *among* the king's *fideles*. See Garnett's work cited above.

[38] See below, p. 187, for the beginning of this historiographical tradition.

horizon of European legal development. Instead, the beginning, and the lack until the beginning of the law of alien status have been explained with reference to the fortuitous events that England was conquered by the Normans and that the descendants of the conquerors happened to lose their overseas possessions at some point. One wonders whether other European kingdoms, which did not share the same military fortune with England, could ever have the beginning of their law of alien status. Also, any war fought at any time has the potential to sharpen the group identity of the parties involved. One wonders again why the law of alien status appeared, if it did, at that particular moment in English history rather than much earlier or later. Attributing the beginning of the law of alien status to the loss of Normandy made it impossible to appreciate the historicity of the law of alien status.

Military confrontation, therefore, is not a fruitful place to look for the beginning of the law of alien status. The beginning must instead be sought in the shift of focus in the law of personal status from concrete, itemised and marketable *libertates* and *privilegia* to the abstract notion of political faith and allegiance. The new approach marked the end of an era in European legal development and opened up a new age where the kingdom or the State became the constant and ultimate point of reference by means of which an individual's identity is legally defined, and interpersonal relationships are legally analysed. The emergence of the English law of alien status must be viewed as a 'European' event whose novelty and historicity must be studied from a European perspective. It had nothing to do with the Norman Conquest or the loss of Normandy.[39]

---

[39] There is a considerable amount of literature stressing the merits of comparative history. Marc Bloch, 'Pour une histoire comparée des sociétés européennes', 46 *Revue de Synthèse Historique* (1925) 15–50; W. H. Sewell, 'Marc Bloch and the logic of comparative history', 6 *History and Theory* (1967) 208–18; G. M. Frederickson, 'Comparative history' in *The past before us*, ed. M. Kammen (Ithaca, 1980), pp. 457–73; John Elliott, 'National and comparative history', an inaugural lecture in the Oxford University, 10 May 1991. The necessity for a European approach to legal history in particular is strongly argued in Reiner Schulze, 'European legal history – a new field of research in Germany',13 *Journal of Legal History* (1992) 270–95. For a concise explanation of why the study of the birth of European modern States must take account of the changes appearing not only in one particular country but all over western Europe in the late Middle Ages, see the introduction by J.-Ph. Genet in *L'Etat moderne: genèse – bilans et perspectives* (Paris, 1990).

THE INTER-DISCIPLINARY APPROACH

Basing themselves on the assumption that the beginning of the law of alien status must be viewed as the appearance of sharpened psychological and legal categories (allegedly resulting from the loss of Normandy), legal historians have searched for precedents to which the appearance of such categories may be attributed. Once the beginning was located by means of (a) precedent(s), the rest of the story would then be told entirely in terms of how narrowly or widely the precedents were interpreted by later generations of lawyers and judges. Thus, Professor Maitland argues that the war-time 'dilatory' exception against French enemies – which only had the effect of postponing the lawsuit until the war was over – gradually transformed itself into the permanent 'peremptory' exception against aliens in general (conclusively barring their lawsuit regardless of war).[40] Similarly, the precedents of temporary seizures of the Normans' lands upon the loss of Normandy are thought to have somehow transformed into a general law of alien treatment as the military confrontations with French kings dragged on.

It is true that neither the dilatory exceptions nor the seizures of the Normans' lands are viewed in themselves as the examples of the law of alien status. They are offered as the precedents containing, as it were, a germ for the metamorphosis. The precise moment of the beginning of the law of alien status is therefore lost somewhere in the development process which is described as 'an exaggerated generalization' of the precedents. Nevertheless, the beginning – understood as a concoction of judicial manoeuvring of precedents – is believed to be lying wholly within the realm of legal logic.[41]

In my view, the beginning of the law of alien status was not the result of the appearance – whether gradual or abrupt – of new psychological or legal categories. The beginning must be explained by a *changed use* of the known categories and concepts such as faith and allegiance to the king. The new way of using the old concepts was made possible because the analysis of

---

[40] The 'dilatory' exception postponed the suing of the claim only until the cessation of the hostilities. *Bracton*, III, 361 (fo. 298), IV, 292 (fo. 415 b), IV, 328–9 (fo. 427 b), IV, 331–2 (fo. 428 b).

[41] Pollock and Maitland, *The history of English law*, I, 462–3.

personal legal relationships began to be conducted on an entirely
different platform. It was a change of paradigm. Such a change
does not form part of the textual contents of legal discourse.
Rather, it was a change of the non-discursive context in which
the legal discourse of the time was practised. Therefore, the
beginning itself cannot be explained by precedents or their
judicial interpretation. It lies outside. Herein lies the need for
an inter-disciplinary study. At the same time, although the
beginning itself may lie outside the realm of legal logic, its
indications can be observed in precedents and they may be
studied to illuminate the history of the law of alien status. To
this extent, the study of our topic has something to offer to –
and just as much to learn from – those who are investigating
various institutional and intellectual changes of late medieval
Europe, of which legal change was an integral part. If an
interdisciplinary study between legal history and social and
political history is at all possible, we would not be able to find a
more appropriate topic anywhere else.[42] So far, such an enterprise has been impossible because the orthodox view failed to
externalise the beginning of the law of alien status from the
realm of legal logic.[43] Probably, a history portrayed as an
exaggerated generalisation of precedents 'will not seem strange
to those who have studied the growth of the king's preroga-
tives'.[44] But, certainly, it has been regarded as strange and
irrelevant by other historians who do not purport to study the
technicalities of legal history.

---

[42] About the need and possibility of the inter-disciplinary enterprise between legal
history and social and political history in general, see a note by Julius Kirshner
in *Storia sociale e dimensione giuridica*, ed. Paolo Grossi (Milan, 1986) p. 357.
Professor Kirshner kindly provided me with this reference. I wish to thank him
for his advice and warm encouragement.

[43] The mode of legal argument prevalent in case law countries has the tendency to
incorporate the result of historical legal changes into the present legal argument.
Thus incorporated, historical legal changes are often overshadowed by the
power of judicial logic. The point was lucidly argued by Professor Maitland
himself. See his inaugural lecture delivered in the University of Cambridge on
13 October 1888, 'Why the history of English law is not written' in *The collected
papers of F. W. Maitland*, ed. H. A. L. Fisher, 3 vols. (Cambridge, 1911) I,
p. 491.

[44] Pollock and Maitland, *The history of English law*, I, p. 463.

THE SCOPE AND AIM OF THE PRESENT WORK

Lest I should raise readers' expectations too high by the foregoing discussion of the potentials of our topic, it is necessary to state at the outset what I do and do not propose to undertake. This book is not intended to be an interdisciplinary study. Our focus is on *legal* arguments only. The lawyer's viewpoint expressed in the pages of his law book does not necessarily have an immediate impact on the way things are. Nor is it always an accurate and timely reflection of the changes in the real world. What it does, however, is to assign a particular order of priority among competing methods of legal analysis. The method of legal analysis enjoying the highest priority among members of the legal profession at a given time will become the chief means by which social relations are legally conceptualised and conflicts and problems are legally defined. The distinction between legal argument and political, scientific or other non-legal argument turns on whether a system of discourse has at its disposal the institutionalised means of coercion. Not every new proposal or argument regarding distribution of resources is translated into the language of law. Throughout the fourteenth century, for instance, Parliament repeatedly heard the vehement protest of the Commons that because foreigners were taking so many ecclesiastical benefices in England, competent English clerks were losing the opportunity for promotion.[45] However, it took more than a century before the legal profession finally accepted the urgent plea that the mechanism for allocation of ecclesiastical benefices should be changed in the interest of the king's liege-clerks. Only then was the Commons' political argument provided with the institutionalised means of coercion, and could therefore systematically alter the patterns of forcible distribution of resources among individuals (if the reform was vigorously enforced). This is what we call a legal change. And the focus of this book is exclusively on such legal changes. If we do discuss some of the non-legal works of the time, we do it mostly to emphasise the gap between lawyers' outlook and non-lawyers' outlook.

---

[45] *Rotuli Parliamentorum*, 6 vols. (London, 1767–77) II, pp. 141–3 ('les aliens tiegnent tantz des benefiz en vostre terre . . . et voz lieges clers suffisantz par decea le meyns avances . . .': 1343). See below, ch. 3, for further discussion.

Study of the law of alien status requires an investigation into when and how lawyers began to subscribe to a new argument which could carry out the double task of enhancing the juridical homogeneity of those deemed to be 'within' (by removing the existing legal divisions among them) and systematically discriminating against those deemed to be 'without' (by imposing legal restrictions upon their access to local resources). We have some evidence which tends to show how foreign claims to the control of English resources abruptly encountered a flat denial towards the end of the fourteenth century. This book offers a textual analysis of these late medieval legal documents. Such an effort will help bring to light a dramatic change of legal approach on whose legacy we all live now. The birth of a modern State must be sought in these mundane documents which closely record how resources were actually allocated among various contenders. The birth story should no longer remain in the highly speculative domain where only the 'contributions', 'influences', and 'implications' of some historical events or political–philosophical tracts are discussed. Neither the vehemence of political rhetoric, nor the naked power of armed forces or violent uprisings can sustain the continuous functioning of the modern State apparatus.

This book does not aim to offer a comparative study of medieval European legal development either. Apart from a few passing remarks on the situation across the Channel, all my efforts are concentrated on explaining the English experience. The pressing task, as I see it, is to release the history of the English law of alien status from the narrow historiographical confines of the military struggles between two kings separated by the Channel. Once this is done, the topic can be placed on a broader horizon of European legal development and will reveal its rich potential for those who wish to embark on a comparative study of European legal and institutional history. This book aims to do no more than prepare the ground for such comparative studies. My attempt, it is hoped, may also prove useful to those who are interested in studying the emergence and the future course of development of the modern States in Europe and beyond. It is from this standpoint that I propose to study the beginning of the English law of alien status.

Part I

HISTORY

2

FOREIGN MERCHANTS

'Foreign merchants' may be discussed from two different angles:
(1) as a sub-category of foreigners; or (2) as a sub-category of
merchants. The former approach relies on a juxtaposition of
foreigners and Englishmen as contrasting categories. No doubt
such an approach will be useful for a medievalist who wishes to
understand the group psychology of medieval English society. But
it is of little use for our purpose. It is not our aim to study the
popular sentiments regarding the presence and activities of foreign
merchants in medieval England. The aim of the present chapter is
to investigate the *legal* environment in which these merchants
lived and conducted their business. As far as personal legal status
is concerned, I see no point in comparing foreign merchants to
English serfs; or foreign slaves (some Italian merchants, for
example, brought them for their personal use) to English knights.
I therefore choose the latter approach; that is, foreign merchants
will be discussed as a sub-category of merchants. This does not
mean that I postulate a legal category of merchants. I use the term
'merchants' as a factual, economic category of traders. We may
begin by posing the following questions:

(1) What was the legal environment for commercial activities in
    general in medieval England?[1]
(2) What were the differences between the legal status of English
    merchants and that of foreign merchants?

Medieval England – like elsewhere in Europe – offered two

---

[1] It is unnecessary for our purpose to attempt a rigorous definition of 'commercial
activities'. The expression is used to indicate various profit-making activities
typically conducted by those who were normally referred to as *mercatores* in
medieval Europe.

23

distinctively different sets of legal environment for commercial activities: fairs and cities. The contrast is worth stressing.

MERCHANTS IN FAIRS

Merchants (*mercatores*) in medieval Europe were often classified as travellers (*peregrini, viatores*).[2] Until the thirteenth century, the important bulk of commercial activities was carried out by these wayfaring merchants, who were calling at fairs at regular intervals.[3] The legal environment of fairs must be understood in light of the fact that fairs were important sources of income for the lord who had feudal claims over them.[4] The revenues from fairs comprised (1) tolls levied from incoming merchants; (2) rents from stalls, booths and houses; and (3) perquisites of the fair court (piepowder court). The value of a fair – from the viewpoint of the lord – depended on its popularity.[5] The lord, it may be assumed, had a good reason to strive to offer an attractive legal environment for *all* incoming merchants.

In certain cases, fairs were held in urban locations. These cases illustrate that the urban legal regime was temporarily suspended during the fair. The surviving records of the fair at Chalon-sur-Saône show that from the first day of the summer fair, the usual toll (*grand peaige*) ceased. In other words, the burgesses' privilege to collect tolls was temporarily superseded by the special toll

---

[2] Gratian, *Decretrum*, C. 24, q. 3, c. 23. For further references, see Vito Piergiovanni, 'La "peregrinatio bona" dei mercanti medievali: a proposito di un commento di Baldo degli Ubaldi a X. I. 34', 105 *Zeitschrift der Savigny-Stiftung für Rechtsgeschichte*, Kan. Abt. (1988) 348–56. However, we do not agree with all his interpretations.

[3] See, in general, Jacques Le Goff, *Marchands et banquiers du moyen âge* (Paris, 1972). For the recent state of research in this area, see Jean Favier, *De l'or et des épices: naissance de l'homme d'affaires au moyen âge* (Paris, 1987).

[4] P. Huvelin, *Essai historique sur le droit des marchés et des foires* (Paris, 1897) p. 184.

[5] See E. W. Moore, *The fairs of medieval England: an introductory study* (Toronto, 1985) in general. I thank Professor T. H. Lloyd for drawing my attention to this work. The grants of messuages and rows of houses near the market place were often qualified with the clause 'frons vero tempore ferie domino reservetur'. The lord of the fair could therefore charge rents to merchants who were obligated to have their stalls there. Trading in the rear of the houses needed special permission. *Select cases concerning the law merchant, 1270–1638*, vol. I, 23 Selden Society (1908) p. xxxii.

(*pertusaige*) collected by the men of the duke during the fair.[6] During the fair of St Giles in Winchester, the municipal authority was also entirely suppressed. The bishop, who was the feudal lord of the fair, took the keys and custody of the city gates from the burgesses and set up the fair court which took cognisance of all pleas touching breaches of peace, debts, contracts and even the lands and houses in the city.[7] At the opening of the fair in York, the bailiffs of the archbishop – the feudal lord of the fair – came upon the city bridge and received the staves from the bailiffs of the city, which symbolised the transfer of the administrative authority during the fair.[8] While the fair was on, there was a legal environment which was in sharp contrast with that of the city. The following institutional arrangements must be discussed in connection with the legal environment of fairs: (1) safe-conduct; and (2) court of piepowder.

Safe-conduct

Offering a safe passage to an individual or to a group of individuals by providing an armed escort or an official document had a long history dating back from the Antiquity.[9] But the growth of commerce in the twelfth century changed the nature of this ancient institution. Merchants became its heaviest users. From then on, the institutional arrangement known as safe-conduct was frequently used to safeguard the movement of merchants and their goods.[10] Henry I, for example, granted the fair of St Ives to the abbot of Ramsey in 1110. The grant was accompanied by a guarantee of safe-conduct that all, while going and remaining

---

[6] *Les Péages des foires de Chalon-sur-Saône*, ed. Sven Andolf (Göteborg, 1971) pp. 36–7, 80.

[7] E. Lipson, *The economic history of England*, vol. I, *The Middle Ages*, 9th edn (London, 1947) p. 241.

[8] *Placita de Quo Warranto*, ed. W. Illingworth, Records Commission (London, 1818) pp. 221–3; Francis Drake, *Eboracum: or the history and antiquities of the city of York* (London, 1736) p. 218.

[9] On this topic in general, see C. De Craecker-Dussart, 'L'Evolution du sauf-conduit dans les principautés de la Basse-Lotharingie du VIIIe au XIVe siècle', 80 *Le Moyen Age* (1974) 185–243.

[10] Renée Doehaerd, 'Féodalité et commerce: remarques sur le conduit des marchands, XIe–XIIIe siècles' in *La Noblesse au moyen âge, XIe–XVe siècles*, ed. Philippe Contamine (Paris, 1976) p. 206.

there and returning thence, should have the king's firm peace: 'et
volo et praecipio ut omnes ad eam venientes et in ea existentes et
inde redeuntes firmam pacem in eam habeant'. The 'firm peace'
was often manifested in the form of the extremely severe punishment imposed on those who broke the peace of the fair.[11]

For mercantile purposes, safe-conduct did not mean exemption
from tolls. Safety of transportation was promised on condition
that due customs were paid. In 1224, for example, the family of
Petrus de Conti obtained a safe-conduct. We find the following
text in the Patent roll: '[the recipients] shall have the letters of
safe-conduct in coming to England with the goods and merchandises of the said Petrus upon payment of just and due customs'.[12]
Much attention has been paid to a text (c. 991–c. 1002) which set
forth differential rates of tolls payable by various foreign merchants at Billingsgate, London. Merchants from Rouen, Picardy,
Normandy, Huy, Liège, etc. were mentioned in the document.
This may be regarded as an example of the tolls which were
usually described in contemporary legal documents as 'recta et
debita' or 'antiqua et recta'.[13]

The preferred status of the merchants who later became known
as Hanse merchants is reflected in the Billingsgate document:

---

[11] The above-quoted passage and other similar ones are to be found in *Chronicon
Abbatiae Rameseiensis*, Rolls series, ed. W. D. Macray (1886), pp. 221, 226, 286.
British borough charters, 1042–1216, ed. Adolphus Ballard (Cambridge, 1913)
pp. 197–9 also gives a number of examples regarding Winchester, Cambridge
and Portsmouth. See also Philippe de Beaumanoir, *Coutumes de Beauvaisis*, ed.
Amédée Salmon, 2 vols. (Paris, 1899–1900) I, pp. 367, 432: 'celui qui se bat un
jour de fete ou de marche, en allant et en venant au marche payera une amende
. . . Car tuit cil qui sont ou marchie ou en alant ou en venant du marchie, sont
ou conduit le conte et doivent avoir sauf aler et sauf venir.' For various examples
of severe punishment which were imposed to maintain the peace of fairs, see
Doehaerd, 'Féodalité et commerce', p. 206.

[12] *Patent rolls of Henry III, 1216–1225*, p. 434 ([the recipients] 'habent litteras de
conductu in veniendo in Angliam cum rebus et mercandisis ipsius Petri,
faciendo inde rectas et debitas consuetudines').

[13] The Latin text appears in British Library, Cottonian MS A. 140. It is printed in
Benjamin Thorpe, *Ancient laws and institutes of England*, 2 vols. (London, 1840)
I, p. 127; *Hansisches Urkundenbuch*, 11 vols. (1876–1939) I, 1–2; *Die Gesetze der
Angelsachsen*, ed., Felix Liebermann, 3 vols. (Halle, 1903–1916) I, pp. 232–4.
Liebermann suggests that the text was originally from c. 991–c. 1002. Henry T.
Riley discusses the text in detail in *Munimenta Gildhallae Londoniensis: liber
albus, liber custumarum et liber Horn*, Rolls series, 3 vols. (London, 1859–62) I,
introduction. An English translation of the text is given in Lipson, *The economic
history of England*, I, p. 512.

they were held worthy of all good laws equally with London merchants. A charter issued by Henry II to the merchants of Cologne in 1157 may be discussed in this connection. It provides that the persons and possessions of the merchants, including their house in London, shall be 'in my custody and protection (*in custodia et protectione mea*)' and that they shall be protected 'as if they were my men and friends (*sicut homines meos et amicos*)'. The charter was confirmed repeatedly afterwards. Some of these confirmation charters state that the safe-conduct is granted because the recipients are the king's men: 'quia homines et fideles mei sunt'.[14]

How are we to understand these charters? Are they the 'precursors' of the letters of denization? Did the merchants of Cologne purchase these charters because they were foreigners? Had they been Englishmen, would it have been unnecessary to purchase such protection? Consider the following passage of a charter issued in 1215: '[the recipients] shall come and go in all our land with all their merchandises, buying, selling and transacting well and in peace freely and quit of all exactions (*Quod eant et veniant per totam terram nostram cum omnibus mercandisis suis emendo et vendendo et negotiando bene et in pace libere quiete et honorifice*)'. The charter promises, among other things, the safety of transportation of goods and persons within the realm. The recipients were the burgesses of Swansea. Like the merchants of Cologne, the burgesses of Swansea had to go through the trouble and expenses of acquiring the charter. Was it because they were Welsh? What about the burgesses of Cambridge, Colchester, etc.? Did they purchase similar charters because they were foreigners?[15]

But what about the passage, 'because they are my men (*quia homines et fideles mei sunt*)'? Did the merchants of Cologne become the king's subjects – or were they to be so regarded – because of these charters? If so, how are we to explain the numerous confirmation charters, which would mean that they were 'repeatedly' naturalised? Had they become the king's subjects and, after a

---

[14] *Hansisches Urkundenbuch*, I, 8 (1157), 16 (1175), 22 (1194), 37 (1210), 43 (1213); *Calendar of charter rolls*, I, 214 (1235). For the expression 'quia homines et fideles mei sunt', see *Hansisches Urkundenbuch*, I, 8, 16, 22.

[15] Ballard, *British borough charters, 1042–1216*, p. 216 gives many similar examples pertaining to various other cities.

while, lapsed again into the status of aliens? Obviously, the term
fidelis poses serious problems of interpretation.[16]

As I have pointed out already, the same 'fidelis' was used in
numerous writs and charters during the period to refer to the
king's subject.[17] In 1194, however, Richard I granted a safe-
conduct to 'dearest friend, kinsman and our *fidelis* (*karissimo amico
et consanguineo et* fideli *nostro*)', who was William the king of
Scotland.[18] Does that mean that the king of Scotland sought, and
the king of England granted, denization by this document? Of
course, it may be argued that the king of Scotland became a vassal
of the king of England as evidenced by the treaty of 1174, and that
this should suffice to make him a subject; hence, the expression
'fidelis'. This line of argument, however, did not appear until the
sixteenth century.[19] May we rely on a sixteenth-century argument
in interpreting a twelfth-century text? May we alternatively rely
on the familiar thesis of 'feudal anarchy' and persuade ourselves
that the feudal lordship was all important and that the subject
status, as distinct from the vassal/tenant status, was left in
obscurity and confusion? The use of *fidelis* in these documents
would then be regarded as a reminder of the supposed imprecision
and incoherence of medieval jurisprudence: although William the
king of Scotland may be rightly called *fidelis*, referring to the
merchants of Cologne as *fideles* would be rather 'anarchical' and
'confusing'. One may also note in this connection that in ancient
Rome, safe-conduct was often called 'diploma' or 'fides'.[20] 'Fides'
was sometimes used in this way in the Middle Ages. We find, for
example, the following document which was issued in 856: 'If
some of you dare not travel to that place, we shall give you the
God's and our lord Charles' *fides*.'[21] Also, in 1217, a safe-conduct

---

[16] See, however, Doehaerd, 'Féodalité et commerce', p. 215 ('le privilège' [specifi-
cally granted by a charter] 'vaut mieux que la coutume dans la société médiévale:
le privilège est un contrat entre personnes ou groupes identifiés et comporte de
ce chef un pouvoir contraignant autrement efficace que la *lex*').

[17] See above, p. 14.

[18] E. L. G. Stones, *Anglo-Scottish relations 1174–1328*, 2nd edn (Oxford, 1970)
pp. 16ff.

[19] See below, p. 170.

[20] De Craecker-Dussart, 'L'Evolution du sauf-conduit', p. 189.

[21] Capitula ad Francos et Aquitanos missa de Carisiaco, *M. G. H., LL. Capitularia*, vol. II, p. 282 ('Et si aliquis . . . de vobis . . . non audeat ambulare ad
illum, nos vobis damus Dei et nostri senioris Karoli fidem'). Quoted from de
Craecker-Dussart, 'L'Evolution du sauf-conduit', p. 189.

was mentioned in the following terms: 'Safe-conduct: know that Hugo de Lascy shall come [to England] with our peace and *fides*.'[22]

I refrain from discussing the precise meaning of 'fidelis' in the present chapter. At this stage, I simply point out the possibility that the term 'fidelis' might not have been used in quite the same way as we would use the term 'subject'. Suffice it to emphasise the danger of approaching the institution of safe-conduct with our habitual frame of mind formed by a sharp division between aliens and subjects. The interpretative problem posed by the term *fidelis* in these documents should not prevent us from seeing the crucially important point: that is, *all* merchants – regardless of their allegiance or national origin – had to pay for the king's protection in one form or another. Further research may well reveal that some difference in economic terms might have been maintained between the English and the foreign merchants in pricing the privileges. But as far as the formal legal reasoning is concerned, all merchants had specifically to acquire the necessary privileges. No one was freely given unsolicited privileges, whether an Englishman or a foreigner.

Court of piepowder

The existence of special courts and trial procedures intended to provide fast and effective legal remedies for merchants is well documented. *Bracton* mentions 'justitia pepoudrous' and explains that it is for merchants who ought to have quick legal remedy: 'propter personas qui celerem habere debent justitiam, sicut sunt mercatores quibus exhibetur justitia pepoudrous'.[23] The author of *The mirror of justices* also states that 'speedy remedy should be provided from day to day for foreign plaintiffs *in fairs and markets* in the court of piepowder according to the law merchant'.[24] The court of piepowder sat all day and cases could be adjourned from

---

[22] *Patent rolls of Henry III, 1216–1225*, p. 34 ('De conductu: . . . sciatis quod Hugo de Lascy venit ad fidem et pacem nostram').

[23] *Bracton on the laws and customs of England*, trans. Samuel Thorne, 4 vols. (Cambridge, Mass., 1968–77) IV, p. 63 (fo. 334).

[24] Our translation is based on *The mirror of justices*, 7 Selden Society (1893), p. 9 ('de jour en jour se hastast droit destranges pleintifs *en feires e marchiez* cum pe poudrous solom lei marchande'). Emphasis supplied.

hour to hour. Fewer essoins (lawful excuses for not appearing in court) were allowed in order to expedite the procedures. There were special provisions regarding default judgment and sale of attached goods.[25]

The custumal of Torksey (*c.* 1238) offers a vivid contrast between a borough court and a piepowder court. According to the custumal, the latter is for merchants and wayfaring foreigners (*pro mercatoribus et forencecis transeuntibus*). No one who dwells, or has lands or tenements in Torksey, shall be impleaded or amerced in the piepowder court except upon voluntary consent to appear in that court. The piepowder court had distinctive procedures of inquest where the jury would be empanelled by foreign, as well as native, merchants of the town: 'If the pleadings lead to an inquest, it will be taken from foreign and native merchants then present in town.'[26]

Although the piepowder court was initially developed to meet the special needs of markets and fairs only, the procedural arrangement appears to have become more widely available for foreign merchants later on. *Liber albus* of London, for example, has the following passage (*c.* 1285) which promises a mixed jury for certain types of cases without any reference to markets or fairs:

If an inquest is joined between a foreigner and a native in cases of contract, debt or trespass of which foreign merchants can have cognisance, it will be done by twelve men, of which one half shall be natives and the other half, foreigners staying in town.[27]

The procedures of the staple court may also be discussed in this connection. The aim of the staple court was to offer 'speedy trial . . . from day to day and hour to hour'. If an inquest had to be taken, it ought to be composed wholly of foreigners when both parties were foreigners, wholly of denizens when both parties were

---

[25] For procedural details of the piepowder court, see *Select cases concerning the law merchant, 1270–1638*, I, introduction.

[26] The Latin text is printed in ibid., pp. xxxvii–xxxviii ('Et si placitat ad inquisicionem, capta erit de mercatoribus forincecorum et intrinsecorum tunc in villa existencium'). The editor, Charles Gross, suggests that the text was composed in *c.* 1238 (p. xxxvii). Mary Bateson thought that the custumal was compiled after 18 Edward III. *Borough customs*, vol. I, 18 Selden Society (1904) p. lii.

[27] *Borough customs*, I, p. 201 ('Et enqueste jointe denzein et forein, soit fait par xii dount la moitee soit de denzeines et l'autre moitee des foreins demurrantz en ville, si ceo soit de contract, de dete ou trespas, dount marchauntz foreyns puissent aver conusaunce').

denizens, and half of foreigners and half of denizens when one party was foreign and the other was not.[28] The staple court, therefore, had a closer affinity with the piepowder court than with a borough court. As far as we know, no borough court professed to hear pleas from day to day and from hour to hour.

The procedures of the piepowder court do not seem to contain anything particularly unfavourable to foreign merchants. It appears that fairs provided a legal environment for commercial activities which was based on the notion of fundamental fairness. A systematic legal discrimination against aliens, if such a thing did exist, played no part in the judicial framework of fairs. Of course, fairs lasted no more than about a week.[29] But that was not a serious problem for wayfaring merchants. They could pack and leave. Somewhere nearby, another fair would be waiting for them with an equally attractive legal environment.

FOREIGN MERCHANTS IN CITIES

The importance of fairs, however, sharply declined in the fourteenth century.[30] By the end of the thirteenth century, cities became the most important centres of commercial activities. The legal environment of cities, as we shall see, was widely different from that of fairs. All unenfranchised outsiders − including foreign merchants − had to be prepared to meet ruthless legal discrimination. But the permanent business opportunities

---

[28] Statute 27 Edward III st. 2 (1353); Statute 28 Edward III *c*. 13 (1354). I wish to thank Dr Marianne Constable, Department of Rhetoric, University of California, Berkeley for kindly sending me a proof copy of her book, *The law of the other: the half-alien jury and changing conceptions of citizenship, law and knowledge* (Chicago, 1994). Her book contains a discussion on the early history of the mixed jury (ch. 1). Some discussion of the arrangement of the staple court can be found in Spencer Brodhurst, 'The merchants of the staple', 17 *Law Quarterly Review* (1901) 56–76.

[29] The lord of the fair often insisted that no merchant should linger once the fair was over. This was to achieve maximum concentration of commercial activities during the period of the fair. Once the fair was over, the lord could no longer claim the revenues (tolls, rents, judicial fines, etc.) from the merchants, hence the need to make sure that no commercial activities took place outside the period of fair.

[30] Regarding the decline of English fairs, see Lipson, *The economic history of England*, I, pp. 260–63. The comparable situation in France is explained in Le Goff, *Marchands et banquiers*, pp. 18ff.

available in cities – as opposed to the periodic opportunities for commercial activities in fairs – proved irresistible to foreign merchants. Accordingly, they began to obtain charters which allowed them the possibility to 'buy and sell in town (*emere et vendere in villa*)' in addition to the guarantee of safe-conduct, 'that they shall be able to travel to the fairs throughout all our land (*quod libere possint ire ad ferias per totam terram nostram*)'. What then was the legal environment '*in villa*'?

'*Liberties*' of a city

The law of the merchants of lower Lotharingia (*c.* 1130) gives us a detailed account of the legal conditions under which various groups of foreign merchants did their business in London. The text sets forth how their ships shall approach London Bridge; how the king's chamberlain and sheriffs shall take certain luxury items and wine for the king's use while these merchants are obliged to wait for two ebbs and a tide before commencing their business; when they shall be allowed to sell their merchandise, and in what quantity; to whom they can sell these goods and in what order; when and according to what procedures they may go outside the four boundaries of London to trade; the procedures to be observed in unloading the goods from their ships and carrying them into the city for sale; the tolls to be paid in doing so; the procedures for lodging and unpacking of their goods; what they shall be allowed to buy, and how much. There are further provisions stating that they shall not stay in London for more than forty days and that they shall answer all claims in the court of hustings of London. Again, certain groups of Hanse merchants appear to have negotiated better conditions: they may lodge wherever they will within the walls of the city. According to the text, merchants from Tiel, Bremen, Antwerp, Norway and Denmark may sojourn in the city for one whole year. Danes, in particular, have the same privilege as London merchants in that they may, by the law of the city of London, go anywhere in England to trade in fairs and markets.[31]

---

[31] The text is printed and discussed in *Liber custumarum*, Rolls series (1859–62) part 1, pp. xxxv–xxxix, 61–3. *Hansisches Urkundenbuch*, III, p. 391 also printed the same text. Mary Bateson printed a slightly different text from BL Add. MS 14252 (fos. 99b–101a) with a parallel text from a Guildhall MS, *Liber Ordinacionum*. Mary Bateson, 'A London municipal collection of the reign of John', 17

Other groups of texts, which are known respectively as *Libertas Londonienses* (*c.* 1133–54) and *Consuetudines* (not earlier than 1155), also confirm that tight control was exercised against foreign merchants who came to London to do business.[32] Why were these foreign merchants under such restrictions? Had they been English, would they have been immune from these restrictions? There is nothing original about our claim that the 'liberties' of a medieval city were extended only to its burgesses and their heirs.[33] Liberties of a city meant, among other things, that its burgesses enjoyed monopolistic control of commercial activities within the city. The records of the borough court of Norwich support the conclusion that 'in the early Leet Rolls, [the liberty of the city] refers exclusively to trade. One who is "de libertate" may freely trade; no one else may.'[34] According to *Liber albus* of London, merchants who were not of the liberty of London (*mercatores qui non sunt de libertate etc.*) were prohibited

---

English Historical Review (1902) 495–502. H. T. Riley, who edited *Liber custumarum*, thought that the text belonged to the first half of the thirteenth century. Höhlbaum in *Hansisches Urkundenbuch* suggested that the law dated from *c.* 1130. Christopher Brooke et al., *London, 800–1216: the shaping of a city* (London, 1975) pp. 258–92 contains a general discussion about foreign merchants' commercial activities in medieval London.

[32] Benjamin Thorpe thought that the *Libertas Londonienses* dated from the reign of Edward the Confessor (1042–66). Thorpe, *Ancient laws and institutes*, I, pp. 463–4. Felix Liebermann corrected this view and suggested that the text dated from *c.* 1133–54. *Die Gesetze der Angelsachsen*, I, p. 673. The *Consuetudines* appears under the heading 'Quedam civitas consuetudines sive libertates' in BL Add. MS. 14252. It is generally thought to be slightly later than the *Libertas Londonienses*. The text is printed in Bateson, 'A London municipal collection', 711–18. Terence H. Lloyd, *Alien merchants in England in the high Middle Ages* (Brighton, 1982) pp. 10–11 contains a brief discussion of the customs of London which is based on these texts.

[33] Borough charters normally stipulated that the liberties were granted to the burgesses and 'their heirs'. This was probably because it was not entirely clear whether burgesses formed a 'corporate' body which has the eternal existence transcending the deaths of its component individuals. In the absence of the legal notion of corporation, the most important legal device to cope with time was inheritance.

[34] *Leet jurisdiction in the city of Norwich during the thirteenth and fourteenth centuries*, 5 Selden Society (1891) p. lxxxvi. For various examples, see ibid., pp. xxxvii, lxxxviii, 48, 72. Ballard, *British borough charters, 1042–1216*, pp. 211–14 gives a number of clauses from the twelfth-century borough charters which also support this conclusion. On this topic in general, see Charles Gross, *The gild merchant: a contribution to British municipal history*, 2 vols. (Oxford, 1890).

from selling wine or other wares by retail within the city.[35] As far as this clause is concerned, there was little legal difference between merchants from Torksey and merchants from Antwerp in the sense that neither of them were of the liberty of London. Whether the former group of merchants were in a better legal condition than the latter is a question which cannot be answered until the contents of each merchant group's privileges have been carefully compared. To know that merchants from Torksey were an English king's subjects does not help. If merchants from Norwich, Colchester or Leicester could do business in London under fewer restrictions than merchants from Norway, it was not because they were English, but simply because they had acquired better and more comprehensive privileges.[36] In 1373, for example, the burgesses of Beverley were asked to pay tolls in York. Their goods were seized upon failure to comply with the demand. The burgesses had to defend their liberty by confronting the mayor of York with the following provision of their charter which exempted them from tolls in all of Yorkshire: 'Et sciatis quod sint liberi et quieti ab omni theloneo per totam schiram Eboraci sicut illi de Eboraco'.[37] Whether or not these merchants of Beverley were English was irrelevant. No one was asking whether they owed allegiance to the English king. All that mattered was whether they had specifically acquired the necessary liberty, and how they could prove it.

   The Norwich customs document (*c.* 1340) summarises that all this was, after all, a question of being *liberi* or *serui*: 'No one who resides in the city shall conduct mercantile activities unless he is in scot and lot of the said city and contributes to the communal aid because all those who are received into the citizenry are *liberi* and no *serui* of anybody.'[38] All other categorical divisions – such as

---

[35] *Liber albus*, Rolls series (1859) p. 143.

[36] Burgesses of royal boroughs were often granted the liberty to trade free from tolls throughout England. Borough charters for non-royal boroughs usually contain a provision which exempts the burgesses from tolls within the territory controlled by the grantor of the charter. There is no need to multiply the examples, which may be perused in Ballard, *British borough charters, 1042–1216*, pp. 180–90.

[37] *Beverley town documents*, 14 Selden Society (1900) p. 44.

[38] *Leet jurisdiction in the city of Norwich*, p. lxxxvi ('Item nullus mercandizet in ciuitate qui in eadem facit residentiam nisi sit ad lottum et scottum illius civitatis et ad communia eiusdem auxilia contribuat et quia omnes qui recipientur in parem ciuitatis sint liberi et non servi alicuius').

foreigner/Englishman; alien/subject – lose significance in light of such a text. One must not forget that a great number of people who were born in medieval England lived all their life and died without ever having been able to claim the status of *liberi* as understood by the author of the Norwich customs document. This is why Bracton could still follow Gaius and, amidst the highly patriotic current of the time,[39] say that the division between *liberi* and *serui* was the *prima diuisio personarum*.

Merchant groups' access to a city

Throughout the Middle Ages, foreign merchants kept coming to England. The volume and intensity of their contact with England may well have fluctuated depending on the economic, military and political circumstances. But the legal framework in which the contact was made remained more or less stable, though it was not static. In the remaining pages of this chapter, I shall attempt to identify this legal framework. Initially, foreign merchants' contact with the urban business centres of England seems to have taken the form of seeking an access to the liberties of a city. In 1194, for example, the merchants of Cologne obtained a charter which contained the following passage: 'that [they] shall be able freely to go to fairs in all our land and to buy and sell in London and other cities'.[40] We have already discussed the earlier charters issued to them in 1157 and 1175. The earlier ones did not contain this passage. The latter half of the passage (*emere et vendere et in villa London. et alibi*) suggests, in particular, that they managed to acquire the liberty to trade in cities. We note that the charter was not qualified by a proviso regarding the pre-existing liberties of third parties. Compare, for example, the following item of liberty which was conceded to the burgesses of Leicester in 1199: 'That they may freely and without hindrance go and return and trade throughout the whole of our land with all their goods and wares *saving to us and others our due and just customs.*'[41] Whether it was

---

[39] See in this connection Ernst Kantorowicz, '*Pro patria mori* in medieval political thought', 56 *American Historical Review* (1950–1) 472–92; Gaines Post, 'Two notes on nationalism in the Middle Ages', 9 *Traditio* (1953) 281–320.

[40] *Hansisches Urkundenbuch*, I, 22 ('quod libere possint ire ad ferias per totam terram nostram et emere et vendere et in villa London. et alibi').

[41] Ballard, *British borough charters, 1042–1216*, p. 216 ('Quod libere et sine

due to carelessness or excessive generosity, the omission of such a proviso might have put the merchants of Cologne in an exceptionally privileged position. However, the confirmation charter of 1210 put an end to this situation. We find that the grant of liberty was qualified by the proviso, 'salva libertate civitatis nostre Londoniensis'.[42] London merchants seem to have succeeded in keeping a check on the advance of Cologne merchants.

In the following decades, we see many more groups of foreign merchants obtaining the same items of liberties as were usually granted to burgesses of English boroughs. In 1230, for example, merchants from Nantes obtained a charter which provided that they might trade freely in all the king's dominions quit of all customs in coming, staying or returning, saving the liberties of the city of London and of others who had grants of earlier date.[43] A charter issued to 'all merchants of Gutland' in 1237 promises that the recipients shall be quit of all regional tolls in England.[44] In 1255, merchants of St Omer in Flanders secured a charter which provided that in all the king's lands and dominions, they and their goods, wherever they were found, should be free from arrest for any debt, unless they themselves were sureties or principals of the debt.[45] Burgesses were usually entitled to carry out summary arrest of the goods and persons of unenfranchised *extranei*.[46] Moreover, in their dealings with burgesses, *extranei* were deemed collectively responsible for debts of their colleagues from the same area.[47] Exemption from the collective responsibility was an important item of mercantile liberty which a good borough charter should not fail to mention. Burgesses of Bristol, for

---

impedimento omni eant et redeant et negotientur per totam terram nostram cum omnibus rebus et mercandisis suis *salvis nobis et aliis debitis et justis consuetudinibus'*). Emphasis supplied.

[42] *Hansisches Urkundenbuch*, I, p. 37. The proviso may have referred to the charters issued to the burgesses of London in 5 Richard I (1193), and in 1 John (1199). These charters are printed in *Liber custumarum*, part 1, pp. 248–9, 251.

[43] *Calendar of charter rolls*, I, 124–5.

[44] Ibid., 227.

[45] Ibid., 441. Regarding a similar privilege conceded to merchants of Ypres in 1232, see Lloyd, *Alien merchants*, p. 107.

[46] The distress between burgesses required a licence of the reeve. See Ballard, *British borough charters, 1042–1216*, p. 162 ('Burgensi cum Burgense namiare non liceat sine licentia prepositi'; from a charter to Wearmouth 1162, 1186).

[47] Pierre-Clément Timbal, 'Les lèttres de marque dans le droit de la France médiévale' in *L'Etranger*, part 2 (Brussels, 1958) pp. 112–13.

example, obtained the privilege as evidenced by the following clause in their charter of 1188: 'that no burgess be distrained anywhere in my land or realm for any debt unless he be the debtor or a surety'.[48]

In my view, these charters issued to foreign merchants in the earlier half of the thirteenth century indicate that foreign merchant groups were gaining access to the business opportunities of cities. Had they been concentrating on fairs only, why would they have taken the trouble to obtain these burghal liberties? Fairs did not usually involve the liberties of cities. Even if some fairs were held in urban locations, the liberties of burgesses, as we saw, were superseded by the seigneurial authority during the fair.

The *Carta mercatoria* of 1303 was the culmination of this legal development. The charter was issued to the merchants of 'Alemannie Francie Ispanie Portugalie Navarre Lumbardie Tuscie Provincie Cathalonie ducatus nostri Aquitannie Tholosanie Caturtinii Flandrie Brebantie et omnium aliarum terrarum et locorum extraneorum'.[49] In addition to the routine promise of safe-conduct, the charter specifically provides that these foreign merchant groups shall have the liberty to trade in cities: 'in civitatibus burgis et villis mercatoriis possint mercari'. Moreover, the charter abolishes the restrictions on lodging and the usual forty-day limit on the sojourn in cities: 'quod predicti mercatores in civitatibus burgis et villis predictis pro voluntate sua hospitari valeant et morari cum bonis suis'.[50]

The charter reveals further advances in foreign merchants' attempts to infiltrate into the protectionist legal regime of cities.

---

[48] There are many similar examples in Ballard, *British borough charters, 1042–1216*, pp. 161–6. The text quoted here is from p. 165 ('quod nullus burgensis alicubi in terra vel potestate mea namietur vel distringatur pro aliquo debito nisi sit debitor vel plegius').

[49] The text is printed in Norman Gras, *The early English customs system* (Cambridge, Mass., 1918) pp. 259–64.

[50] Regarding this clause, Norman Gras makes the following comment: 'Foreign merchants were to be free to live in the towns but at the pleasure of their hosts, a qualification which would easily leave open many a loophole of supervision and restraint' (ibid., p. 137). He does not seem to have taken full account of the previous legal situation where foreign merchants had to leave after forty days regardless of whether they pleased their host or not. Whether the clause could lead to arbitrary supervision and restraint was not the point. The point was that foreign merchants were now enabled to stay in cities *as long as* they kept their host satisfied.

For instance, it is provided that disputes involving the foreign merchants must be quickly resolved on a daily basis if such disputes could be dealt with by law merchant: 'celerem justitiam faciant de die in diem sine dilatione secundum legem mercatoriam de universis et singulis que per eandem legem poterunt terminari'. We may recall that the merchants of lower Lotharingia were required to answer all claims at the court of hustings of London, which was held only once a week.[51] *Liber albus* confirms that this had indeed been the practice in London and that it had caused some degree of inconvenience to foreign merchants. According to this source, one of the questions raised during the eyres of London in 5 and 15 Henry III concerned the resolution of disputes involving wayfaring merchants. The question began as follows: 'whether or not the Bailiffs of the city could determine the disputes brought by wayfaring merchants who would not be able to stay. . .'. We are told that the hearing of the case had to wait until the weekly session of the court of hustings: 'quod non solent teneri extra Hustengum'. But during those eyres, it was agreed that, from then on, the mayor and sheriffs, assisted by two or three aldermen, should hear such plaints from day to day and provide legal remedies without delay.[52] The concession offered by the *Carta mercatoria* was, therefore, not unprecedented in London. However, we may not jump into a conclusion that the concession was superfluous because we do not know the situation in other cities. Moreover, the concession of the *Carta mercatoria* had the additional merit of specifying that the trial ought to be conducted 'according to law merchant (*secundum legem mercatoriam*)'.

The *Carta mercatoria* further provided that in all cases involving foreign merchants, except criminal cases carrying a death penalty, the inquest must be done by a mixed jury as long as there was a sufficient number of foreign merchants: 'inquisicio fieri debeat sit medietas inquisicionis de eisdem mercatoribus et medietas altera de aliis probis et legalibus hominibus loci illius ubi placitum illud esse contigerit'. As we saw, foreign merchants had already been enjoying these trial procedures during the fairs.

---

[51] See above, p. 32. On the frequency of the court of hustings in London, see Ballard, *British borough charters, 1042–1216*, p. 142 ('Et husteng sedeat semel in hebdomada, videlicet die lunae'; London charter of 1131).

[52] *Liber albus*, p. 67.

When the fair was over, however, they must have been at the mercy of the borough court, whose procedures were rather biased against all unenfranchised 'extranei'. The following text of *Quedam ciuitatis consuetudines siue libertates* of London (*c.* 1155) provides a good insight:

> If a non-citizen brings a lawsuit against a citizen, the proof shall not be by non-citizens [presumably by non-citizen witnesses or oath-helpers] unless one of the witnesses or oath-helpers be of the city; and if a citizen brings a lawsuit against a non-citizen who does not have a land in the city either, the proof shall not be by [citizen] witnesses unless one of them be of the county where resides the non-citizen.[53]

The procedural arrangement described in this text must not be confused with the mixed inquest. The mixed inquest promised by the *Carta mercatoria* required that one half (*medietas*) of the jurors were to be empanelled by foreigners if one party was a foreigner. The above-quoted passage only requires that the proof shall not be by an all citizen or all non-citizen panel. If the half-foreign inquest was intended to guarantee a maximum level of fairness, the procedures described in the above passage are aimed only at a minimum level of protection from ruthless discrimination rampant in a borough court.[54]

As we saw, foreign merchants in London had already been benefiting from the procedural guarantees of a half-foreign jury in cases of contract, debt or trespass.[55] The *Carta mercatoria* extended the promise to *all* cases involving foreign merchants except criminal cases carrying a death penalty (*in omnibus generibus placitorum salvo casu criminis pro quo infligenda sit pena mortis*). In short, the *Carta mercatoria* promised that foreign merchants were to be provided with a fair and speedy legal remedy not only in

---

[53] BL Add. MS 14252, fo. 119a. The Latin text is printed in Bateson, 'A London municipal collection', 713 ('Si quis forensis hominem civitatis implacitaverit, non poterit comprobare eum per forenses nisi alter de civitate sit; et si homo civitatis forensem implacitaverit, qui [de] civitate non sit, neque in ea terram habeat, cum testibus eum probare non poterit, nisi alter sit de comitatu in quo manet').

[54] Charles Gross' explanation of the procedures of the piepowder court is not entirely satisfactory because the procedural differences – which must have existed before the *Carta mercatoria* was introduced – between a borough court and a piepowder court were not sufficiently stressed. See *Select cases concerning the law merchant, 1270–1638*, I, introduction.

[55] We quoted a passage dating from *c.* 1285 on p. 30 above.

certain limited commercial cases in fairs, but also in cities, in a
wider range of cases, and throughout the year.

Norman Gras finds it hard to believe that foreign merchants
could possibly have been given such a wide range of liberties:
'[t]he exact extent to which the merchants were permitted by local
influences to enjoy these and other similar benefits granted cannot
. . . be reckoned. Certainly the merchants received something
short of the full measure of the grant.' But he offers no evidence to
support his incredulity. Professor Maitland, on the other hand,
attempted to belittle the importance of the *Carta mercatoria* for
the study of the law of alien status: '[i]t will interest rather the
economist than the lawyer, and rather the student of the fourteenth and fifteenth centuries than the student of earlier times'.
Since he believed that the English law of alien status was the result
of military confrontations with French kings, the materials relating to peaceful commercial activities – which often contain
embarrassingly favourable treatments for foreign merchants –
were regarded as something which is best ignored. 'Mere common
law has little to do with these foreign merchants', he said. But we
see no reason to steer away from foreign merchants in studying the
law of alien status. Foreign merchants formed, after all, the most
important bulk of foreigners that came to England in the Middle
Ages. The legal problems they posed and the solutions proposed
and adopted by lawyers of the time must be studied as an
important part of the history of the law of alien status.[56]

It is true that the foreign merchants agreed to pay a higher rate
of customs duty in exchange for these liberties. Payment of higher
customs duty is clearly a legal disadvantage. Is this the beginning
of the legal discrimination against aliens? The apparent similarity
between this and the alien's legal disability is, however, deceptive.
The higher rate of customs duty, known as *Nova custuma* of 1303,
was portrayed by the contemporaries as resulting from negotiation
and mutual agreement – whether fictitious or real – between the
king and the foreign merchants. As far as the legal argument is
concerned, therefore, the unequal treatment embodied in the new
customs duty is not fundamentally different from the legal inequality between merchants of London and merchants of South-

---

[56] See Gras, *The early English customs system*, p. 259; Pollock and Maitland, *The
history of English law*, I, pp. 464–5, respectively.

ampton, for example. In all these cases, there existed legal inequality stemming from negotiation and the ensuing agreement between the grantor and the recipients of mercantile liberties. There is nothing in the nature of such a regime to distinguish foreign merchants from English merchants in a systematic manner. Sometimes, foreign merchants managed to secure a better deal than the English merchants. Always, some merchants, whether English or foreign, managed to secure a better position than others. The introduction of *Nova custuma* of 1303 did not change this fundamental structure in any way.[57]

What becomes clear, I hope, from the texts examined so far in this chapter is that the legal condition of merchants in medieval England was defined solely in terms of 'liberties'. The *Carta mercatoria* was, of course, focused solely on the liberties specifically acquired and specifically granted. Payment of higher or lower customs duty; enjoyment or loss of monopolistic control of trade in the city; imposition or removal of restrictions upon commercial activities; payment of tolls, and exemption from tolls, etc. can all be explained as a question of acquiring liberties and the degree of comprehensiveness of the liberties thus acquired. Liberties in the Middle Ages were acquired through purchase, inheritance, marriage or gift. We have no evidence yet to suppose that ethnic identity (Englishness) or political allegiance (fidelity to the king) was deemed to be a sufficient ground to claim and enjoy liberties.

Individual settlement (from the 1250s)

In the middle of the thirteenth century, there was an important change in the pattern of long-distance trade in Europe. Charter rolls provide some evidence which allows us to describe the change. In 1252, for example, a Florentine merchant, Deutayutus Willelmi, obtained a charter which provided that he and his family members might freely buy, sell and carry on business throughout the king's dominions 'just as any citizens of London (*sicut aliquis*

---

[57] Having successfully negotiated an advantageous rate of customs duty from the foreign merchants mentioned in the *Carta mercatoria* of 1303, Edward I attempted to negotiate a similarly increased rate of customs duty from some of the English merchants. This attempt was unsuccessful. See W. Stubbs, *The constitutional history of England*, 3 vols., vol. II, 3rd edn (Oxford, 1887) p. 164.

civum nostrorum London.)'. It was further provided that he and his heirs should be in the gild merchant of the city and that they should have other liberties and free customs which the citizens of London had.[58] In short, the charter confirmed that the recipient was given all the liberties of a citizen of London. From then on, we find many similar examples. Alwyn Ruddock mentions a few Italian merchants known to have held lands and houses in Southampton in the latter half of the thirteenth century. Fornari de Lucca, for example, was married to the heiress of a leading burgess of the city. T. H. Lloyd gives references to one John Brilond who was styled as citizen of Lübeck and London in the 1260s, and to one Gerard Merbode, son of Merbode of Dortmund, who was styled as citizen of London in the 1280s. Professor Lloyd also mentions certain Flemmings who were reputed 'denizens' in *c.* 1270. Alice Beardwood too notes that Peter Bonyn of Flanders became a citizen of London in 1271.[59]

These cases seem to allow us to make the following generalisation: until the first half of the thirteenth century, mercantile liberties were negotiated by groups of foreign merchants themselves. Those merchants actually came to England, secured the necessary liberties and carried out commercial activities themselves. By the middle of the thirteenth century, this practice seems to have lapsed into disuse. Instead, foreign merchant groups began to rely more and more on resident agents in England rather than coming to England and trading for themselves. This explains the increasing number of *individual* foreign merchants settling down in cities permanently. In short, merchants ceased to be travellers. They became city-dwellers. Sooner or later, the urban power structure was to be in their hands. Their transformation

---

[58] *Calendar of charter rolls*, I, 407. See also Public Record Office, Charter roll, 37 Henry III m. 21, which gives the following text: 'quod ipsi cum propria familia sua adeo libere et quiete emere possint vendere et negotiari . . . per totam potestatem nostram sicut aliquis civum nostrorum London'. The reference to the gild merchant is enigmatic because London did not in fact have a gild merchant. Professor T. H. Lloyd kindly drew my attention to this point.

[59] See, respectively, Alwyn Ruddock, *Italian merchants and shipping in Southampton, 1270–1600* (Southampton, 1951) pp. 120–1; T. H. Lloyd, *England and the German Hanse, 1157–1611: a study of their trade and commercial diplomacy* (Cambridge, 1991) pp. 44–5; Lloyd, *Alien merchants*, p. 13; Alice Beardwood, 'Mercantile antecedents of the English naturalization laws', 16 *Medievalia et Humanistica* (1964) 69.

(from wayfarers to city-dwellers) was accompanied by remarkable changes in their lifestyle and business pattern.[60]

The new trend was also reflected in the *Carta mercatoria* of 1303. The foreign merchant groups enumerated in the charter were permitted to do wholesale trade 'as well with the native, indigenous merchants as with the foreign, non-citizen merchants or agents (*tam cum indigenis seu incolis eiusdem regni et potestatis nostre predicte quam cum alienigenis extraneis vel privatis*)'. Until then, I suppose, foreign merchants' commercial activities in cities were limited to wholesale transactions with the native merchants (*cum indigenis*). Why then did foreign merchants want to do wholesale trade with *alienigenis extraneis vel privatis* as well? The word 'agent (*privatus*)' provides a clue.[61] Permission for wholesale trade 'cum alienigenis extraneis vel privatis' meant that foreign merchant groups were allowed to transfer their goods to their resident agents. These resident agents, as we saw in the case of Deutayutus Willelmi, might have already acquired the liberties to do retail business in a city 'just as any citizen (*sicut aliquis civum*)' of the same city. Probably not all foreign merchant groups had their own resident agent in England. Some merchant groups from Spain, for example, may have hired, on an *ad hoc* basis, an Italian merchant who had acquired the liberties of, say, London. Also, foreign merchant groups certainly did not have a resident agent in *every* city in England. There may have been occasions when a Hanse merchant who was resident in Sandwich, for example, was requested to go to Southampton to act as an agent of Portuguese

---

[60] Alwyn Ruddock calls it a 'revolution' in the method of long-distance trade. *Italian merchants and shipping*, p. 117. See also Lloyd, *Alien merchants*, p. 77; and, generally, R. S. Lopez, *The commercial revolution of the Middle Ages, 950–1350* (New Jersey, 1971). The development of the banking system may also be discussed in this connection. By the late thirteenth century, merchants completely took over the position of the urban ruling class. Rodney H. Hilton, *English and French towns in feudal society – a comparative study* (Cambridge, 1992) p. 18. Regarding the situation in Florence, Genoa, Venice and Milan, see Yves Renouard, *Les Hommes d'affaires Italiens du moyen âge* (Paris, 1968) pp. 110ff. During the preceding centuries, however, it is debatable whether the urban patricians were mainly composed of merchants. Henri Pirenne argued that the origin of medieval European towns must be sought in the revitalisation of the merchant population. Henri Pirenne, *Les Villes et les institutions urbaines*, 2 vols., 2nd edn (Paris, 1939). Paul Hohenberg et al., *The making of urban Europe, 1000–1950* (Cambridge, Mass., 1985) question Pirenne's thesis.

[61] According to the *Revised medieval Latin word-list from British and Irish sources*, ed. R. E. Latham (London, 1965), *privatus* meant 'close friend' or 'confidant'.

merchants. The phrase 'cum alienigenis extraneis vel privatis'
adopted by the *Carta mercatoria* can be interpreted to encompass
all these possible situations.[62]

The impact of allowing the foreign merchants to trade with
their resident agents can be better appreciated when we look at the
sources which appeared in Edward II's reign. The impressive
range of privileges granted by Edward I to a large number of
foreign merchant groups was certainly not well received by
English merchants. Soon after the death of Edward I, therefore,
the *Carta mercatoria* was declared illegal by the Ordainers in 1311
in a rather chaotic political climate. Both the privileges enumerated in the charter and the burdens of the higher rate of customs
duty (*Nova custuma*) fell in abeyance thereafter, only to be
selectively restored in the reign of Edward III.[63] Consider, then,
the following passage from *Liber albus* of London: 'that inquiry
shall be made each year, if any persons enjoying the freedom of
the city have traded with the property of others who are not of the
freedom, avowing that such goods are their own. And those who
shall be lawfully convicted thereof, shall lose the freedom.'[64] This
clause is from Edward II's charter to the burgesses of London. It
clearly indicates that London merchants would no longer put up
with the wholesale transfer of goods between foreign merchants
and their agent who was *de libertate civitatis* of London, which
was precisely what the *Carta mercatoria* allowed. Although the
precise date of this charter of Edward II is not available, I believe
that it appeared when the *Carta mercatoria* was no longer in
effect.[65]

The economic advantage of having resident agents has already
been noted by Alwyn Ruddock: 'Whereas the visiting merchant

---

[62] A foreign merchant who had acquired the liberties of a city might still be
perceived as *alienigena*. The term 'alienigena' referred to the ethnic identity of a
person. It did not have much to do with the person's legal status as a free-man of
a city.

[63] Stubbs, *The constitutional history of England*, pp. 344–5.

[64] *Liber albus*, p. 142 ('quod quolibet anno inquiratur si qui de libertate civitatis
exercuerint bona aliorum qui non sunt de libertate, advocando bona illa sua
propria bona esse. Et illi que inde legitime convicti fuerint, libertatem amit-
tant'). The translation is from *The white book of the city of London*, trans. Henry
T. Riley (London, 1861) p. 127.

[65] See also *Calendar of letter-books ... at the Guildhall, Letter Book E, c.
1314–1337*, ed. R. R. Sharpe (London, 1903) pp. 42, 45 (both entries are
datable as post-1314) and *Liber albus*, p. 264 (undatable).

was obliged to let his goods go comparatively cheaply when the arrival of a ship with a large cargo brought down prices in the neighbourhood, the resident agent could bide his time and hold back his merchandise until prices reverted to normal again'.[66]

Hildebrand Suderman – a case study

Individual settlement of foreign merchants in English cities continued well into the fourteenth century. In this connection, we will discuss the letters patent issued during 1324–35 to an influential Hanse merchant, Hildebrand Suderman. Unlike earlier letters patent to foreign merchants who had similar requests to Suderman's, the letters patent issued to this Hanse merchant contain no reference to the liberties of any particular city. In June 1324, for example, Suderman obtained the liberties to trade as the king's merchant (*ut mercator noster*). It was further provided in the charter that he should be able freely to carry out other business of his own as if he were a native of the kingdom (*velut indigena regni et potestatis*). The same liberties were promised again in 1335.[67]

So far, these documents have been treated as 'precursors' of the letters of denization. Clive Parry, for example, argued that the letters patent issued to foreign merchants in the fourteenth century should be viewed as the 'innominate forerunners' of later letters of denization. According to Alice Beardwood, these documents would form the 'mercantile antecedents' of later letters of denization. The same attitude can be found in the writings of Philippe Dollinger, who regarded these documents as evidence of

---

[66] Ruddock, *Italian merchants and shipping*, p. 119.

[67] *Calendar of patent rolls, 1321–1324*, p. 280 (1323, safe-conduct), p. 407 (April 1324, safe-conduct as well as exemption from the arrest of goods on account of others' debt), p. 434 (June 1324, grant, during pleasure, of liberties to trade 'velut indigena'); *Calendar of patent rolls, 1324–1327*, p. 128 (1325, the previous grant extended for life); *Calendar of patent rolls, 1327–1330*, p. 448 (1329, grant of 1325 reconfirmed); *Calendar of patent rolls, 1334–1338*, pp. 187, 192 (exemption from the higher rate of customs duty). As a leading Hanse merchant in London, he is a well-known figure both then and now. Alice Beardwood, *Alien merchants in England 1350–1377: their legal and economic position* (Cambridge, Mass., 1931) p. 61 and Lloyd, *England and the German Hanse*, p. 35 discuss various materials relating to him in great detail. See also Public Record Office, Patent rolls, 17 Edward II, part 2, m. 5; 9 Edward III, part 2, m. 4 for the original Latin text which contains the phrase 'velut indigena regni et potestatis'.

the mechanism of acquiring English nationality.[68] The expression
'velut indigena' seems to have encouraged such an interpretation.
However, to translate 'indigena' into 'denizen' and to treat these
documents as precedents of the letters of denization would
amount to abandoning the task of historical analysis and replacing
it with an uncritical lexicographical operation. Words do not carry
fixed values which can be transferred into another language across
a long span of time. Not only do we need to examine the precise
circumstances under which the term 'indigena' began to appear in
these documents, but also the legal reasoning underlying the
deployment of this particular word would have to be explained
before a decision is made to translate 'indigena' into 'denizen'.

We have already encountered the word *indigena* in the *Carta
mercatoria*: 'tam cum indigenis seu incolis eiusdem regni . . .
quam cum alienigenis extraneis vel privatis'. There is no doubt
that 'indigenae' did not mean *all* native Englishmen. A large
number of native Englishmen had never enjoyed the mercantile
liberties, and they could under no circumstances be included in
the referent of the term 'indigenae' here. Can the word 'denizen'
adequately bring out this situation? The expression 'denizen' or
'denization' comes with an implicit suggestion that the division
between alien and denizen should be of superior importance
compared to other personal legal divisions among the inhabitants
of England. This can hardly be the case during the period that
concerns us here. From the legal point of view, to be a 'denizen' in
medieval England could not have meant much. On the other
hand, whether one was an unfree tenant of a farm land or a
merchant free-man of a city did make a big difference. No sensible
person would have paid good money to obtain the 'denizen status'
in medieval England even if such a thing did exist. Mercantile
liberties, on the other hand, were worth paying for. In fact, the
above-mentioned documents were about the mercantile liberties
acquired by Hildebrand Suderman. This Hanse merchant was
therefore no different from Deutayutus Willelmi, who, as we saw,

---

[68] Clive Parry, *British nationality law and the history of naturalization* (hereafter,
History of naturalization) (Milan, 1954) pp. 9, 18, 24–5. Beardwood, 'Mercantile
antecedents'. Philippe Dollinger, *La Hanse, XIIe–XVIIe siècles* (Paris, 1964)
p. 77: 'L'acquisition de la nationalité anglaise, dont l'exemple le plus ancien
connu remonte à 1309, se fit d'abord sous la forme de l'admission à la
bourgeoisie d'une ville.'

obtained the same kind of liberties in 1252 which permitted him to trade freely just as any 'citizens' of London (*sicut aliquis* civum *nostrorum London.*). If that was the case, why did the letters patent in the early fourteenth century choose the word '*indigena*' rather than '*civis*'?[69]

The following events may be considered in this connection. In 1312, the free-men of London petitioned that unknown strangers should be admitted only upon production of a certificate of London merchants whose trade they wished to enter.[70] In 1319, London merchants managed to impose the requirement that the admission to the liberty of the city should be effected only in the hustings with the consent of the free-men of the city.[71] In 1326, all foreigners who had been admitted to the liberty of London were removed from it. It was further ordained that henceforth the admission should be on the security of six reputable men of the trade through which the person sought entry into the liberty of the city.[72] These events indicate that the free-men of London were increasingly sensitive to the king's practice of selling mercantile liberties to foreign merchants. Suderman's letters patent (1324–35) were drawn up in these years when it was politic to avoid a specific mention of London. But the legal rigour of the concept of 'civis' in medieval England did not allow the possibility of using the word unaccompanied by a specific reference to a particular city. *Civis* had always to be accompanied by a reference to 'such and such a city' because the contents of the liberties differed from city to city.[73] Under these circumstances, 'velut

[69] There are plenty of examples where the recipient of mercantile liberties was specifically referred to as a 'burgess' of a particular borough rather than as an 'indigena' of the realm. See *British borough charters, 1216–1307*, ed. A. Ballard and James Tait (Cambridge, 1923) pp. 137–8. Beardwood, 'Mercantile antecedents', p. 69 also gives a couple of examples.

[70] *Calendar of Letter Book E*, p. 13. The reference is from Beardwood, *Alien merchants*, p. 68.

[71] *Calendar of Letter Book E*, p. 214; *Liber albus*, p. 142 ('quod nullus alienigena in libertatem civitatis praedictae admittatur, nisi in Hustengo').

[72] *Liber albus*, p. 142 ('quod indigena, et praecipue Anglicus, mercator de certo mistero vel officio in libertatem civitatis praedictae non admittatur, nisi per manucaptionem sex proborum hominum de certo mistero vel officio, etc.'). See Beardwood, *Alien merchants*, p. 68 for further references.

[73] For this reason, we find it preferable to render 'civis' into 'burgess'. The word 'citizen' – if it is used without a reference to a particular city – is prone to confusion. The modern concept of 'citizen' must be sharply distinguished from the medieval notion of 'civis'. Different medieval cities had different legal

indigena' must have proved preferable precisely because of its vagueness. The protest of London merchants was effectively dealt with by replacing the precise legal term 'civis' with a deliberately ambiguous term 'indigena'. This point has already been noted by Philippe Dollinger.[74]

A comparison with the *lettres de bourgeoisie* issued in France during the same period produces some good results. The trend of individual merchants' settlement in cities appears to be confirmed in France as well. From the middle of the thirteenth century, we find references to 'bourgeois du roi'.[75] Many of them were foreign merchants who managed to obtain mercantile liberties from the king.[76] Both in England and in France, the essential contents of the letters patent issued during this period were mercantile liberties. For example, the *lettre de bourgeoisie* issued to Jacques Barthélémy of Florence (1325) promised the liberties 'to remain, come and go, to be engaged in commerce and other legitimate transactions'.[77] Unlike in England, however, the French *lettres de bourgeoisie* did not opt for the vague expression 'velut indigena'. We find unequivocal statements that the recipient was to have these liberties 'ut burgens'.[78] Why?

environments for business. T. H. Lloyd, for example, notes that London handled considerably less than half of all foreign trade until the end of the thirteenth century. He suggests that it was probably because of the particularly restrictive legal environment for business in London compared to other cities. Lloyd, *Alien merchants*, p. 12.

[74] He recognised that foreign merchants in England initially obtained mercantile liberties 'sous la forme de l'admission à la bourgeoisie d'une ville'. He then went on to point out, 'La pratique ayant suscité des difficultés, la couronne en vint, depuis 1324, à conférer à des étrangers l'"indigénat" leur reconnaissant l'égalité des droits et des privilèges économiques avec les marchands anglais dans toute l'étendue du royaume.' Dollinger, *La Hanse*, pp. 77–8.

[75] Jacques Boizet, *Les Lettres de naturalité sous l'ancien régime* (Paris, 1943) p. 22.

[76] More details can be found in Léon Mirot, *La Colonie lucquoise à Paris du XIIIe siècle au XVe siècle* (Paris, 1927); C. Piton, *Les Lombards en France et à Paris*, 2 vols. (Paris, 1893); Edmond René Labande, 'De quelques Italiens établis en Languedoc sous Charles V' in *Mélanges d'histoire du moyen âge: dédiés à la mémoire de Louis Halphen* (Paris, 1951) pp. 359–67.

[77] For the entire text and reference, see Boizet, *Les Lettres de naturalité*, p. 169 ('quod . . . morari conservari ire redire incedere mercaturas aliosque contractus licitos exercere valeant').

[78] There are many examples: 'ut ceteri burgenses et mercatores regni nostri tractetur' (1312); 'quod gaudeat omni privilegio libertate qua alii originarii burgenses de Rupella gaudent' (1322); 'quod de inceps non ut Ytalici, sed ut cives et regnicole nostri quantum ad omnia reputentur' (1324); '[q]uodque . . . possint contrahere et quoscumque contractus licitos exercere sicut ceteri nostri

First, there is enough evidence indicating that royal intervention in the affairs of towns and communes in France became a regular event from the end of the thirteenth century.[79] By 1358, we find Charles V, the prince regent, declaring: 'To our father and to us who represent him belongs exclusively the right to create and constitute cities and communes'.[80] As a result of this development, there was no meaningful distinction between royal boroughs and seigneurial boroughs in late medieval France. All towns and communes were under the direct authority of the king. This may be one of the reasons why French kings enjoyed the unchallenged power to sell mercantile liberties to a stranger and make him a *bourgeois du roi*.

Second, one may turn to the very concept of *bourgeois du roi*, that is, a burgess of no particular borough. In England, the political and administrative power of the kings during the twelfth and thirteenth centuries allowed them to make impressive promises. Burgesses of a royal borough in England could obtain mercantile liberties which were effective throughout the kingdom (*per totam terram et potestatem Regis*). French kings, on the other hand, were not in the position to make such promises during that period. Consequently, *bourgeois* of various seigneurial boroughs often entered into an agreement (*traité d'entrecours*) whereby one's 'parochial' liberties were recognised in the other's borough, and *vice versa*.[81] That, of course, was one way of coping with the increased business need within the fragmented legal environment of medieval France. Another method which became popular from the middle of the thirteenth century was to obtain the *lettre de bourgeoisie* and become a *bourgeois du roi*. Jacques Boizet notes that in many cases, the recipient of the *lettre de bourgeoisie* had already

---

burgenses dicti loci' (1328); 'et qu'ils jouissent et puissent et doyent jouir de toutes et teles franchises, privileges, libertez et coutumes come ioissent et ont accoustume a ioir nos autres bourgeois de Paris et de nostre dit royaume' (1341). All these *lettres de bourgeoisie* are printed in Boizet, *Les Lettres de naturalité*, pp. 165–80.

79 On this topic in general, see C. Petit-Dutaillis, *Les Communes françaises: caractères et évolution des origines au XVIIIe siècle* (Paris, 1947).

80 *Ordonnances des roys de France de la troisième race* . . ., vol. III (1355–64), ed. D.-F. Secousse (Paris, 1732) 305 ('Au roi notre père et à nous qui le représentons appartient exclusivement le droit de créer et de constituer des consulats et des communes'). Quoted from Achille Luchaire, *Les Communes françaises à l'époque des Capétiens directs* (Paris, 1911) p. 271.

81 Boizet, *Les Lettres de naturalité*, p. 30.

been enjoying the mercantile liberties of his own borough. But
these merchants wanted to expand the horizon of their business
activities. *Lettre de bourgeoisie* was, therefore, a personalised mercantile institution whereby the recipient obtained the liberties to
carry out the business in most part of the kingdom of France
('ubicumque in regnis nostris . . . exceptis terris et locis rebellium
nostrarum'[82]). Du Cange seems to have been aware of this history.
He noted that the essence of being *'burgenses regis'* was to have the
freedom of movement within the realm: 'Burgenses de percursu
iidem qui burgenses regis'.[83] This, we believe, is why merchants,
whether foreign or not, could continue to acquire mercantile
liberties 'ut burgenses' without causing any legal problems in
France. As the concept of *bourgeois du roi* – burgess of no
particular borough – was firmly in place, there was no need to seek
a subterfuge in the vague expression 'velut indigena'.

At any rate, the expression 'velut indigena regni' quickly fell out
of use in England. Consider, for example, the letters patent issued
to a Lombardian merchant, Benedict Zacharie, in 1365.[84] The
document is similar to the letters patent issued to Suderman in
1335 in the sense that it is focused on the exemption from the
higher customs duty. But the mention of 'indigena' is now
completely dropped. The text is composed entirely in terms of the
'liberties' of London. Benedict Zacharie is described as a merchant
free-man of London (mercator London. . . . liber homo eiusdem
civitatis') permanently dwelling there with a house, a wife and
children. It is further recited that he is in scot and lot of the city
and pays other dues touching the city just like any other citizens of
London. In consideration thereof, he is exempted from the higher
rate of customs duty as long as he remains a citizen of London.
The logic is that he should not pay more than what other citizens
of London pay: 'quod plus quam alii cives dicte civitatis indigene

---

[82] From the *lettre de bourgeoisie* issued to Jacques Barthélémy of Florence (1325).

[83] Quoted from Boizet, 'Les lettres de naturalité', p. 30. The same business need
was met in England in a different way. In 1275, for example, the Statute of
Westminster I *c.* 23 formally ended the system of inter-municipal reprisals
against English merchants in England. See *The charters of the borough of
Cambridge*, ed., F. W. Maitland and M. Bateson (Cambridge, 1901) p. xix. As a
result, there never developed the concept of 'burgenses regis' in England (except
for occasional references to 'mercator noster').

[84] *Calendar of patent rolls, 1364–1367*, p. 103. The Latin text is printed in
Beardwood, 'Mercantile antecedents', pp. 74–5.

pro custumis mercandisarum et aliorum bonorum suorum nobis solvunt solvere non teneantur'. There is nothing new about this argument. Already in 1252, Deutayutus Willelmi was promised that he would not be tallaged any more than other citizens of London. In all these cases, the question has always been about the liberties of a city, and the most important division was between those who had these liberties and those who did not. Allegiance to the king, ethnic identity, alien or subject status had no role to play in this legal approach.[85]

Our argument may be summarised as follows. The remarkable change of business strategy for intra-European long-distance trade in the mid-thirteenth century required many individual foreign merchants to settle down in English cities. The charters we have examined show how these foreigners, now finding themselves in the position of permanent residents of a city, coped with various problem situations arising in connection with their settlement and trade in the restrictive urban legal environment. From the beginning to the end, the most important concept was 'liberties' of a city; and the most important legal distinction was between 'liberi' (who had liberties) and 'serui' (who did not have them). It would, of course, be wrong to imagine that the contemporaries could not tell the difference between foreign and English merchants. Moreover, there is some likelihood that this difference may have resulted in dissimilar legal treatments. For example, English merchants of a city who went to another city in England on business did not have to go to a host or leave the city after the forty-day period as foreign merchants had to. As these visiting English merchants were no doubt unenfranchised outsiders of the city they were visiting, like any foreign merchants, the absence of the lodging restriction applicable to them may suggest that some legal distinction was being made between English visiting merchants and foreign visiting merchants.[86] But this does not under-

---

[85] For more examples indicating that the exemption from the higher rate of customs duty was 'propter libertatem civitatis', see Beardwood, *Alien merchants*, p. 69.

[86] Professor Terence Lloyd kindly pointed this out to me. I believe, however, that one must not rule out the possibility that the Statute of Westminster I *c.* 23, though it was mainly about the cessation of inter-municipal reprisals, might have been understood in a broader manner to cover the question of sojourn and lodging as well. If that was the case, the differential legal treatment between the visiting English merchants and foreign merchants can be satisfactorily explained

mine our conclusion that the legal consequences stemming from the division between Englishmen and foreigners were implicit, ill-defined and unsystematic. No attempt was made to explain or justify the differential treatment other than by the immediate obviousness of the perceived difference. The difference was not objectified; it was not expressed in an explicit and coherent argument. We must wait until the discriminatory legal treatment of foreigners is backed by a consistent and explicit argument before concluding that the law of alien status has begun.

We do not propose to take issue with those who wish to see the 'English nation' taking shape in the collective imagination of medieval London merchants. Nor does it matter to us whether the fourteenth-century customs collectors began to realise their true identity as the natural-born subjects of the English king. Whether or not that was the case, our point is simply that the basic framework of legal analysis did not show any sign of departure from the *summa diuisio personarum* between *liberi* and *serui*.

A NEW APPROACH

What separates the letters patent issued in the reign of Richard II – especially after the 1380s, when Canon lawyers dominated the Chancery staff[87] – from the ones we have so far examined defies all attempts at a rational explanation. Alice Beardwood has noted that the letters patent issued in the reign of Richard II were considerably different from the earlier ones. But her studies were based on the assumption that the English law of alien status began with the loss of Normandy and that it was already well in place by the late thirteenth century. Therefore, her aim was not to investigate the beginning of the law of alien status itself, but to trace the beginning of denization – an institution which she assumed to

---

in terms of the 'liberties' of a city. No reference to ethnicity or allegiance would be necessary then. It is also possible that the absence of the lodging restriction applicable to the visiting English merchants was simply due to the fact that it was unusual for English merchants to stay in another English town for such a long time.

[87] John H. Baker, *An introduction to English legal history*, p. 119. See also A. L. Brown, *The early history of the clerkship of the Council* (Glasgow, 1969) who observes that the records of the King's Council were 'dramatically transformed' (p. 1) in the reign of Richard II.

have appeared *after* the law of alien status had been well established. In 1911 William Shaw had undertaken a study with the same assumptions and aim, and suggested that the settled form for the letters of denization first appeared at the beginning of the fifteenth century.[88] Alice Beardwood merely attempted to argue that the date proposed by Shaw should be moved back by a quarter of a century. Before Alice Beardwood's article appeared in 1964, Clive Parry had also taken issue with Shaw's article and suggested that the mid-fourteenth-century letters patent granting the liberties of a city should all be regarded as 'forerunners' of later letters of denization. Philippe Dollinger, as I pointed out earlier, went even further and claimed that the first instance of denization in England began to appear as early as 1309. We have already discussed the inadequacy of these arguments.[89] I believe that the letters patent issued to foreign merchants from the 1380s onwards must be analysed from a fresh perspective. They may be able to show how the argument for systematic legal discrimination against alien merchants was introduced for the first time. We may be able to see that its introduction took the form of a rupture, a sudden and complete departure from the existing pattern of legal argument.

Among a number of letters patent issued during this period, I choose – mainly for ease of reference – to discuss the one issued to John Swart (1397).[90] The focus of John Swart's letters patent was that he was to be treated just as one of the king's liege-men: 'ipse decetero tractetur et in omnibus teneatur sicut unus de veris et fidelibus ligeis nostris'. Of course, this passage alone will not

---

[88] *Letters of denization and acts of naturalization for aliens in England and Ireland 1603–1700*, ed. William A. Shaw (Lymington, 1911) p. iii.

[89] Parry, *History of naturalization*, pp. 24–5. Beardwood, 'Mercantile antecedents', *passim*. See also Beardwood, *Alien merchants*, p. 65. Dollinger, *La Hanse*, pp. 77–8. See note 68 above.

[90] The full Latin text can be found in Beardwood, 'Mercantile antecedents', p. 75. Alternatively, see *Calendar of patent rolls, 1381–1385*, p. 413 (letters patent issued to Adam Hill in 1384), p. 581 (Henry Kerle, 1385); *Calendar of patent rolls, 1385–1389*, p. 53 (John de Hill, 1385); *Calendar of patent rolls, 1388–1392*, p. 23 (Edmond Arnaud, 1389), p. 318 (Henry Shafot, 1390), p. 361 (John Moner, 1390); *Calendar of patent rolls, 1391–1396*, p. 9 (Bartholomew Basan of Luca, 1391), p. 285 (Godfrey van Upstall of Brabant, 1393); *Calendar of patent rolls, 1396–1399*, p. 84 (John Swart, 1397), p. 176 (John Banam of France, 1397), p. 463 (Ernest Ruden of Germany, 1399). Most of these entries have already been mentioned by Parry, *History of naturalization*, p. 24.

justify our claim that his letters patent marked an abrupt and complete departure from the well-established trend. On the surface, there is little difference between 'sicut unus de . . . fidelibus ligeis nostris' and 'velut indigena regni et potestatis nostris' (from Suderman's letters patent of 1324). We need to look further.

(1) John Swart's letters patent went on to state that he was to be able to acquire lands, tenements, rents and other possessions in England, having and holding them permanently for himself, for his heirs and assignees: 'et quod ipse terras et tenementa redditus et alias possessiones quecumque infra idem regnum nostrum adquirere possit habenda et tenenda sibi heredibus et assignatis suis imperpetuum'. Does this mean that he was unable until then to acquire lands, tenements, etc.? If foreign merchants had all along been able to acquire lands, tenements, etc., then what was the point of making such a statement? Should we therefore conclude – as most historians have done – that foreigners were unable to acquire lands, etc. in England?

The immediate obstacle to such a conclusion would be the letters patent issued to Benedict Zacharie in 1365. There, Zacharie was described as having already acquired the status of a free-man of London when he applied for the letters patent. If he had not been able to acquire some form of burgage tenement, we wonder how he acquired a house and became a free-man of the city. By breathing the air of the city for over a year? T. H. Lloyd gives numerous examples of Italian merchants in the late thirteenth and early fourteenth centuries who were citizens of London and elsewhere.[91] Alice Beardwood put together a list of some seventy-five foreign merchants who were free-men of London and other cities during 1350–77.[92] We also note a passage from *Liber custumarum*, which provides that 'merchant strangers good, lawful, and sufficient who shall wish to enjoy the franchise of London shall have the same'.[93] How did they all become free-men of a city, remain in scot and lot, and pay subsidies levied on the

---

[91] Lloyd, *Alien merchants*, pp. 174ff.
[92] Beardwood, *Alien merchants*, appendix.
[93] *Liber custumarum*, part 1, pp. 220–1.

immovable if they were unable to acquire lands and tenements? Were they all 'exceptional' cases? Had they all secured
'denization' before they became free-men of a city? Or were
burgage tenements given a different legal treatment so that
foreigners could acquire them without restriction? We are able
to offer at least one example which seems to disprove all these
suppositions.

John Adam was an apothecary from Lucca. In 1350, he and
John Pynselegle of Genoa appeared in the Surrey feet of fines
as the parties to a transaction of land.[94] Two years later, he
appeared in the patent roll. He obtained the letters patent to
be exempt from the higher rate of customs duty applicable to
foreign merchants.[95] In other words, he was engaged in a land
transaction *before* he obtained the exemption from the higher
rate of customs duty – a measure which is usually regarded as
the evidence of 'denization'. The land was probably not a
burgage tenement either. Surrey and Middlesex were the
favourite counties for London merchants. When they felt that
they had become sufficiently rich, they went there to acquire
land to provide for the future of their wives and children.[96]

(2) John Swart's letters patent continue to state that he shall be
able to have all kinds of actions, real as well as personal, and to
bring or answer complaints in whatever manner: 'et quod ipse
omnimodas acciones tam reales quam personales in quibuscumque querelis habere possit ac placitare et responderi modo
quo'. Does this mean that he was unable to bring any lawsuit
until then? Even personal actions such as covenant, debt,
trespass, etc.? What about the procedures of piepowder court
which we have discussed? What about all those provisions

---

[94] Frank Lewis, Pedes finium; *or fines relating to the county of Surrey* (Guildford,
1894) p. 121. Ralph Nevill, 'Surrey feet of fines', 13 *Surrey Archaeological
Collection* (1897), pp. 139–40.

[95] *Calendar of patent rolls, 1350–1354*, p. 196 (13 January 1352).

[96] Sylvia Thrupp, *The merchant class of medieval London, 1300–1500* (Chicago,
1948) pp. 122, 284. In the county of Surrey alone, the names appearing in the
feet of fines strongly suggest that a further search and comparison with Patent
rolls will produce more examples of foreign merchants' land acquisition.
However, multiplication of examples is not of vital importance to our argument
that foreigners were under no legal restriction in purchasing and holding land in
medieval England. We approach this topic from a different perspective in the
following chapters.

about the mixed jury?[97] Should we understand that the above-quoted passage was focused exclusively on the king's court; and, therefore, the legal remedies of the piepowder court were irrelevant? Alice Beardwood's work (1931) makes it unnecessary for us to go over this ground again. We rely on her conclusion that foreign merchants were free and able to sue all manner of personal actions in the king's court as well as in the Chancery and in the Exchequer until the end of Edward III's reign.[98]

What about real actions? Should we follow the universally accepted opinion that foreigners were unable to bring real actions in England?[99] That would mean that even if they could acquire houses (burgage tenements), they had no means of defending or claiming them. Take the passage from the *Carta mercatoria* of 1303 which promises a mixed inquest for foreign merchants 'in all cases (*in omnibus generibus placitorum*) involving foreign merchants except criminal cases carrying a death penalty'. Are we to believe that real actions were not among the *omnibus generibus placitorum*? Or should we just say – as many historians do – that foreign merchants were simply not interested in real property while domestic merchants were obsessed with land?[100]

(3) Finally, John Swart's letters patent promise that he shall be as free and entire (*libere et integre*) as any of the king's liege-men originating from this kingdom, unencumbered by distur-

---

[97] See above, pp. 30–1, 38–9.

[98] Beardwood, *Alien merchants*, pp. 80ff. See also *Select cases in the court of King's Bench under Edward I*, vol. I, 55 Selden Society (1936), pp. 78–7 (1281).

[99] Beardwood argues as follows: 'aliens had practically the same rights in private law as subjects had, excluding, of course, real actions'. See *Alien merchants*, p. 80. Even though she herself noted that foreigners were bequeathing lands in London (ibid., p. 61), she did not think it necessary to question the canonical view that aliens were unable to bring real actions.

[100] Professor Maitland suggested as follows: 'they [foreign merchants] do not come here to settle; they do not want land; they would be well content were they permitted to lodge where they pleased'. Pollock and Maitland, *The history of English law*, I, p. 464. Beardwood, *Alien merchants*, pp. 61–2, 78, repeats the same view: '[foreign merchants] were not likely to be concerned in cases arising out of the ownership or possession of land'. On the other hand, the overwhelming importance of land for London merchants is demonstrated by Thrupp, *The merchant class*, pp. 122ff. Jacques Le Goff also mentions 'préoccupations terriennes des hommes d'affaires médiévaux'. Le Goff, *Marchands et banquiers*, p. 8.

bances and demands made by the king, his heirs or his servants: 'adeo libere et integre sicut unus de ligeis nostris infra dictum regnum nostrum oriundus absque perturbacione seu impeticione nostri vel heredum nostrorum aut ministrorum nostrorum quorumcumque'. The mention of mercantile liberties such as 'emere et vendere' or 'negotia sua facere possit' is silently dropped from Swart's letters patent. Instead of the tedious, but precise enumeration of 'thelonio, pontagio, muragio, etc.', we find only the vague expression, 'perturbacione seu impeticione'. It appears moreover that the 'perturbacione seu impeticione' referred only to the customs and other demands made by the king or his officers. In fact, the mention of regional tolls was completely deleted. Does it mean that England suddenly became a 'toll-free' zone? Also, instead of the well-established cliché 'the recipient shall be free and quit (*libere et quiete*) of tolls, pontages, etc.', we see a different expression, 'free and entire (*libere et integre*)'. It is no longer a question of whether one would or would not have to pay particular tolls and customs. The question now is whether one's very existence, one's whole being, is free and entire, or somehow lacking in perfection and fullness. According to the letters patent, John Swart was to be as 'free and entire' as any of the natural-born liege-men. Does that mean that all natural-born liege-men were already 'free and entire'? What about the English-born villeins? Were they also legally free, complete and entire? Or, legally speaking, were they not persons?

CONCLUSION

We begin our investigation with these questions in mind. We aim to solve at least some of these puzzles by the end of this book. Letters patent appearing from the 1380s onwards, of which John Swart's were an example, seem to have been composed by a person who held very different assumptions about mercantile liberties and exemption from the higher rate of customs duty. The clauses which we have examined indicate that the drafter was either completely ignorant of the previous legal development, or was determined to ignore all that had gone on in the preceding centuries. The text was no longer focused on mercantile liberties. We no longer hear anything about being a free-man of a city. Previously, the letters patent would enumerate specific items of liberties dispassionately bought and sold. John Swart's letters patent, on the other hand, are full of passionate claims about the relationship of faith and allegiance which binds the king and his subjects together. The text leads us to imagine that as long as John Swart remained faithful to the king, his legal existence would be complete and entire. He would no longer have to haggle over this or that item of liberty. The plenitude of his legal existence would guarantee the ability to enjoy the *full* range of liberties available. He would no longer have to pay for the liberties either. The king would freely give out all the liberties as long as John Swart fulfilled the following conditions:

(1) to do liege-homage to the king ('quod prefatus Johnnes nobis homagium ligeum faciat'); and
(2) to dissociate himself from his countrymen ('quod non sit de societate mercatorem alienigenarum').

We have never encountered such requirements before. Perhaps, from now on, it might not be entirely unreasonable to expect that *every* body, as long as he remained faithful to the king, might be able to claim liberties. Our lord the king seemed to be suddenly imbued with a new sense of liberality and started to give liberties to *all* his beloved subjects (*fideles*) as a matter of grace (*gratis*). All he would ask in return was that they be faithful to him. Foreigners, however, were now running the risk of being 'unfree and incomplete' as they lacked faith and allegiance to our lord the king.

John Swart was probably no different from other foreign merchants of the previous reign. He probably did not ask for something radically different from previous foreign merchants' usual demand: commercial liberties and exemption from the higher rate of customs duty. We have no ground to suspect that the factual circumstances surrounding his application have much altered. But the response suddenly took on a grandiose tone. It now contained pointed assertions about general and far-reaching legal issues (property holding, access to legal remedies and fullness of legal standing). Exemption from the higher rate of customs duty – probably the main reason for John Swart's application – was more or less drowned amidst these powerful statements, most of which must have sounded rather odd to this merchant as they were affirming what he had already been enjoying. Strange as they may have sounded to the applicant, these lofty statements indicate that faith and allegiance have now been brought to bear the awesome weight of the legal edifice, which the concept of *libertas* used to bear for such a long time. John Swart's letters patent became the model of the letters patent to be issued in the following centuries.[101]

[101] For many references and the full text of a few exemplary letters patent of the fifteenth century, see Parry, *History of naturalization*, pp. 25ff. For the sixteenth century, see *Letters of denization and acts of naturalization for aliens in England, 1509–1603*, ed. William Page (Lymington, 1893).

3

FOREIGN CLERKS

'Ecclesiastical property', wrote John of Paris in the first years of the fourteenth century, 'has been given to communities, not to individual persons. So therefore, no one person has proprietary right and lordship over ecclesiastical property. It is the community concerned which itself has these.' If an individual person has a right of usage over the property for his maintenance commensurate to his needs and rank, 'he has this not as an individual in his own right but purely as part and member of the community'.[1] Professor Maitland also recognises that throughout the Middle Ages, 'it is never forgotten that the bishop who as bishop holds lands . . . holds these lands as head of a corporation of which canons or monks are members'. It is not to be doubted either that the parson of a parish church exercises his right over the church and its appurtenances in a rather peculiar way.[2] Obviously, churchmen's landholding poses a number of technical and theoretical issues which make it distinct from laymen's legal control of land.[3]

This, however, is not the topic I propose to discuss in the present chapter. Whether a person's access to the control of land is categorised as ownership or usufruct, whether such a control is

1 John of Paris, *On royal and papal power*, trans. J. A. Watt (Toronto, 1971) pp. 96–7.
[2] F. W. Maitland, 'Corporation sole' in *Maitland – selected essays*, ed. H. D. Hazeltine et al. (Cambridge, 1936) pp. 82–9. The situation in medieval France is discussed by P.-C. Timbal, 'La vie juridique des personnes morales ecclésiastiques en France aux XIIIe et XIVe siècles' in *Etudes d'histoire du droit canonique dédiées à Gabriel Le Bras* (Paris, 1965) pp. 1425–45.
[3] For a useful guide on this subject, see Janet Coleman, 'Property and poverty' in *The Cambridge history of medieval political thought, c. 350–c. 1450*, ed. J. H. Burns (Cambridge, 1987) pp. 604–48. Coleman, 'Medieval discussions of property: *Ratio* and *Dominium* according to John of Paris and Marsilius of Padua', 4 *History of Political Thought* (1983) 209–28.

exercised by the person in his own right or in right of a community: these are questions which do not have immediate relevance
to our argument. Categorisation of a person's legal position has no
doubt the effect of determining the variety and range of the legal
remedies the person can have recourse to in protecting and
promoting his interests. But as long as all relevant remedies are
sufficiently reliable and effective, which category they belong to is
of little importance to us. Ownership or usufruct is not an end in
itself. It is merely a means – a legal device with practical
procedural consequences – to satisfy one's needs and desires.
Churchmen, whether English or foreign, were not in a position to
make use of all the legal devices which lay landholders had at their
disposal. But they were using other remedies suited to their
particular legal position. The question which I pose in this
chapter is whether foreign clerks were denied all or some of the
remedies which English clerks were allowed to use in securing an
access to ecclesiastical property in England. I propose to discuss
this question with particular reference to the distribution and
conferment of ecclesiastical benefices in the thirteenth and fourteenth centuries.

It is tempting to present this narrow topic in a sweeping
language of the 'struggles' between the Church and the State, or
the 'conflicts' between the universalism of the medieval Catholic
Church and the localism of a 'national' church, or the 'tension'
among the papacy, lay magnates and secular rulers. The tempta-
tion is even greater for the fourteenth century because papal
provisions were then playing a decisive role in regulating churchmen's access to ecclesiastical property and it has been a long-
standing interpretative tradition to see in the mechanism of papal
provision a conflict structure generating the momentum for the
constitutional changes of the late-medieval Western Church.[4] But
the broadly sketched 'conflicts' and 'struggles' are not entirely
suited to an analysis of the legal framework within which ecclesias-

---

[4] See, for example, the excellent works of Colin Morris, *The papal monarchy, the
western Church from 1050 to 1250* (Oxford, 1989); Kenneth Pennington, *Pope and
bishops, the papal monarchy in the twelfth and thirteenth centuries* (Pennsylvania,
1984); Jean-Philippe Genet and Bernard Vincent, eds., *Etat et Eglise dans la
genèse de l'état moderne* (Madrid, 1986); Stuart Mews (ed.) *Religion and national
identity* (Oxford, 1982).

tical benefices were distributed. A brief explanation is necessary to clarify this point.

Examples of conflict over ecclesiastical benefices are not lacking, of course. Patent rolls for the years 1343–5, for instance, show that the church of St Peter, Staunford became vacant while the priory of St Fromund was seized in the king's hands due to the war with the French king. The king presented his candidate Richard Martyn to fill the vacancy. The king's claim was presumably that if the vacancy occurred while the priory was seized in his hands, he should be entitled to present in right of the prior. The prior disagreed and appointed Simon Benet, a papally provided candidate, to the vacant church. A lawsuit between the king and the prior ensued and, upon the judgment in the king's court in favour of the king, the king's writ was issued to arrest those who were pursuing Simon's claim in derogation of that judgment. Simon's brother, John Benet, who was himself a notary public and was probably involved in securing his brother's appointment, was arrested by the king's officers. But Stephen Benet, another brother of Simon, and several other supporters of the Benet brothers fought against the king's officers and managed to rescue John Benet.[5]

Another example of conflict may be mentioned. The prebend of Bere and Cherministre in the diocese of Salisbury was simultaneously claimed by Thomas de Hatfield, the king's clerk, and William de Veyraco and Robert de Turre de Adria, both of whom were papally provided candidates. The case was brought to the king's court and a judgment was entered in favour of the king's appointee. But the papally provided candidates would not give in, and made a number of appeals to Court Christian. Thomas de Hatfield was therefore repeatedly cited to papal curia. But the king's beloved clerk would not capitulate either. He appealed to the king, and the king issued his letters close on 10 May 1343 prohibiting the bishop of Durham, who was involved in pursuing the claims of William de Veyraco, from doing anything in derogation of the judgment of the king's court favouring Thomas de Hatfield. The king's letters close were delivered to the bishop on

---

[5] *Calendar of patent rolls, 1343–1345*, pp. 406, 426–7, 579, 584–5. More examples of violent struggles for benefices are to be found in F. Cheyette, 'Kings, courts, cures, and sinecures: the statute of provisors and the common law', 19 *Traditio* (1963) 295–349 at 334–5.

13 May, who then found himself in London on another business. On 15 May, if we are to believe the bishop's account of the event, the king' officers, with bludgeons in their hands, confronted the bishop and demanded of him with rough, loud voices immediately to stop meddling with the judgment of the king's court.[6]

As far as the question of conflict is concerned, what can safely be stated with regard to these cases is that a conflict existed between contending claimants. Whether, on the other hand, John Benet in our first example can be described as seeing himself engaged in a struggle between the Church and the State, and whether the bishop of Durham in our second example believed that he was caught up in a conflict between the centralising papacy and the resilient English king, or between the local church hierarchy and the secular power structure, are questions which cannot be answered unless one commits oneself to a particular methodological stance requiring a lengthy, but not necessarily convincing, explanation. There are, no doubt, examples of immediate personal confrontation between the pope and a secular prince, or between the king and the bishops. The strained relationship between Philip the Fair and Boniface VIII is well enough known. The dealings between the popes and the Holy Roman Emperors in the fourteenth century would be difficult to describe if one is not at all to use the image of conflict. England was no exception to this trend. The clash of opinions regarding taxation of the property of the clergy led Edward I to outlaw all prelates of his realm. But the legal framework for the regulation of churchmen's access to ecclesiastical benefices remained unaffected by these sensational events. What mattered to individual claimants was the routine legal procedures, not the impressive conflicts and sensational struggles between high profile figures.

For quite some time already, historians have attempted to bring to light aspects of compromise and co-operation among major players of medieval church politics to complement the images of conflict and struggle which have characterised the historiography

---

[6] *Richard d'Aungerville of Bury, Fragments of his register and other documents*, ed. G. W. Kitchin (London, 1910) 30–3 ('nonnulli praedicti domini Regis nostri servientes ad arma clavas suis tenentes in manibus coram nobis personaliter constituti, nobis dixerunt alta voce . . .'). *Calendar of entries in the papal registers relating to Great Britain and Ireland*, Papal letters, vol. III (1342–62) pp. 79, 86, 88, 149, 257. *Calendar of close rolls, 1343–1346*, pp. 118–19.

for centuries. Such an effort will no doubt contribute to our
understanding of medieval history in general and the history of
church politics in particular.[7] But it does not seem to be of much
help to an analysis of the technical legal arguments, which still
remain largely unexplored. This is not at all to suggest that
historians in general should abandon the task of identifying and
describing general trends and macroscopic forces underlying the
contemporaries' actions and arguments. But legal historians, particularly those wishing to investigate foreign clerks' access to
ecclesiastical property in medieval England, would need more
than an appreciation of large-scale confrontations and compromises. Crucial to an investigation of this kind is an understanding
of how individual clerks sought and fought for the control of
ecclesiastical property in various legal forums.

Legal argument is perhaps not the most convenient means of
expressing one's overall outlook or the urgent issues of the time.
Legal argument has to be presented under the formal constraints
imposed by the accepted practice of the profession. Lawyers and
judges do not have the liberty to have a free-style conversation in
court where any and every issue that may interest the parties can
be raised in an unstructured manner. The parties' claims need first
to be formulated according to the formal requirements currently
recognised by the profession. These formal requirements show a
great deal of stability and are not necessarily affected by the short-
lived conflicts and compromises. If materials relating to foreign
clerks in the thirteenth and fourteenth centuries are approached

---

[7] To cite but a few, Peter Heath, *Church and realm, 1272–1461: conflict and
collaboration in an age of crises* (London, 1988); J. R. Wright, *The Church and the
English crown, 1305–1334* (Toronto, 1980); W. A. Pantin, *The English church in
the fourteenth century* (Cambridge, 1955); J. R. L. Highfield, 'The relations
between the Church and the English crown from the death of Archbishop
Stratford to the opening of the Great Schism, 1349–1378', Oxford Univ. D.Phil.
thesis, 1951; Robert N. Swanson, 'Universities, graduates, and benefices in later
medieval England', 106 *Past and Present* (1985) 28–61; E. F. Jacob, 'On the
promotion of English university clerks during the later Middle Ages', 1 *Journal
of Ecclesiastical History* (1950) 172–186; Margaret Harvey, 'The benefice as
property: an aspect of Anglo-Papal relations during the pontificate of Martin V,
1417–1431' in *The church and wealth*, ed. W. J. Sheils and Diana Wood (Oxford,
1987) pp. 161–73; Jane Sayers, *Papal government and England, during the
pontificate of Honorius III, 1216–1227* (Cambridge, 1984); Jean Gaudemet, 'Un
point de rencontre entre les pouvoirs politiques et l'église: le choix des évêques'
in *Etat et Eglise dans la genèse de l'état moderne*, ed. J.-P. Genet and B. Vincent
(Madrid, 1986) pp. 279–93.

without knowledge of the formal constraints under which the late medieval lawyers operated, it would be difficult to obtain a balanced assessment of the vehement rhetorical claims of their contemporaries.

By shifting the focus from the broad pictures of gigantic struggles and shrewd compromises to individual claimants actually involved in concrete disputes, one can investigate more closely how the parties composed their arguments deploying various rhetorical elements. There is, after all, scope for treating the persistent pleas to uphold the 'dignity and rights of the crown', 'laws of the realm' or the 'liberties of the Church' as rhetorical elements parading in a person's argument rather than as factual descriptions narrating genuine historical clashes. It will also be possible, I hope, to show that these rhetorical elements and the way they were deployed were, for a long time, manifestly unsuited to give rise to a legal argument for systematic discrimination against foreign clerks.

FOREIGN CLERKS AND THE CANON LAW

The fierce attack often repeated against foreigners holding ecclesiastical benefices in England is certainly not a reliable guide to the precise scale of foreign influx in the late medieval English Church. But the existence of such complaints demonstrates beyond doubt that there were foreign clerks holding ecclesiastical benefices in England, and that they were the frequent target of bad publicity.[8] To this extent, one is justified in believing that the category of 'foreign clerks' is not a mere historiographical contrivance, but a category which has some historical basis; but only to this extent. For, as it will be argued, a more detailed analysis of the relevant texts will show that there was hardly any legal ground to separate foreign clerks from English clerks. In so far as conferment of an ecclesiastical benefice is concerned, 'foreign clerks' were a non-category for both Canon lawyers and English common lawyers of the time. This is one of the areas where the discrepancy between

---

[8] Many of the anti-papal or anti-foreign petitions of the thirteenth and fourteenth centuries are conveniently gathered and printed in Johannes Haller, *Papsttum und Kirchenreform* vol. I (Berlin, 1903) pp. 543–52.

popular polemical argument and technical legal argument was most striking. We shall begin with Canon lawyers' argument first.

Ecclesiastical benefices, Canon lawyers would explain, may be acquired in one of the following manners: (1) election, (2) collation, (3) presentment and institution, (4) papal provision.[9] Another way of explaining the same topic is to say that the conferment of an ecclesiastical benefice is carried out through procedures governed by the Canon law and the common law of the country. Although the borderline between the two systems of law was often blurred by jurisdictional disputes between Canon lawyers and secular lawyers, it is still convenient to maintain a distinction for the purpose of exposition. Regarding ecclesiastical benefices, the main concerns of Canon lawyers were the procedures of election, collation, papal provision, examination and institution. In England, disputes arising from presentment of candidates were dealt with by common lawyers in the king's court.[10]

The canonical position on foreigners' access to ecclesiastical benefices has already been studied in detail, and we need only to add a few general remarks. Part of what follows is based on the conclusions of Laprat who has demonstrated that throughout the fourteenth century, there was no Canon legal obstacle to foreign clerks' access to ecclesiastical benefices.[11] As far as Canon lawyers were concerned, foreign provenance of the claimant of an ecclesiastical benefice was a matter subsumed under the question of the clerical candidate's qualification (i.e., whether the foreign prove-

---

[9] Petri Rebuffi, *Praxis beneficiorum absolutissima acquirendi, conservandique illa, ac amittendi, modos continens* (Lyons, 1570) pp. 29ff. For modern works giving a concise outline of this topic, see Jean Gaudemet, *Le gouvernement de l'église à l'époque classique*, vol. II, *Le gouvernement local* (Paris, 1979) pp. 68–76. For a fuller treatment, see Geoffrey Barraclough, *Papal provisions* (Oxford, 1935); G. Mollat, *La Collation des bénéfices ecclésiastiques sous les papes à Avignon, 1305–1789* (Paris, 1921); G. Mollat, 'Bénéfices ecclésiastiques en occident' in *Dictionnaire de droit canonique*, vol. II (Paris, 1937) cols. 406–49; Bernard Guillemain, *La Politique bénéficiale du pape Benoît XII, 1334–1342* (Paris, 1952); K. Ganzer, *Papsttum und Bistumsbesetzungen im der Zeit von Gregor IX. bis Bonifax VIII.: ein Beitrag zur päpstlichen Reservationen* (Cologne, 1968); Louis Caillet, *La Papauté d'Avignon et l'église de France – la politique bénéficiale du pape Jean XXII en France, 1316–1334* (Paris, 1975).

[10] J. W. Gray, 'The *Ius praesentandi* in England from the Constitutions of Clarendon to Bracton', 67 *English Historical Review* (1952) 481–509.

[11] R. Laprat, 'Incapacité bénéficiale des aubains' in *Dictionnaire de droit canonique*, ed. A. Villien et al. (Paris, 1924–65) vol. I (1935) cols. 1332–80.

nance constituted a legitimate cause for disqualifying a candidate). The Canonical requirements for the clerical candidate's qualification were often summarised as follows: (1) maturity of age; (2) good moral character; and (3) sufficient learning.[12] The basic principle that the candidate must be able and suitable (*habilis & idoneus*) for the post can hardly accommodate the suggestion that foreign candidates must systematically be rejected because of their foreign provenance. The decretal *Ad decorum* of Innocent III (1206) contains an explicit statement which supports my argument. The main thrust of the text is that the churches of Constantinople, especially that of St Sophia, must be served by 'learned and suitable candidates, regardless of their provenance (*litterati et alias idonei, undecumque originem duxerint*)'.[13] One of the rules of papal chancery (*regulae cancellariae*) in the late fourteenth century gives a more specific content to this broad principle of suitability (idoneity). According to the rule – commonly referred to as *De idiomata* – parish churches and other ecclesiastical benefices with cure of souls must be given to candidates well versed in the local language.[14] For one thing, this shows that benefices *without* cure of souls were open to all suitable candidates regardless of their command of the local language. For benefices with cure of souls, the rule indicates that all qualified candidates, regardless of their provenance, would be considered as long as they met the linguistic requirement.[15]

The principle of idoneity was generally applicable regardless of whether the ecclesiastical benefice was to be conferred through election, collation, papal provision or institution upon presentment. Bishop Grosseteste of Lincoln left us vivid examples indicating how the principle was at work. A few cases may be mentioned. The bishopric of Chichester became vacant in 1244. Robert Passelew was elected to fill the vacant post. According to Matthew Paris, Bishop Grosseteste undertook the examination of the elected candidate. The candidate was found unfit for the post

---

[12] Rebuffi, *Praxis beneficiorum*, pp. 34–7. See also Gray, 'The *Ius praesentandi*', p. 509.
[13] Laprat, 'Incapacité bénéficiale', col. 1337 (*Decr.* 3. 7. 5).
[14] Ibid., cols. 1340–2.
[15] See also William Watson, *The clergy-man's law, or the complete incumbent* (London, 1701) pp. 147ff. (If the presentee does not understand the English language, the bishop may lawfully refuse the candidate. 'But if he doth understand our language, altho' he be an Alien born, he is not to be refused.')

and the election was annulled.[16] Two years later, the same Passelew, the king's clerk and a forest judge, was presented by the king to the vacant church of St Peter, Northampton. Passelew was again examined by Bishop Grosseteste, found unfit for the post, and was refused to be instituted.[17] Bishop Grosseteste is well known also for his resolute opposition to a number of papally provided candidates. By far the most celebrated case is where the bishop refused to admit Frederick di Lavagna, nephew of Pope Innocent IV, to a canonry in Lincoln. The story obtained notoriety because of a stormy letter which Matthew Paris attributed to the bishop. But, as pointed out by Henry Luard, who edited the bishop's letters, Grosseteste's refusal was not because the candidate was a foreigner, nor because he was a papally provided candidate. The refusal was due to the fact that the candidate was too young and unfit for the post. Henry Luard summarised Bishop Grosseteste's attitude to ecclesiastical appointment in the following terms: 'Englishmen and foreigners, if he knows them to be unfit persons, are alike rejected; and this is the case with all indiscriminately however great their patrons may have been. The nominees of English noblemen, Roman Cardinals, the king, and the Pope met with the same fate.'[18]

Whether one sees in Bishop Grosseteste's many refusals and equally numerous acceptances of recommended candidates an image of confrontation and/or compromise between big players of medieval church politics, or a portrait of an outspoken, steadfast, heroic figure standing out from a troubled time in English church history, the point which must not be missed is that there existed well-established Canon legal criteria for clerical candidates' qualification. This means that all considerations regarding the choice of candidate had to be expressed using these criteria. Those who

---

[16] Matthew Paris, *Chronica majora*, Rolls series, 7 vols., ed. H. R. Luard (1872–83) IV, pp. 358, 401. Robert Grosseteste, *Epistolae*, Rolls series, ed. H. R. Luard (1861) pp. lx–lxi.

[17] Grosseteste, *Epistolae*, p. lxvi. See also Grosseteste's Letter CXXIV ('quod ei justitiario Forestae, fungenti hujusmodi justitiariae officio, curam animarum non traderemus'). The king's vexation on this refusal is mentioned in Letter CXXV. Grosseteste defends his decision to refuse Passelew in a letter (CXXVI) to the Archbishop of Canterbury.

[18] Grosseteste, *Epistolae*, pp. xviii–xix. Grosseteste's refusal of F. Lavagne is also discussed at length by A. L. Smith, *Church and State in the Middle Ages* (Oxford, 1913) pp. 111–13.

compose their argument wishing to rely ultimately on the authority of the Canon law (Bishop Grosseteste was no doubt one of them) must accept and conform to the argument structure recognised by the Canon law of the time. No matter how strong was the anti-papal or anti-foreign sentiment (the above-mentioned letter attributed for some time to Bishop Grosseteste does show that such sentiment existed), when it comes to the question of a candidate's suitability, Canon law allowed no other varieties of argument than *maturitas etatis* (age), *morum honestas* (conduct) and *scientia litterarum* (learning) of the candidate. Unless a radical change is made to this argument structure, there is no room for an argument for rejecting foreign clerical candidates merely because of their foreign provenance. Exclusion of foreign clerks must therefore remain an unfulfilled wish of some (such as Matthew Paris) who unleashed bitter complaints whenever and wherever they could. But in ecclesiastical forums, their complaints found no ready advocates.

The mechanism of papal provision confirms again that foreign provenance of the candidate had no role to play in canonical disposal of ecclesiastical benefices. The so-called papal 'bull' of provision set in motion elaborate canonical proceedings where interested parties were given ample opportunity to dispute and challenge the candidate's claim to the benefice in question. If, for example, it was stated in the papal rescript that the impetrant was a graduate of a university or that he had knowledge of the local language, one can expect that should any doubt exist as to these points, it would be raised by an interested party. But, as observed by Louis Caillet, nationality or political allegiance of the impetrant was never mentioned in papal rescripts for provision. If geographical provenance of the impetrant was sometimes mentioned, that was for identification purposes only.[19] We have no evidence suggesting that the impetrant's foreign provenance was in itself regarded as relevant to his suitability for the post. Examples pointing to the opposite (i.e., where foreign candidates were deemed suitable and were given the ecclesiastical benefice) do not seem to be lacking.

Geoffrey Barraclough has shown that canonical procedures through which an ecclesiastical benefice was conferred were aimed

---

[19] L. Caillet, *La Papauté d'Avignon et l'église de France*, pp. 290–5.

at establishing whether the candidate had the right (*ius*) to claim
and enjoy the benefice. The procedural arrangement in the
ecclesiastical forums was heavily influenced by medieval Roman
law jurisprudence; just as in the ordinary civil litigation, the
highest goal of the canonical procedures *de beneficiis* was the
prevention of injury to the rights of the individual. There was no
room for consideration of public interest as opposed to private
rights of the parties. As far as medieval lawyers were concerned,
there existed no means of promoting public interest except by
upholding private persons' rights and privileges to the utmost
degree permitted in law. The following remarks of Geoffrey
Barraclough are worth quoting at length:

> the canonical rules of civil procedure were marked, from the second half
> of the twelfth century onwards, by an excessive attention to the rights of
> the parties, by the formulation of the minutest regulations for maintaining
> impartiality and by exaggerated regard for forms, which justify us in
> expressing their spirit in the words, no prejudice, no injury to the parties,
> though the heavens fall![20]

Perhaps we may add, 'though the kingdom might also be impover-
ished and threatened by foreign clerks!'. Exclusion of foreign
clerks was manifestly an argument based on public interest.
Indeed, the very basis of the modern law of alien status is that
consideration of public interest must override private persons'
interests and their narrowly defined legal rights. To study the
emergence of the claim that a candidate's foreign status should in
itself be a sufficient ground for denying his access to an ecclesiastical benefice is no less than to study how the law of personal
status came to incorporate questions of public interest.

FOREIGN CLERKS AND THE COMMON LAW

If Canon law procedures were thus focused on the clerical
candidate's right, common law procedures show a striking contrast
in the sense that they were marked by a singular disregard of the
clerical candidate's right. Common law procedures revolved
around the notion of advowson. Advowson was a right, not of a
clerical candidate, but of a patron. In the ecclesiastical court,

---

[20] Barraclough, *Papal provisions*, p. 80.

patrons had no say except to the extent that their claims touched on the clerical candidate's right to the benefice (*ius beneficiale*). In the king's court, the situation was reversed. Clerical candidates were involved only to the extent that they affected the patron's right (*ius patronatus*) – usually as an obstacle to the patron's exercise of advowson. Apart from this limited involvement, clerical candidates had no legal right which the king's court could recognise and enforce. A brief examination of some of the original writs would clarify this point.

Take the example of the writ *Quare impedit*. Suppose a church in lay patronage became vacant and somehow the bishop happened to fill the vacancy with a papally provided candidate. Since papal provision was not deemed effective with regard to churches in lay patronage, the patron might attempt to recover his advowson (the right to present a candidate of his choice to fill the vacant post).[21] The writ *Quare impedit* can be used in this case. The writ contains an allegation that the defendant(s) (the bishop and/or his appointee) unjustly impede the plaintiff's (the patron's) exercise of advowson. The allegation leads to a demand that the defendant(s) must permit the plaintiff, as the one who claims to have the advowson, to present a suitable person to the church in question which is vacant and within the plaintiff's gift (*que vacat et ad suam spectat donacionem*).[22] This rather bland statement has the effect of delimiting the range of arguments which the parties may put forward during the course of the trial. The pleadings in the case will be focused exclusively on whether the church is vacant and whether the plaintiff has the advowson. Other points are irrelevant.

The same original writ can be used in a number of different factual situations. During the vacancy of a bishopric, the temporalities of the episcopal see are in the hands of the king. If a minor benefice belonging to such an episcopal see becomes vacant during

---

[21] On (ineffective) papal provisions to benefices in lay patronage, see Pantin, *The English church in the fourteenth century*, pp. 54, 58; Heath, *Church and realm*, p. 127. Sometimes, however, lay patrons might be harassed by papally provided candidates. See Ann Deeley, 'Papal provisions and royal rights of patronage in the early fourteenth century', 43 *English Historical Review* (1928) 505; *Calendar of patent rolls, 1343–1345*, p. 150. See also A. D. M. Barrell, 'The effect of papal provisions on Yorkshire parishes, 1342–1370', 28 *Northern History* (1992) 92–109 at 93.

[22] *Early thirteenth-century registers of writs*, 87 Selden Society (1970), CA 52, CC 51, R 83–6.

the period, the king, as the lawful custodian of the temporalities, may present a suitable person of his choice to the vacant post (regalian right).[23] But the exact duration of the king's custody of the episcopal see is often difficult to establish, especially if the old bishop's removal or the new bishop's appointment is contested. It may also be that the news of the vacancy of the minor benefice does not reach the king until after the temporalities have been restored to the new bishop. The bishop may, upon recovery of the temporalities, fill the vacant post with a papally provided candidate. But the king could come in at this stage and present a candidate of his choice, disregarding the bishop's appointment. The idea is that once the benefice became vacant while the advowson was in the king's hands, whether it was filled afterwards simply did not matter to him (no time runs against the king). If the bishop turned out to disagree with this idea, the king could rely on a *Quare impedit*.[24]

Quite a few churches belonged to religious houses. Some of the religious houses were deemed to be under the power of the French king (the so-called 'alien priories'). They were frequently taken into the king's hands while the king was at war with the French king. If minor benefices belonging to these religious houses

---

[23] M. Howell, *Regalian right in medieval England* (London, 1962). Regarding the situation in France, see G. Mollat, 'L'Application du droit de régale spirituelle en France du XIIe au XIVe siècles', 25 *Revue d'Histoire Ecclésiastique* (1929) 425–46, 645–76; Jean Gaudemet, *La Collation par le roi de France des bénéfices vacants en régale, dès origines à la fin du XIVe siècle* (Paris, 1935); Gaudemet, 'Régale' in *Dictionnaire de droit canonique*, vol. VII (Paris, 1960) cols. 494–532, cols. 514–19 for the situation in the fourteenth century.

[24] Pantin, *The English church*, pp. 31, 80. *Calendar of patent rolls, 1343–1345*, p. 78 (king's presentment during the vacancy of the see of York), p. 84 (the same during the vacancy of the see of Ely), p. 87 (during the vacancy of the see of Coventry and Lichfield), p. 178 (vacancy of the see of York in the time of Edward I), p. 399 (vacancy of the see of Ely), p. 419 (vacancy of the see of Worcester). These are only a handful of examples out of a vast number of cases. Some attempts were made to limit the king's claims. The Statute 14 Edward III st. 4, c. 2 provided that the king should not present in another's right except within three years after the vacancy occurred. See *Year Book 14 Edward III*, Rolls series (1883–1911) pp. 122–3. This limit, however, was considered injurious to the king in the Statute 25 Edward III st. 6 (Ordinance for the clergy). By this statute, the king's right to present to benefices in right of another was extended, but limited to vacancies which occurred during his own reign. Since then, therefore, the king's ancestor's time could run against the king. For a detailed discussion, see Cheyette, 'Kings, courts, cures, and sinecures', pp. 313–15.

became vacant during the period of seizure, the king could present his candidate to fill the vacancy. As soon as the war was over and peace was signed, however, the seizure must end.[25] The abbots and priors who have been thus reinstated may get on with their usual business and fill the vacant posts with suitable candidates of their choice. But these appointments often proved to be precarious because, here also, the king could recover the advowsons which he omitted to exercise. Numerous cases demonstrate that the king's appointee and a papally provided candidate often ended up in various courts of law hopelessly entangled in all kinds of legal proceedings. The writ *Quare impedit* was the usual means in these cases to bring the parties to the king's court.[26] Factual details of the contesting candidates may be of infinite variety. The king's appointee may be a rich foreign cardinal greedily accumulating a breathtaking number of ecclesiastical benefices. The bishop's appointee may be a poor, honest and competent English candidate. The prior may have been trying to support the well-educated university graduates from Oxford and Cambridge. But all these stories must remain outside of the king's court. The writ *Quare impedit* did not allow any means of bringing these details into consideration. All that mattered was whether the church was vacant and who had the advowson.

Other original writs which were employed to resolve disputes relating to ecclesiastical benefices (*Darrein presentment*, writ of right for advowsons, *Quare non admisit*, etc.) also indicate that

---

[25] Benjamin Thompson, 'The statute of Carlisle, 1307 and the alien priories', 41 *Journal of Ecclesiastical History* (1990) 560; Donald Matthew, *The Norman monasteries and their English possessions* (Oxford, 1962) pp. 85ff.; and Marjorie M. Morgan (Chibnall), 'The suppression of the alien priories', 26 *History*, NS (1941) 209. A more detailed discussion of this topic will be attempted in the next chapter.

[26] Patent rolls reveal the existence of numerous cases of this nature. For example, *Calendar of patent rolls, 1343–1345*, p. 73 (king's presentment while the priory of Brustall is in the king's hands), p. 86 (while the priory of Derhurst is in the king's hands), p. 178 (church of Fen Drayton), p. 406 (priory of St Fromond in the king's hands), p. 499 (priory of Otriton in the king's hands), p. 582 (priory of Lenton in the king's hands). A quick survey of some of the printed year book case reports (Rolls series, 1883–1911) from the reign of Edward III reveals the following: *Year Book 11–12 Edward III*, pp. 550–4; *Year Book 13–14 Edward III*, pp. 286–8; *Year Book 14–15 Edward III*, pp. 340–54; *Year Book 15 Edward III*, pp. 146–52; *Year Book 16 Edward III*, part 2, pp. 226–32, 300–10; *Year Book 17 Edward III*, pp. 158–82; *Year Book 17–18 Edward III*, pp. 126–36, 266–78; *Year Book 19 Edward III*, pp. 58–65, 164–75.

questions regarding clerical candidates' quality or provenance had
no relevance to the outcome of the proceedings. The writ of
Darrein presentment, for example, is designed to obtain the verdict
to the following question: 'which patron in time of peace presented the last parson, who is now dead, to the [church in
question] which is vacant and the advowson of which the [plain-
tiff] asserts to belong to him?'.[27]

Year book case reports, of course, maintain a complete silence as
to the identity of the incumbent or the contesting candidate. This
is not surprising because these reports were generally not interested in the parties' identity anyway. But we can find one exceptional case where the following remark was made in reporting a
Quare impedit case brought by the king: 'Note that the parson was
a provisor and this suit was undertaken *ex cautelâ* in order to oust
him.'[28] It is of crucial importance that the remark did not come
from those who were engaged in the arguing of the case, but rather
from the compiler of the report. This confirms again that the
parties' arguments in the king's court were not designed to
provide any clue to the personal attributes of the parson or the
contesting candidate. It is only from an external source of information (the compiler) that readers of the report can know – should
they wish to know – that the parson was a provisor. Indeed, there
was a good reason why common lawyers did not, and probably
could not, discuss who the parson or the contesting candidate was.
Such a discussion would inevitably lead to the question of the
clerical candidate's suitability for the post. And that was a
canonical matter over which common lawyers never seem to have
attempted to claim jurisdiction.[29]

The parties in the king's court thus had to remain silent as to
the personal attributes of the contesting candidates. Common
lawyers were, therefore, not in a position to distinguish English
candidates from foreign candidates and favour the ones at the
expense of the others. It is against this background that a series of

---

[27] *Early thirteenth-century registers of writs*, CA 40, CC 47–9, R 79, Hib9.

[28] *Year Book 11–12 Edward III*, Rolls series, pp. 654–6 at 655 ('Nota qe cestui qe
fuit persone fut un provisour et ceste seute ordine per cautelam de lui ouster').

[29] See in this connection *Year Book 20 Edward III*, part 1, Rolls series, pp.
362–71. The defendant (the bishop) in a *Quare non admisit* case claimed that the
king's presentee was a layman and was not acquainted with letters (*non able nien
lettre*). It seems that the court, *per* Willoughby, held that the matter should be
tried by Court Christian (p. 370).

parliamentary bans on papal provision, first appearing in 1343, must be analysed.

Soon after the pontificate of Clement VI began, the following ban on papal provision was introduced in Parliament:

1. No one, regardless of his condition, whether alien or denizen (*soit il Alyen ou Denzein*), shall carry or cause to be carried documents relating to papal provisions and reservations which are prejudicial to the king or to his people;
2. No one shall, by virtue of such provisions or reservations, receive any ecclesiastical benefice;
3. No one shall receive documents concerning provisions or reservations; nor shall anyone, by virtue of these documents, carry out institution or induction; and
4. No one shall do or allow to be done anything that can prejudice the king or his people or weaken the rights of his crown.

The ban was accompanied by an order that a diligent search be carried out to arrest (1) those who carry the above-mentioned documents; (2) those who, by virtue of such documents, receive or claim any benefice; (3) those who, by the authority of such documents, make or cause to be made, appeals citations or proceedings against patrons of such benefice, presentees or any other persons in any court.[30] In spite of the clear language which leaves little doubt that the ban was general and indiscriminate, there seems to be a persistent interpretative tradition which sees that the ban was in fact directed against foreigners. Such an interpretation is at odds with our argument that the contemporary common lawyers had no means of discriminating against foreign clerical candidates. It is therefore necessary to examine the relevant texts in some detail.

The parliamentary ban was followed by a number of writs and letters issued by the king. On 20 July 1343, for example, Edward III issued letters close to all prelates reminding them of the ban and giving relevant instructions. The editor who calendared this document obviously thought that foreigners were under attack. We find the following passage in *Calendar of close rolls, 1343–1346*: '[the king's] order not to admit any alien persons or other proctors or envoys to any benefices of the realm by virtue of

---

[30] *Rotuli Parliamentorum*, 6 vols. (London, 1767–77) II, pp. 144–5.

any provisions of the apostolic see . . . or to provide aliens with
such benefices, nor promulgate any ecclesiastical censures against
those resisting such aliens'.[31] The same letters close are recorded
in the register of John Kirkby, bishop of Carlisle (1332–52).
Professor R. L. Storey calendared the register, and he also
described the letters close as a 'writ of Edward III ordering the
bishop not to admit alien provisors to benefices'.[32]

On the same day, the king's letters patent were issued to those
likely to be involved in papal provisions. The excerpt translation
in *Calendar of patent rolls, 1343–1345* shows that the document
was again seen as an anti-alien measure. According to the translation, the prohibition applied to 'delegates, sub-delegates, executors and sub-executors of graces to aliens' and to 'such aliens and
their proctors and envoys and notaries public and others'.[33] Three
days later, another round of the king's letters close was sent to all
the sheriffs of the realm regarding the ban. A description of one of
these letters can be found in *Calendar of close rolls*. According to
the description, the ban was applicable to 'all-delegates, sub-
delegates, executors, sub-executors and commissaries [who]
execute favours to alien persons'. The ban, it is also stated,
required that 'no alien shall pursue favours or make provisions or
process'.[34] Continuing this unchallenged interpretative tradition,
A. D. M. Barrell has suggested again in a recent article that
foreigners were probably the main target of the parliamentary ban
on papal provision of 1343.[35]

However, a closer examination of the relevant manuscript texts
will reveal a rather different picture. For example, the letters
patent of 20 July 1343 were addressed not only to 'delegates, sub-
delegates, executors and sub-executors of graces to aliens . . .' but

---

[31] *Calendar of close rolls, 1343–1346*, pp. 215–16.
[32] *The register of John Kirkby, bishop of Carlisle, 1332–1352 and the register of John
Ross, bishop of Carlisle, 1325–1332*, ed. R. L. Storey, 2 vols. (Woodbridge, 1993,
1995) I, p. 154, no. 734.
[33] *Calendar of patent rolls, 1343–1345*, pp. 164–5.
[34] *Calendar of close rolls, 1343–1346*, p. 220.
[35] A. D. M. Barrell, 'The ordinance of provisors of 1343', 64 *Historical Research*
(1991) 264–77 at 266–7 ('The operative word throughout this letter [Edward
III's letters close of 20 July 1343 recorded in the archbishop's register in York]
is "alienigenae", and it does not appear that Zouche [the then archbishop of
York] was asked to apply the ordinance any more widely than to prevent
provisions to aliens from taking effect'). Also Barrell, 'The effect of papal
provisions', p. 107, note 124.

also to 'all the king's subjects'.[36] This point is obscured by the opaque English rendering in *Calendar of patent rolls*, 'such aliens . . . *and others*'. Few would guess that these 'others' correspond to '*omnibus fidelibus suis*' in the manuscript text. Also, towards the end of the text, the letters patent reproduce the sweeping ban introduced in Parliament prohibiting the addressees (which include all the king's subjects) from doing or attempting to do *anything whatsoever* that may prejudice the dignity and right of the king and weaken the patronage rights and advowsons of the king and of his subjects.[37]

The king's letters close of the same date sent to the prelates pose a rather more delicate problem of interpretation. The tone of the document, it is true, is milder because the king's instruction begins with a clause which specifically concerns 'foreigners, their attorneys and nuncios (*personas aliquas alienigenas vel eorum procuratores aut nuncios*)'. The lack of an explicit reference to 'all subjects of the king' could give an impression that the ban would apply only to provisions for foreigners, which were never numerous in England.[38] The ecclesiastical hierarchy would certainly feel less threatened if such a wording could lead them to believe that papal provisions for English clerical candidates would be tolerated, because that would mean that the main bulk of their appointments would be safe from the king's intervention. But towards the end of the letters close, the same sweeping clause as used in the letters patent discussed above appears again and prohibits anything whatsoever done or attempted in this connection publicly or secretly by the archbishop or others that could otherwise redound to the prejudice of the dignity and right of the king, and to the disregarding, weakening and diminution of the

---

36 Public Record Office, Patent roll, 17 Edward III, part 2, m. 32v ('Rex delegatis subdelegatis executoribus & subexecutoribus gratiarum personis alienigenis de beneficiis ecclesiasticis regni nostri Angliae vacantibus vel vacaturis per sedem Apostolicam concessarum ac ipsis alienigenis & procuratoribus & nunciis eorum & eorum substitutis ac notariis publicis & omnibus fidelibus suis salutem').

37 Ibid. ('nec vos vel aliquis vestrum per vos seu alios quicquam in hac parte faciatis vel attempte[re]tis per vos seu alios publice vel occulte quod in preiudicium dignitatis et iuris nostri regii ac enervacionem iuris patronatus & advocacionis nobis et fidelibus nostris contemptum possit aliqualiter redundare'). The author wishes to thank Professor J. H. Baker for his help in the reading of the manuscript text.

38 Pantin, *The English church*, pp. 62–3. Cf. Barrell, 'The effect of papal provisions', pp. 92–109.

patronage rights and advowsons of the king and his subjects.[39] The *Calendar of close rolls*, for some reason which is not known to us, omits precisely this clause. Similar editorial discretion is exercised in calendaring the same letters close recorded in the register of Ralph of Shrewsbury, bishop of Bath and Wells (1329–63). There, the editor chose to print the full text of the relevant part of the letters close. But the patience of the editor seems to have worn out where the final sweeping clause begins. The first three clauses concerning foreigners are carefully transcribed in full. But the last clause is reduced to 'etc.'.[40]

The full text of the king's letters close of 23 July 1343 sent to all the sheriffs of the realm is printed in *Foedera, conventiones, literae et . . . acta publica.* The inadequacy of the summary translation given in the *Calendar of close rolls* is easily discernible when it is compared with the printed full text. It is true that the letters close contain passages specifically directed to foreigners and their proctors, substitutes or nuncios. Nevertheless, there is no doubt that the ban was after all applicable to both foreigners and Englishmen ('Prohibuerimus . . . ipsis alienigenis . . . et omnibus aliis fidelibus nostris' . . .).[41]

To believe that Edward III's letters patent and close, unlike the parliamentary ordinance, were aimed only against foreigners is to suppose that the king, of his own accord, has somehow drastically reduced the scope of the sweeping ban introduced in Parliament (papal provisions for foreigners were far less numerous than provisions for English candidates). Such a move – if there was one – might well be regarded as not wholly inconceivable. One may even speculate that it would have been 'politic' of the king to tone down the blunt aggressiveness of the parliamentary ban. But the

[39] Public Record Office, Close rolls, 17 Edward III, part 2, m. 29v. I have also consulted the letters close of the same date recorded in the registers of the archbishop of York, bishop of Carlisle and bishop of Ely. They all contain this sweeping clause. Borthwick Institute, York, Reg. 10, fo. 255v; Cumbria County Record Office, Carlisle, DRC/1/1, fo. 240; Cambridge University Library, G/1/1 (Ely diocesan records), fo. 89v. The scribe of the York register chose to add the following title in the margin of the text: 'Breve regium super non admissione alienigenarum ad aliqua beneficia'. This title, however, does not appear in the other MSS.

[40] *The register of Ralph of Shrewsbury, bishop of Bath and Wells, 1329–1363*, ed. Thomas S. Holmes, 2 vols. (London, 1896) I, p. 405.

[41] *Foedera . . .*, ed. T. Rymer, Records Commission, 4 vols. (London, 1816–69) II, p. 1230.

surviving manuscripts just do not provide enough textual support
for the imaginative interpretation. The king's letters close issued
on 30 July 1343 to mayors and bailiffs of all ports of England
further demonstrate the impossibility of such an interpretation.
The king's instruction was to search and confiscate *all* bulls and
letters prejudicial to the king or to his lieges. The letters close
show no interest in knowing who the beneficiaries of these bulls
and letters were.[42] A few months later, we find orders to arrest
Thomas de Askham, John Furnaux de Bereford and Nocolas de
Hethe who apparently sought papal provision to obtain ecclesiastical benefices. There is, of course, no ground to suppose that they
were all foreigners. More importantly, the relevant texts show
complete indifference as to the provenance of these clerks. There
are a few more cases where the arrest order was challenged by
those accused of having violated the ordinance of 1343. The
defence was all based on an argument that their use of papal
provision was anterior to the 1343 ordinance and that the ordinance was not meant to be retroactive. None of the accused clerks
were claiming that they were Englishmen and should therefore be
allowed to use papal provision.[43] Should we then conclude that
they were all foreigners?

A. D. M. Barrell lays great emphasis on the recurring phrase
'prejudicial to the king or to his people' and suggests that this
clause must have had the effect of singling out foreigners as the
main target of the seemingly broad ban of 1343.[44] He seems to
suppose that papal provisions for English candidates were not
prejudicial, or somehow less prejudicial to the king and his
subjects compared to papal provisions for foreign candidates. This
is where modern historians' prejudice is hampering the analysis of
medieval source materials. On what ground can one suppose that
papal provisions for English candidates were less prejudicial to the
king and his subjects? As I shall argue, the truth may be rather
that papal provisions for English candidates were all the more
detrimental to the rights of the king and his subjects (patrons) just
because they were so much more numerous than papal provisions
for foreign candidates. A. D. M. Barrell was certainly right in

---

[42] *Foedera*, II, p. 1230; *Calendar of close rolls, 1343–1346*, pp. 220–1.
[43] *Calendar of patent rolls, 1343–1345*, pp. 279, 289, 293, 320. See also the
references cited in Barrell, 'The ordinance of provisors', pp. 266, 268, 270.
[44] 'The ordinance of provisors', p. 266.

stressing the clause, 'prejudicial to the king or to his people' because the ban on papal provision was based precisely and wholly on that ground. The argument in the king's court and in Westminster Hall *had to* rely on the 'prejudice to the rights of the king and his subjects' because these rights – the patronage rights (advowsons) – were the only foothold common lawyers had in matters of ecclesiastical benefice. But it is wrong to imagine that the clause could be used to distinguish English candidates from foreign candidates and selectively promote the former. *All* papal provisions are prejudicial to the rights of the king and other non-papal patrons. Prejudice to the patronage right is a matter determined solely by looking at who is entitled to appoint the candidate. Who shall be appointed is irrelevant.

The same argument structure underlies the statute 25 Edward III st. 4 (commonly known as 'the statute of provisors'). The statute mentions, as a matter of principle, free election by the chapter, free collation by the prelates and free exercise of advowsons by religious houses. But the kernel of the statutory remedy was that if the pope made reservations or provisions for major or minor benefices, the privileges of free election, free collation and free exercise of advowsons would be removed from the Church or from the religious houses; and the king or other lay patron, as the case might be, should be entitled to give each such benefice to a suitable candidate of his or her choice. The reason was that the privileges of free election, etc. had originally been granted by the ancestors of the king and magnates as gifts to the Church and to religious houses; but the gifts were made under the condition that the king and his heirs should be entitled to give the licence to elect and the approval for the appointment. Since such conditions would be violated by papal provision, the conditional gifts should revert to the donor and his heirs.[45]

This statute does not allow any room for arguing that if papal

---

[45] *Rotuli Parliamentorum*, II, p. 233 ('dessicome les Elections furent primes grantes par les Progenitours le Roi sur certeins forme et condition, come a demander du Roi conge d'elire . . . Lesqueles conditions nient gardees, la chosse doit par reson resorter a sa primere nature'). See also the statute 25 Edward III st. 4, c. 3 (regarding elective benefices); c. 4 (benefices belonging to religious houses); c. 5 (collative, minor benefices). The statute of 1351 developed the theme which had already been put forward in the Carlisle parliament of 1307. The 'patronal attitude' which lies behind these arguments was noticed by Thompson, 'The statute of Carlisle', pp. 546–7.

provision was made for an English candidate, the king and other patrons would tolerate it.[46] Nor is there any promise that the king and other patrons would use the rights thus recovered to appoint English clerical candidates only. Nowhere in the statute do we find any possibility of differentiating English candidates from foreign candidates. The central concern of the argument is the protection of patrons' rights. *Any* attempt at papal provision, whether it is for the benefit of an English candidate or for a foreign candidate, encroaches upon these rights, and is therefore prejudicial to the king and his subjects who have these rights. It is unfortunate that the statute is known as the statute of 'provisors' because it is not so much about provisors as about patrons. The rationale for the strangely archaic claim of this statute is not to be intelligible from the standpoint of provisors or clerical candidates. The statute is best understood as an exaltation of patronage right (advowson). It is about how patrons parted with their advowsons and how they now asserted to recover them.

Until the end of Edward III's reign, common lawyers' argument showed no sign of departure from patrons' rights. In the eyes of the common lawyers, clerical candidates, foreign or English, had no legal right that could be proven in the king's court and enforced through the writ system. Clerical candidates merely had expectations which might be fulfilled or frustrated depending on the patron's success in the king's court. We have seen that Canon lawyers, in their earnest endeavour to protect the individual candidate's right, completely failed to take into account the question of public interest. Common lawyers were no less earnest in believing that their noblest mission was to protect and assert individuals' rights to the fullest degree permitted in law. They were no more likely to allow the consideration of public interest to interfere with their rigorously individualistic legal approach. Why should the king's and other patrons' rights to present a candidate of their choice be subjected to the restriction that the choice must only be made from English candidates? Why should the bishop's right to make appointments through the canonically sanctioned

---

[46] Not only on the level of legal argument, but also on the level of sentiments, a patron who lost the opportunity to support his favourite candidate because of a papally provided candidate would not find it consoling that the intruder was not a foreigner but an Englishman. In the vast majority of cases, the struggle was between English candidates anyway.

procedures be circumscribed by the condition that only English candidates should be eligible? Why should the king allow English candidates to seek papal provisions when his and his other subjects' rights and advowsons would be thereby infringed upon? If medieval lawyers offered no argument to promote English candidates and to discriminate against foreign candidates, it was not because they could not tell the difference between Englishmen and foreigners. They were operating under a fundamentally different system of legal arguments.

One can imagine that the king's court had little sympathy for the claims of bishops and their candidates even though their argument may have been well founded from the viewpoint of the Canon law. The losers in the king's court might therefore turn to Court Christian where their legitimate claims would not be ignored. However, the appeal to the authority of ecclesiastical jurisdiction is, from the viewpoint of common lawyers, an attempt to obstruct the king's law enforcement mechanism. This must not be tolerated if the common law system was to function effectively and reliably. Patent rolls in the fourteenth century are full of arrest orders directed to those who were pursuing appeals in Court Christian in derogation of the king's rights and judgments of the king's court. The statute of *Praemunire* was rooted in this tradition.[47] As Pantin pointed out, the fact that the papal court came under attack should not mislead us into exaggerating the modernity of the statute. Appeal to the papal court was condemned not because it was an alien court, but because it was an ecclesiastical court.[48] It did not matter whether the party resorting to the ecclesiastical court was a foreigner, an Englishman, a clerk or a layman. All that mattered was that the king's law enforcement mechanism should be maintained at the highest possible level of reliability and effectiveness. The improved dependability of the king's law enforcement mechanism was for the benefit of *anyone* whose claim was duly proven in the king's court. The provenance of the users of this mechanism remained irrelevant.

---

[47] See, for example, the statute 27 Edward III st. 1. On the writ of prohibition, which forms the background to this statute, see G. B. Flahiff, 'The writ of prohibition to Court Christian in the thirteenth century', 6, 7 *Medieval Studies* (1944–5) 261–313, 229–90.

[48] Pantin, *The English church*, pp. 84–7.

A NEW APPROACH FOR COMMON LAWYERS

One year before the death of Edward III (1376), the Commons in Parliament demanded exclusion of foreigners from benefices with cure of souls.[49] They were told that their demand was already met by the two major statutes on this matter ('Ceste Bille est aillours responduz, c'est assavoir en les deux autres grosses Billes de ceste matire'). The 'two major statutes' probably referred to the statute 25 Edward III st. 4 (the statute of 'provisors') and the statute 27 Edward III st. 1 (the statute of *Praemunire*). In the Parliament immediately following the death of Edward III (1377), the Commons raised the same issue again. A different response came: 'The Lords of the Great Council will ordain due remedy on this matter (*Les Seignors du Grant Conseil ordeigneront due remede sur la matire*).'[50] Six years later, it was enacted as follows:

if any alien has purchased, or from henceforth shall purchase any benefice of Holy Church, dignity, or other thing, and in his proper person takes possession of the same, or occupy it himself within the realm, [he shall be severely punished] whether it be to his own proper use or to the use of another.[51]

The argument contained in this statute has a few points which need to be discussed. First, there was a change of viewpoint. Until the end of Edward III's reign, the central question for common lawyers involved in legal disputes over ecclesiastical benefices was, 'who has the advowson?'. We now see a different question being posed: 'who shall have the benefice?'. The conflict situation was now approached from the viewpoint of the clerical candidates, rather than from the viewpoint of patrons.

Second, the candidate's provenance (whether he is an alien or not) has become vitally important in the new approach. So far, we have seen that if a person was lawfully elected or collated and found to be suitable for the post, he would be given the ecclesiastical benefice regardless of his provenance. Likewise, if a person was presented and, having satisfied the canonical requirements, instituted, there was no legal obstacle to his holding of the

---

[49] *Rotuli Parliamentorum*, II, p. 341 ('q nul Cardinal, ne Aliene hors de Roialme demorant, avera Benefice curee deinz les Esglises Cathedralx, ou Dignitez, ou Offices, lezqueux requirent residence').

[50] *Rotuli Parliamentorum*, III, p. 19.

[51] Statute 7 Richard II c. 12 (1383). *Rotuli Parliamentorum*, III, p. 162.

benefice. The only requirement, according to the contemporary lawyers' terminology, was that all these steps should be taken 'par deuwe proces' of the Canon law and the common law.[52] No one seems to have asked whether the candidate was an alien or not. This is not to suggest that the contemporaries were incapable of drawing a distinction between aliens and non-aliens. Our argument is simply that such a distinction was not regarded as relevant to the conferment of an ecclesiastical benefice. If, for example, a person was elected or collated to a benefice by due process of law, he would receive the temporalities upon doing of homage or fealty as required by the established law and practice.[53] He might not be an Englishman, but that did not make it impossible for him to enter into the contractual relationship expressed by homage or fealty. The person's foreign provenance and his contractually defined position as benefice-holder simply co-existed. The above-quoted statute indicates that such a situation would no longer be tolerated. According to the statute, the provenance of the clerical candidate would *first* have to be examined before deciding whether he was entitled to hold the land. This is a significant departure from the earlier legal argument structure where the candidate's provenance was not allowed to be discussed in connection with the conferment of ecclesiastical benefices.

Third, the statute offers a good opportunity to see how the question of public interest was being incorporated in common lawyers' argument. Unlike the ordinance of 1343 whose sole aim was to protect the 'patronage rights and advowsons of the king and his subjects (*iuris patronatus et advocationis nobis et fidelibus nostris*)', the above-quoted statute makes no mention of anyone's rights. Aliens, according to the statute, should be prohibited from holding ecclesiastical benefices. On what ground? We have already seen that the protection of the king's and his subjects' rights could provide no ground for discriminating against foreign clerical candidates. Like any other rights (*iura*) in medieval jurisprudence,

---

[52] For the expression 'par deuwe proces' in this context, see Anthony Fitzherbert, *Graunde Abridgement* (*c.* 1514–16), Quare non admisit, pl. 7.

[53] Although the investiture controversy made it unnecessary for consecrated bishops to do homage, the oath of fidelity was nevertheless required to receive the temporalities. Minor benefice-holders, *a fortiori*, were not exempted from the oath. *Glanvill*, lib. 9, c. 1; Gaudemet, *Le gouvernement de l'église*, II, p. 154.

advowson (*ius patronatus*) knew no barrier of ethnicity or provenance of the rightful claimant. The king and other patrons might, if they wished, use their advowsons to appoint foreign candidates. By doing so, they were exercising, not prejudicing, their rights and privileges. In fact, what the statute 7 Richard II purported to do was something which the traditional argument based on individuals' rights could never do: that is, to promote the interest of English clerical candidates by suppressing foreign candidates' expectations. That the king and his subjects should all exercise their rights in a way conducive to the 'common utility' was no doubt an idea which had long existed. But its enforcement seems to have depended largely on the sense of moral obligation. Now the statute of 1383, relying on the division between aliens and non-aliens, could provide a legal means of enforcing the noble obligation. Surely, the statute would demand the sacrifice of some of the individual patrons' well-established rights to promote whomever they saw fit. As any modern lawyer would agree, public interest requires some sacrifice of individuals' rights.

Parting with advowson and attempting to incorporate public interest into the legal argument, however, was bound to have a consequence which few common lawyers of the fourteenth century would readily accept: they would lose their unique foothold in matters of ecclesiastical benefice. Advowson, it must be recalled, was the only means of justifying common lawyers' involvement in the distribution of ecclesiastical benefices. No wonder the anti-foreign statutes of Richard II's reign were quietly stifled. Even after the radical constitutional changes introduced in the reign of Henry VIII, it was still not entirely clear whether foreigners might be disqualified from holding ecclesiastical benefices in England.[54]

---

[54] Watson, *The clergy-man's law*, ch. 20 states that an alien priest may be presented. Watson was relying on Henry Rolle (d. 1656), *Abridgment des plusieurs cases*, 2 vols. (London, 1668) II, p. 348. Edward Coke, on the other hand, claimed that if an alien was presented, the bishop ought not to admit him but might lawfully refuse him. *The Institutes of the laws of England*, IV, p. 338. He offered a similar opinion in *Waller's case* (1610), *Godbolt* 179. Rolle's *Abridgment* is generally regarded as not very trustworthy. But we believe that Coke is no more reliable on this point. Further details should await a separate treatment which is yet to be undertaken.

CONCLUSION

There is no need to discuss whether the statute of 1383 had actually been applied. The mechanisms for the distribution of ecclesiastical benefices, the patterns of legal disputes arising therefrom and the methods of resolving them remained unaltered throughout the fourteenth century and in the fifteenth century. Also, the statute was focused exclusively on the *conferment* of ecclesiastical benefices. Of course, the problems related to ecclesiastical benefices did not end there. Once a benefice was conferred, there arose another set of problems relating to the enjoyment of revenues from the benefice. I have refrained from discussing the legal difficulty which the non-resident benefice-holders (who were often foreigners) had to encounter in receiving revenues from their benefices in England. The scope of this chapter is thus very limited. It only deals with *one* aspect of foreign control of English ecclesiastical resources. Admittedly, the statute of 1383 had little impact even in this narrowly defined area.

Nevertheless, I believe that the statute is significant. The striking contrast it poses against the previous legal arguments contributes to a better understanding of the argument structure of the fourteenth-century lawyers. We also note with interest the statute's chronological proximity to the radical change of legal approach regarding foreign merchants (see chapter 2 above). We shall attempt a fuller discussion of the nature of these legal changes in the chapters that follow. In the remaining pages, I offer a few general remarks relevant to this chapter's discussion.

The emergence of the law of alien status has often been explained in terms of the growth of monarchical power. Professor Maitland suggested that 'an exaggerated generalisation of the crown prerogative' would explain the development of the English law of alien status. Professor M. Boulet-Sautel also argued that the French law of alien status must be studied against the backdrop of the political changes of the late medieval France which she characterised as 'an episode of the king's reconquest over the seigneurial authority'.[55] However, the actual circumstances in which lawyers began to rely on the division between foreigners

[55] See ch. 1 above; M. Boulet-Sautel, 'L'Aubain dans la France coutumière du moyen âge' in *L'Etranger*, part 2 (Brussels, 1958) pp. 68, 69, 88.

and non-foreigners do not seem to render support for these explanations. For instance, the systematic ban on foreign clerical candidates' access to ecclesiastical benefices would not necessarily bring gains to the king or enhance his dignity. It would not be entirely beneficial to the magnates or ecclesiastical institutions either. Indeed, the blanket ban against aliens was *infringing* upon the rights and liberties of the king and his subjects. If the new legal argument had been generally accepted and applied, the immediate beneficiary would have been the aspiring English clerical candidates, not the king, nor the magnates, nor the ecclesiastical institutions.

The growing awareness of national identity has been another favourite theme associated with the development of the law of alien status. Professor Maitland was arguing on this line when he conjectured that there could hardly be such a thing as English nationality in post-Conquest England, and that the starting point for the English law of alien status must be sought in the loss of Normandy. No doubt, the fourteenth-century source materials would offer a rich ground on which one might pursue and develop the topic of national identity. But our question is how such a mode of perception could be translated into a legal argument. We have seen that the repeated political attack on foreign clerks did not bring about an immediate change of legal argument. We need not ask whether the unresponsiveness of the lawyers was due to their inability or unwillingness. It is sufficient to point out that a legal argument based on allegiance or national identity would be repugnant to the fundamental legal values consistently upheld by medieval common lawyers. To say that the law of alien status resulted from the growing awareness of national identity is to run the risk of psychological determinism. We reject such an argument for the same reasons for rejecting an argument that economic relations alone would be sufficient to explain various historical changes.

It may seem attractive to argue that the statute of 1383 must be understood in light of the 'historical context' of the Great Schism and the death of Edward III. The appearance of several popes fiercely antagonising each other was no doubt a momentous political event which could provide an impetus for important reform movements. The end of the long reign of Edward III and the minority of his successor was no less significant. However,

how the parties involved would actually make use of this opportunity is something which the so-called historical context cannot
always tell. We know that the magnates and prelates, as well as
Edward III, were not entirely happy with the mechanism of
distribution of ecclesiastical benefices,[56] and repeated attempts
were made during his reign to change the situation. But the
systematic ban against aliens suggested by the statute of 1383
shows no connection or continuity with the blunt measures
attempted during the reign of Edward III. The new argument is
something that cannot be predicted or explained by looking at the
historical context. The systematic ban against foreign candidates
would infringe upon the rights of the magnates and prelates, not
to mention the king's rights. It would be strange to suppose that
the magnates and prelates would want such a measure now that
the powerful king was dead and the papacy was in deep trouble.
Rather, we are inclined to believe that the so-called historical
context does not allow us to predict the precise direction in which
the lawyers' creativity would take its course at the moment of a
revolutionary legal change. Once the change took place, one may
perhaps explain why it took place in the way it did. In doing so,
however, one may easily lose sight of the fact that at the actual
moment of the change, there could well have been viable alter-
natives. Repeated historiographical attempts to explain the whys
of a change might have the tendency to tint the change with an
aura of inevitableness which was probably not there at the time of
the change.

We do not wish to deny the eloquence of the exhortation that
legal changes should be studied in light of the 'real' motives.
Again and again, we have been told that in order to understand the
true meaning of the contemporaries' arguments, we must first of
all study who would gain and who would lose in real terms. But
the vice of explaining a legal change as if it is wholly explainable in
terms of the political, economic, psychological and other contextual parameters, is that we are often left with a wrong impression
that lawyers could say whatever they were asked to say.

---

[56] Cheyette, 'Kings, courts, cures, and sinecures' demonstrates that the clergy had
good reason to be unhappy about the legal remedies offered by the common
lawyers during Edward III's reign.

4

FOREIGN RELIGIOUS HOUSES

The one and a half centuries that followed the Norman Conquest were marked by 'a stupendous resurgence of monasticism' in England. The number of monasteries increased from 61 to about 700 between 1066 and 1215. Countless manors and estates were transferred to newly created or existing religious houses on both sides of the Channel for the spiritual well-being of the donor or the transferor.[1] In this chapter, we examine the foreign control of English lands resulting from these monastic endowments. It may be a delicate issue to determine the degree of 'foreignness' of the English daughter-houses of various foreign religious orders. We know that an alien prior could bring an action and the defendant's plea that the prior was an 'alien born' was not allowed. The reason was that the prior was bringing the action in right of the religious house, not in his own right (*car il port l'action come prior in iure domus et non in iure proprio*).[2] Whether cases like this can be interpreted as showing the existence of a theory of 'corporation' in medieval English law is not an easy question. But at least the case clearly shows that priors and abbots were regarded as holding the

---

[1] J. C. Dickinson, *The later Middle Ages: from the Norman Conquest to the eve of the Reformation – an ecclesiastical history of England* (London, 1979) p. 95. On the growth of monasticism during this period in general, we rely on D. Knowles, *The monastic order in England 940–1216*, 2nd edn (Cambridge, 1966). On the monastic endowments of the Norman kings in particular, see E. Mason, '*Pro statu et incolumnitate regni mei*: royal monastic patronage 1066–1154' in *Religion and national identity*, ed. S. Mews (Oxford, 1982) pp. 99–117. For the organisational details of the Religious (including canons regular and mendicant orders), see J. Hourlier, *L'Age classique, 1140–1378: les Religieux* (Paris, 1973).

[2] R. Brook, *Graunde Abridgement*, Denizen & alien, pl. 15 (39 Edward III). It may be inferred from this case that if a foreign-born person (*alien née*) brought an action in his own right (*in iure proprio*), the defendant could successfully bar the action by the plea of 'alien born'. We discuss the precise meaning of 'alien born' more fully in the following chapter.

land not in the same manner as a lay landholder.[3] For the purpose
of this chapter's discussion, it is sufficient to note that a prior or
monks, as individual human beings, might be born abroad but
that the religious house itself could not be said to be born as
human beings are born. If one envisages a regime (not necessarily
a legal regime) where the place of birth is closely connected to the
distinction between foreigners and non-foreigners, the foreign or
non-foreign status of a religious house is bound to pose difficult
questions.

Nevertheless, English daughter-houses of certain foreign religious orders were frequently referred to as 'alien priories'. It
seems that their foreign affiliation, personal composition, organisational and financial dependence were considered as the factors
contributing to their foreignness.[4] More importantly, the contemporary references to the 'alien priories' often include what are
known as 'dative priories'. These dative priories acted as bailiffs or
agents of a foreign abbot of a foreign abbey located overseas who
held English lands. All revenues from these lands were collected
and sent abroad by the proctor or bailiff resident in England.
Foreign control of English land was beyond doubt in these cases.[5]

So far, the history of the law of alien status has been studied
without taking due account of the foreign control of monastic
endowments.[6] Of course, the vicissitudes of the English possessions of foreign religious houses have been studied by many
historians.[7] But these studies were not focused on the development

---

[3] For further details, see F. W. Maitland, 'Corporation sole' in *Maitland – selected
essays*, ed. H. D. Hazeltine et al. (Cambridge, 1936) especially at pp. 86–7.

[4] For details, see D. Knowles, *The religious orders in England*, vol. II (Cambridge,
1955) pp. 127, 135; Dickinson, *The later Middle Ages*, p. 196.

[5] The head of a 'dative priory' who merely had the custody of the land as a proctor
or bailiff could not even be a party to a lawsuit touching the land. The lawsuit
had to be brought by, or against, the foreign abbot himself. The foreign abbot
could, of course, appoint his attorney in England to whom writs could lawfully
be directed. *Year Book*, Mich. 15 Edward III pl. 7.

[6] Clive Parry simply alluded to the 'curious phenomenon of denization of alien
priories' without any discussion. Parry, *British nationality law and the history of
naturalization* (Milan, 1954) p. 19.

[7] We refer to Chester New, *History of the alien priories in England to the confiscation
of Henry V* (Chicago, 1916); Rose Graham, 'Four alien priories in Monmouth-
shire', 35 *Journal of British Archaeological Association* (1929) 102–21; Graham,
'The papal schism of 1378 and the English province of the order of Cluny' in her
English ecclesiastical studies, (London, 1929) pp. 46–61; Marjorie M. Morgan,
'The suppression of the alien priories', 26 *History*, NS (1941); Morgan, *The*

of legal argument. Moreover, since their understanding of the 'alien' status of the foreign religious houses was based on an uncritical acceptance of the conventional view, their otherwise admirable works turn out to be rather a burden to an accurate understanding of the law of alien status. We propose to examine the *legal* aspect of what has so far been studied as the suppression of alien priories.

SEIZURES *IN MANU REGIS*, 1204–1413

The ecclesiastical terrae normannorum

The English lands of the Norman religious houses were taken into the hands of John on the occasion of the loss of Normandy. It was probably because the Norman abbots did fealty to Philippe Auguste and, to use the contemporary legal description, became '*inimici*' of John.[8] Henry III's seizure of the lands of Norman religious houses in 1244 appears to have had an identical legal structure.[9] Renowned jurists of the seventeenth century have argued that the seizure of the Normans' land indicated the subject status, rather than the alien status, of the Norman tenants. Had they been aliens, thus reasoned Sir Edward Coke in *Calvin's case* (1608), they would not have been able to hold any English land in the first place. That the king seized their English land only shows

---

English lands of the abbey of Bec (Oxford, 1946); Donald Matthew, *The Norman monasteries and their English possessions* (Oxford, 1962); Benjamin Thompson, 'The statute of Carlisle, 1307 and the alien priories', 41 *Journal of Ecclesiastical History* (1990). The list is by no means exhaustive.

[8] The seizure of the lay and ecclesiastical *terrae Normannorum* in or about 1204 is recorded in *Rotuli de oblatis et finibus* . . ., ed. T. D. Hardy, Records Commission (1835) p. 335; *Rotuli Normanniae* . . ., ed. T. D. Hardy, Records Commission (1835) pp. 122–37. The seizure *occasione Normannorum* was also mentioned in a case brought to the king's court a few years later. In that case, payment of money to Norman monks was described as payment 'ad inimicos domini regis ultra mare'. *Curia regis rolls*, vol. VI, pp. 85–6 (1210). Philippe Auguste's policy to demand fealty from the Norman lay and ecclesiastical lords is indicated in the pope's reply to the Norman bishops dated 7 March 1205. *Regesta pontificum Romanorum, 1198–1304*, ed. August Potthast (Berlin, 1874) no. 2435.

[9] The seizure is mentioned in *Matthew Paris, Chronica majora*, Rolls series, 7 vols., ed. H. R. Luard (1872–83) IV, 288; *Close rolls 1242–1247*, p. 337; F. M. Powicke, *The loss of Normandy 1189–1204* (Manchester, 1913), p. 423. A detailed discussion of the legal structure of these seizures will be attempted in ch. 6 below.

that they *did* hold land in England and, therefore, were the subjects of the English king. A few decades later, Sir Matthew Hale observed that the temporary seizure of the Normans' land became a permanent removal of land as the war with the French kings became almost perpetual. This, of course, was the beginning of the unchallenged historiographical tradition which Professor Maitland was relying on when he suggested that the English law of alien status must probably have begun with the loss of Normandy.

We shall discuss these points in some detail later on. For the purpose of this chapter's discussion, we simply note that the seizure of the Normans' lands can be understood *primarily* as a feudal legal measure based on the relationship between a lord and a tenant. Neither Coke nor Maitland seem to have denied this.[10] We therefore take this as the starting point of our discussion. It appears that the seizure *in manu regis* was one of the most commonly occurring procedures in the king's legal dealings with his tenants. For instance, upon the death of a lay tenant-in-chief, the fief was taken into the king's hands until the procedures of inheritance were completed. Upon the death of a bishop or an abbot who was a tenant-in-chief, the lands were taken into the king's hands until they were returned to the new bishop or abbot. Also, all tenants-in-chief, lay or ecclesiastic, foreign or English, who incurred the king's displeasure had to be prepared to have their land taken into the king's hands. Edward I's frequent seizures of the temporalities of the English as well as foreign abbots and prelates also seem to have been carried out on this ground.[11] In all these cases, there does not appear to have been

---

[10] When Maitland suggested that the starting point of the English law of alien status must be sought in the loss of Normandy, he was not arguing that the seizure of the Normans' land was in itself a legal measure based on alien status. The seizure was treated as an event providing the momentum for later legal development which he described as 'an exaggerated generalisation of the crown prerogative'. F. Pollock and F. W. Maitland, *The history of English law before the time of Edward I*, 2nd edn, 2 vols. (Cambridge, 1968), I, 463.

[11] In 1294, foreign and English abbots and the clergy recovered the king's protection in return for the grant of a moiety of their benefices and goods (*Calendar of patent rolls, 1292–1301*, pp. 89–95). The seizure of temporalities of all the clergy of the realm on 30 January 1297 is recorded in *Annales Monastici*, Rolls series, 5 vols., ed. H. R. Luard (1864–9) III, p. 405 (*Annales de Dunstaplia*); Bartholomew Cotton, *Historia Anglicana*, Rolls series ed. H. R. Luard (1859) pp. 318–19. See also Jeffrey H. Denton, *Robert Winchelsey and the*

any legal difference between the taking of an English tenant's land and that of a foreign tenant's land. They were tenants all the same.

The seizure did not mean irrevocable loss of the land. During the period of the seizure, the lands were under royal management. The king's bailiff would reap all the revenues except for some allowances necessary to avoid wasting of the lands. If the seizure was carried out against monastic endowments, suitable provision had to be made for the sustenance of the monks during the period of seizure.[12] To put an end to such an arrangement and to recover the seisin of the land, payment of a sum of money, among other things, was necessary. This was in order to have the goodwill of the king (*pro benevolentia regis habenda*).[13] Abundant records show that the king's goodwill knew no limit which a modern-day lawyer's notion of alien or subject status might impose. The seizure of the Norman religious houses was quickly ended and the lands, together with the king's goodwill, were restored upon payment of a fine.[14] The following case indicates that the seizures of John and Henry III did not throw any trace of doubt on the Norman abbot's ability to hold lands in England. When a Ralph de Cuylly claimed the manor of Edston (Aetherstone) in Warwickshire in 1275, the abbot of Bec-Hellouin vigorously defended his and his abbey's right in the manor. Through his attorney Richard de Flaunville,[15] the abbot put himself on the grand assize to prove his right. Upon default of Ralph de Cuylly, judgment was entered

Crown 1294–1313 (Cambridge, 1980) pp. 60, 107–33. The increasingly frequent seizures of the temporalities of the clergy during the reign of Edward III are discussed in J. R. L. Highfield, 'The relations between the Church and the English crown from the death of Archbishop Stratford to the opening of the Great Schism, 1349–1378', Oxford Univ. D.Phil. thesis, 1951, pp. 264–72.

[12] M. Howell, 'Abbatial vacancies and the divided mensa in medieval England', 33 *Journal of Ecclesiastical History* (1982) 181–7. I wish to thank Dr Martin Brett for kindly drawing my attention to this work.

[13] Matthew, *The Norman monasteries*, p. 77. Morgan, *The English lands of the abbey of Bec*, p. 120.

[14] Immediately after John's seizure, the prior of Ogbourne recovered the lands of the abbey of Bec-Hellouin upon payment of £100 and a promise that no issues would be sent abroad. *Rotuli de oblatis et finibus*, p. 314. In the same year, the prior of Frampton paid 100 marks to recover the custody of the abbey of Caen's manors. *Ibid.*, p. 199 (5 Oct. 1204). Numerous similar examples are given in Matthew, *The Norman monasteries*, p. 73; Powicke, *The loss of Normandy*, p. 425.

[15] On 6 January 1275, Richard de Flaunville was appointed the abbot's attorney and proctor-general in England for five years. *Calendar of patent rolls, 1275–1281*, p. 75.

for the abbot of Bec-Hellouin and the said Ralph was amerced. Throughout the case, no one thought it necessary or useful to investigate the alien or subject status of the abbot or the abbey of Bec-Hellouin.[16]

War-time seizures

The outbreak of the war between Edward I and Philippe IV led to the introduction of tight security measures against certain suspected foreigners. In September 1295, the monks who were under the power of the French king and of his allies were removed from places near the sea or navigable waters and relocated to other houses situated inland. Suitable English clerks were appointed to watch over them and to make inventories of their assets and revenues. Their lands and goods were taken into the king's hands.[17] In less than two months, the lands began to be restored on condition that a fixed sum of money should be paid yearly during the war.[18] When a definite peace was concluded in 1303, the situation came back to normal again. Most of the arrears of the heavy yearly farms were pardoned.[19]

If John's or Henry III's seizures of the land of the Norman religious houses were examples of feudal legal measures which were based on the relationship between a lord and a tenant, Edward I's seizure was a war-time sequestration of enemy assets. In neither case does the notion of alien status seem to have played any part. Edward I's seizure of 1295 was applicable to the foreign religious and laymen who were under the power of the French king or his allies only. It has already been carefully studied and

---

[16] *Select cases in the court of King's Bench under Edward I*, vol. I, 55 Selden Society (1936), pp. 16–19.

[17] *Calendar of fine rolls, 1272–1307*, pp. 362–6; *Calendar of close rolls, 1288–1296*, pp. 458–9. Details of the financial contribution exacted from these priories in 1294 are discussed in Thompson, 'The statute of Carlisle', pp. 554–5.

[18] On 14 November 1295, the bailiff of Warminghurst recovered the lands of the abbey of Fécamp upon payment of a fine. PRO E 106/3/19, mm. 4, 5. The reference is from Matthew, *The Norman monasteries*, p. 86. On 15 December 1295, the prior of Ogbourne recovered the lands of the abbey of Bec-Hellouin on a similar condition. Numerous other 'alien' priories followed suit. *Calendar of patent rolls, 1292–1301*, pp. 175–7.

[19] PRO E 106/4/18, PRO Ancient correspondence, XXVIII, 75. The reference is from Thompson, 'The statute of Carlisle', p. 555. See also Morgan, *The English lands of the abbey of Bec*, p. 122.

demonstrated that manors, churches and hospitals belonging to the mother-house or abbey which was not under the power of the French king were not treated as 'alien' priories.[20] The so-called 'alien' priories were in fact 'religiosi alienigena de potestate regis Franciae'.[21] Sometimes, *alienigena* was dropped and they were called simply 'religiosi de potestate regni Franciae'.[22] The reason for the seizure appears to have been their *enemy* status, which must be sharply distinguished from their alien status.

It may be unwise, it is true, to emphasise too much that the war-time seizure was not applicable to the foreign religious houses which were not deemed to be under the power of the French king. The relative security enjoyed by the daughter-houses of the Cistercian, Premonstratensian or Carthusian orders may equally be explained by the fact that their monks were mostly English. But the following remarks of D. Knowles must not be overlooked either: '[T]he Cistercians here never attempted – as the Cluniacs . . . attempted with success – to cut themselves loose from overseas control.' 'The provinces, and in particular the English Province [of the Carthusian order], never became self-consciously nationalistic and independent.'[23] The point is that during the period which concerns us, there was simply no clear-cut legal distinction between alien and subject status applicable to foreign religious houses in England. There was no such legal distinction because the existing rules derived from the feudal legal relationship and the ancient rules of war-time seizure and reprisal already provided a sufficient ground to seize the lands belonging to the religious houses concerned. It is a truism requiring no emphatic assertion that until and unless there arises a pressing need, no new legal rule will be invented. But, nevertheless, the truth needs recalling from time to time.

In time of peace, however, the French abbeys, not to mention other foreign religious houses, enjoyed full rights in their English lands.[24] The contemporary records provide ample evidence. We

[20] New, *History of the alien priories*, ch. 2.
[21] PRO E 106/3/10, 11. Quoted from Thompson, 'The statute of Carlisle', p. 555.
[22] Cotton, *Historia Anglicana*, p. 259.
[23] Knowles, *The religious orders*, II, pp. 127, 135.
[24] Thompson, 'The statute of Carlisle', p. 560; Matthew, *The Norman monasteries*, pp. 85ff.; and Morgan, 'The suppression of the alien priories', p. 209 all agree that French abbots could recover their lands upon concluding of a peace.

refer to an instruction which the prior of Frampton gave to his attorney in 1303. The attorney was told to receive the lands belonging to the abbot of Caen from the Chancellor and to do all other things which the concluding of the peace dictates and requires (*que forma pacis inter dictos reges . . . exigit et requirit*).[25] A similar war-time seizure was carried out in 1324–7. Again, we see that in May 1328, the abbot of Ivry was restored to his lands with their issues as from 11 April 1327, because, on that day, peace had been signed between England and France.[26] These cases make it impossible to establish any connection between the war-time seizure and the law of alien status. One of the essential features of the legal treatment of aliens is that the argument for the denial or restriction of their access to local resources is self-sufficient, and does not depend on military or other external events.

The war with French kings broke out intermittently in Edward III's reign. Similar war-time measures were repeated in 1337–60 and 1369–77.[27] The underlying legal reasoning remained unchanged. It is important to note that throughout this period, numerous foreign religious houses and their daughter-houses continued to buy English lands in intervals of peace. In short, '[t]he war did not fill them [Norman monasteries] with foreboding or make them less optimistic that they would enjoy their English property for ever'.[28]

Letters patent issued to Cluniac cells in the reign of Edward III must be understood against the backdrop of these war-time measures. In 1351, the prior of Lewes obtained exemption from war-time aids after having endowed the king with several advow-

---

[25] PRO Ancient correspondence, XXVIII, 75. Quoted from Matthew, *The Norman monasteries*, p. 86.

[26] For the seizure during 1324–7, see *Foedera* . . . , ed. T. Rymer, Records Commission 4 vols (London, 1816–69) IV, pp. 87, 96; PRO E 106/5/2 mm. 1, 3. Regarding the restoration of lands to the abbot of Ivry, see *Calendar of close rolls, 1327–1330*, p. 284.

[27] For 1337–60: *Foedera*, IV, 777; *Calendar of fine rolls, 1337–1347*, pp. 28ff.; *Calendar of patent rolls, 1334–1338*, pp. 483–4. For 1369–77: *Rotuli Parliamentorum*, 6 vols. (London, 1767–77) II, p. 302. These seizures generated a number of year book cases concerning the king's exercise of the advowsons belonging to the 'alien' priories while their lands were in the king's hands because of the wartime seizure. For references, see note 26, ch. 3 above.

[28] Matthew, *The Norman monasteries*, p. 103. From *Patent rolls* between 1282 and 1350, he finds many examples of 'alien' priories obtaining the licence to acquire lands in mortmain.

sons worth 200 marks per year.[29] Letters patent issued to the prior
of Thetford in 1376 make it clear that the burden of seizures and
aids, from which the prior sought exemption by paying £100, was
to last during the war only.[30] In both cases, it is true, the letters
patent stated that the recipient shall be reputed *'indigene'*.[31] This
term has been translated into 'denizen', and these letters patent
have been unquestioningly regarded as letters of denization.
However, as we have already argued at some length, it would be
quite inappropriate to render 'indigena' into 'denizen'.[32] No
definite set of privileges or disabilities was yet attributable to the
concept of 'indigena' or 'alienigena'. These terms were used as
factual epithets describing one's provenance. The precise legal
effects to be given to this factual attribute depended on the
particular circumstances in which these descriptions were used. In
the case of the letters patent issued to Cluniac cells, the legal
significance of the term 'indigena' must be understood in connection with the war and the enemy status of the recipients. It had
little to do with alien status.

The death of Edward III in June 1377 brought some change. As
soon as Parliament met on 13 October 1377, the Commons
succeeded in implementing a proposal which had been put
forward for quite some time. The following measures were agreed
upon in that Parliament: (1) certain Frenchmen, monks as well as
laymen, were to be expelled from the realm and were not to be
allowed to return while the war continued; (2) the religious service
to be performed in the priories thus evacuated was to be performed by English monks during the war; (3) the parish churches
belonging to these foreign religious houses were to be farmed out
to suitable (English) clerics for the duration of the war; and (4) the
lands of these foreign religious houses were to be farmed out for
the duration of the war to anybody offering the highest bid.[33]

---

[29] *Calendar of patent rolls, 1350–1354*, pp. 47–8.
[30] *Calendar of patent rolls, 1374–1377*, p. 301. In addition to the exemption from
the wartime aids, the letters also provide that 'in time of war they [the prior and
convent of Thetford] shall render to the king the 1 mark which in time of peace
they *ought to* pay yearly to the house of Cluny' (emphasis supplied).
[31] See PRO Patent rolls, 25 Edward III, part 1, m. 27; 50 Edward III, part 1, m. 5.
[32] See above, p. 46.
[33] *Rotuli Parliamentorum*, III, pp. 22–3. The proposal for expulsion of Frenchmen
to make way for English monks had already appeared in 1346. Ibid., II,
pp. 162–3. It was repeated in 1376: 'pur le temps q la Guerre se dure q touz les

Perhaps the harshness of these measures reflected the chaotic situation which followed the death of the long-reigning king and the minority of his successor. The expulsion of foreign monks and the regrant of the temporalities to lay farmers probably went beyond the established pattern of war-time treatment of alien priories which was particularly concerned about meticulous guarding of landholders' interests and protection of spiritual services by keeping the possessions of the Church from the hands of laymen.[34] Still, however, these measures were subject to the proviso, 'during the war (*durant la Guerre*)'. The essential similarity with Edward I's war-time seizure was thus maintained.

To confuse the war-time treatment of enemy with the permanent discrimination of alien is to miss the point altogether. Also, it is not of much use and, in our view, is probably wrong, to say that the law of alien status grew out of the war-time measures applicable to enemies. Wars have existed ever since the beginning of history. Seizures of persons and properties based on the notion of retaliation or reciprocity have an equally long history.[35] We wonder why the 'metamorphosis', if any, from the war-time treatment of enemy to the permanent discrimination of alien did not take place much earlier or much later.

Upon his accession in 1399, Henry IV vowed that 'it es noght my will that no man thynk yt [= that] be waye of Conquest I wold disherit any man of his heritage, franches, or other ryghtes that hym aght to have, no put hym out of that that he has and has had by the gude lawes and customes of the Rewme'. As part of the general restoration policy, the order of 1377 was rescinded and the lands were restored to the foreign religious houses.[36] A petition submitted by the Commons in 1410 seems to indicate that the 'gude lawes and customes of the Rewme' were still that the foreign abbots were the tenants who could sell or otherwise dispose of the

Franceoys soient bannes & oustes del Roialme'. Ibid., II, pp. 342–3. But none of them were allowed during the reign of Edward III.

[34] Morgan, 'The suppression of the alien priories', p. 207. It is true that the lands of some foreign priories were occasionally regranted to lay farmers during the reign of Edward III. But they were exceptions, rather than the rule. Matthew, *The Norman monasteries*, p. 109.

[35] See Pierre-Clément Timbal, 'Les Lèttres de marque dans le droit de la France médiévale' in *L'Etranger*, part 2 (Brussels, 1958) pp. 108–38.

[36] *Rotuli Parliamentorum*, III, p. 423; *Foedera*, VIII, pp. 101–2; *Calendar of patent rolls, 1399–1401*, pp. 70–2, 80–1.

lands which were seized in the king's hands because of the war.
The petition warns that if the lands were returned to the foreign
abbeys upon concluding the final peace, the king could no longer
expect to enjoy the windfall of wardship, marriage and other
profits because the religious houses never die or have children.
The petitioners suggested, however, that the lands which his
subjects acquired from the foreign abbots during the seizure
would continue to yield such profits for the king even after the
war. Considering this, it was proposed, the king should give
licence to his subjects to cross the sea to bargain and purchase the
English manors, lands, etc. from French abbots (*passer la meer
vers les parties de dela pur la bargaigner & purchacer des ditz Aliens
. . . ascuns des ditz Manoirs, etc.*). It was the best time to buy –
rather than seize – lands from the foreign landholders![37]

A NEW APPROACH – 1414

In 1413, seizure of the lands of the foreign religious houses was
done for the first time without any reference to the war. Instead, it
was proclaimed that the lands were to be seized in relief and
support of the communities of the realm (*en reliefment & supportation de les Communes*). In the following year, it was ordained that
the lands of the alien priories should remain in the hands of the
king and his heirs forever because restoring them to the foreign
religious houses upon concluding peace would be damaging to the
realm and to its people.[38]

Was it a new argument, or an old argument which had until
then been set aside because of some extra-legal considerations?
The question cannot be adequately dealt with until after we have

[37] *Rotuli Parliamentorum*, III, p. 644 ('Et en cas q . . . fynal Pees soit fait . . . Vous
ne prendrez ascune profit des ditz Manoirs, Seigneuries, Terres . . . des Aliens
avaunt ditz, esteantz en lour mayns propres . . . forsq tant soulement de ceux de
voz liege q purront purchacer ascunes des Manoirs . . . come de Gardes,
Mariages, et pur Fyns des Alienations, et plusours autre profitz q adonqs
appartinedront et deviendront a Vous a cause des purchacez').
[38] *Rotuli Parliamentorum*, IV, pp. 13 (1413), 22 (1414). The petition of 1414 also
recites that at the beginning of the war, the English subjects were permanently
disinherited from their possessions in France by a judgment rendered in France.
I did not, however, have the opportunity to verify the accuracy of this
statement.

examined the full range of late medieval common lawyers' arguments employed in dealing with other types of foreigners (i.e.,
foreign merchants, foreign clerks, foreign lay landholders) as well.
However, the theoretical structure of the arguments advanced in
1413 and 1414 deserves a few comments.

First, it is curious to see that those ordinances did not claim that
the king had any 'right' to keep the lands. According to the text,
the lands should remain with the king and his heirs not because
the king had a lawful claim to the lands and therefore to be
deprived of them would constitute an injury to him and his heirs,
but simply because it would be better that way for the people and
for the communities of the realm. This is remarkable all the more
because historians have for so long explained that an alien's
inability to hold English land was the offspring of the crown
prerogative. Since the essential features of the prerogative escheat
(one of the king's proprietary claims as an exceptional feudal lord)
had long been established by the time of those ordinances, we may
expect that a legal argument for permanent removal of lands from
foreign religious houses – if it indeed grew out of prerogative
escheat – should at least make some reference to this 'lawful' claim
of the king. The ordinances of 1413 and 1414 completely fail to
meet the expectation.

Second, the ordinance of 1414 claims that restoring the lands to
the foreign religious houses would be 'damaging' to the realm and
its people (*damage & perde aviendroient a votre dit Roialme & a
votre people*). Damage to others is, of course, a familiar ground for
imposing legal sanctions upon a person responsible for the
damage. But foreign religious houses' control over their lands, as
demonstrated by the petition of 1410, was based on their position
as 'lawful' tenants. In this case, one cannot claim damage or loss
with regard to, or arising from, their lawful control of the land
unless one has an overriding or at least an equally valid legal
claim. Now, what lawful claim could the *communes* or the *people* of
the realm have in regard to the lands belonging to the foreign
religious houses? On what ground could the *people* of the realm
possibly claim 'damage' or 'loss'? What rights (*iura*) did they have
for those lands?

What we see here is again how the rigour and the logical
coherence of medieval jurisprudence were being mollified by
emotional claims invoking 'relief and support of the communities

of the realm'. Foreign religious houses' claim for their English lands was firmly grounded upon their legal position as tenants. This means that they could count on the legal bond instituted by homage. As Glanvill explains, homage creates the 'bond of fidelity (*fidelitatis connexio*) between the lord and the tenant'. Bracton further stresses that this bond of mutual faith is legally recognised and protected. He thus refers to it as a 'bond of law (*vinculum iuris*)'.[39] The lawful tenant's control of the land is guaranteed by the binding power of this personal relationship. The ordinance of 1414 purports to sever this personal legal bond between foreign religious houses and their respective lord so that lands can be permanently removed from the foreign tenants.

Medieval common lawyers recognised two ways in which a tenant might lose control of the land. The first was with a judicial sentence. A formal conviction of felony, for example, would permanently tear asunder the legal bond between the lord and the tenant and, as a result, the latter would lose lawful control of the land. The second way was without a judicial sentence. In this case, the loosening of the legal bond was temporary. If, for instance, there were uncertainties about inheritance, the lord might take the land into his hands until the question of inheritance was lawfully settled. Also, if a tenant was suspected of a wrongdoing against the lord, the lord might, without a judicial sentence, take the land into his hands to compel the tenant to appear in his court.[40] During the war, of course, certain enemy assets might be temporarily taken into the king's hands. The ordinance of 1414, however, introduces a wholly new ground to sever the legal bond created by homage: relief and support of the communities of the realm. According to the ordinance, foreign religious houses were to be permanently (*pur toutz jour*) deprived of the control of their English land without any judicial sentence. This is an innovative and unprecedented argument. As far as I know, it had never before been claimed and openly accepted that the *vinculum iuris* between a lord and a tenant might be torn forever asunder without a judicial sentence. Of course, if a tenant died without an heir, the lord would permanently be released from the tenurial obligation; and

[39] *Glanvill*, lib. 9, c. 4; *Bracton*, II, p. 228. See also *Fleta*, vol. III, 89 Selden Society (1972) p. 38.

[40] For further details and references, see Keechang Kim, 'Etre fidèle au roi: XIIe–XIVe siècle', 293 *Revue Historique* (1995) 241–2.

no judicial sentence would be necessary for this to happen. Religious houses, however, never die.

Legal historians have paid virtually no attention to the significance of the inexplicable 'leap' from the temporary seizures to the permanent removal of the lands of foreign religious houses. Inexplicable as it is, the leap is a clear sign of the revolutionary change of argument structure which distinguishes medieval jurisprudence from modern jurisprudence. The crux of the argument contained in the ordinance of 1414 is that a person's firmly established legal position may be overridden by some such vague consideration as *reliefment & supportation de les Communes*. As far as I know, no medieval jurists would have willingly embraced such a radical claim. Few modern jurists, on the other hand, would find the considerations of public interest too vague and unwieldy for legal analysis.

We cannot stress too much that the idea of systematic legal discrimination against aliens must have been a radically new idea when it was initially introduced. Just like any other radical proposals for social and legal change, its implementation would require a comprehensive change of the existing resource distribution pattern. No new step in the law of personal status may be trodden without trampling on somebody else's vested interest. Each new step would require forcible removal of resources from certain groups of people who, until that moment, had never doubted the validity and legality of their claim. It is idle to expect that such a legal change could be accomplished overnight. As late as the middle of the fifteenth century, we see French abbots attempting to bring their 'lawful' claims as tenants of English lands. They probably did not realise that they were already living in an age where 'law' did not matter as much as 'faith' in our lord the king.[41]

---

[41] Matthew, *The Norman monasteries*, pp. 120–42; Morgan, *The English lands of the abbey of Bec*, p. 131, note 3 for further references to the claims put forward by French abbots. I wish to thank Dr M. Chibnall (Morgan) and Dr Martin Brett who read an earlier draft of this chapter and provided me with valuable comments and warm encouragement.

5

BIRTH BEYOND THE SEA

So far, we have discussed foreign merchants' acquisition of land and mercantile liberties, foreign clerks' control of ecclesiastical benefices and foreign religious houses' legal position as tenants of lands in England. Up until now, we have been able to avoid the question of inheritance because we were focusing on foreign merchants' *initial* acquisition of land and mercantile liberties; because ecclesiastical benefices were not treated as inheritable during the period that concerns us; and because religious houses do not die or have children. Discussion of lay landholding relationships, however, will invariably fall back on the question of descent and inheritance. We discuss it now.

PROOF OF DESCENT

Sir Anthony Fitzherbert, a renowned Common Pleas judge in the sixteenth century, made the following remark on the significance of the writs in the common law: 'Note that the writs are the principal and primary things in our law, by which man recovers what has been wrongly detained from him, and they are the foundation of each lawsuit.' To commence a procedure, the learned judge added, one ought to have a good writ, for otherwise all the rest would be worthless.[1] What is a good writ? The answer will amount to a full history of the development of the common law. Fitzherbert was certainly not interested in the historical

---

[1] *Diversite de courtz et lour iurisdictions et alia necessaria et utilia* (printed by R. Redman in 1523) fo. C.4 ('Nota que les brefes sount les principalx et premer choses en nostre ley, per queux home rec. ceo que a tort luy est deteyn, et le foundation de chescun sute . . . vide quant home comence son sute, que le bref soit bon, ou tout qui ensuer ne vault riens').

investigation of the writ procedures and the development of the
common law. Nevertheless, his statement is broad enough to
throw light on the situation of post-Conquest England, which
must be briefly sketched to prepare the ground for the discussion
of this chapter.

Before royal writs were regularly used for judicial purposes,
they were often used to communicate the king's executive
command in post-Conquest England.[2] The parties involved in a
land dispute often appear to have resorted to this expedient, non-
judicial means of settling the dispute. The executive writ of this
kind would specify the parties, the location of the land in dispute,
the allegation of wrongful detainment and the king's command to
restore the seisin:

William, king of the English, to R[anulf], brother of Ilger, greeting. I
command and order you to let abbot Herbert have the half hide of land of
Sawtry which Ailwin the reeve has held and which Walter de Beaumais
now holds by force, as I have ordered by my writ. And see that I hear no
further complaint thereof for default of right on £10 forfeiture.[3]

The message was clear: instant satisfaction. Perhaps the king was
here exercising his power as the feudal lord of the land under
dispute. In such a case, the line between adjudication and administration was perhaps not always easy to draw. But at least what
one can say with confidence is that the exercise of power to
maintain peace and order did not yet have to be always justified by
formal procedures supervised by the king's justices. The birth of
the common law was yet to be seen.[4]

A common law writ may, to some extent, resemble an executive
writ:

The king to the sheriff, greeting. Command N that justly and without
delay he render to R one hide of land in such and such a vill, whereof the
said R complains that the said N deforces him. And if he does not do this,
summon him by good summoners that he be before me or my justices on
the morrow of the second Sunday after Easter at such a place to show why
he did not do it. And have there the summoners and this writ.[5]

---

[2] *Royal writs in England from the Conquest to Glanvill*, 77 Selden Society (1958–9)
pp. 177–94.

[3] *Royal writs in England*, p. 444, no. 63 (*c.* 1087–91).

[4] R. C. van Caenegem, *The birth of the English common law*, 2nd edn (Cambridge,
1988) ch. 2.

[5] *Royal writs in England*, p. 437, no. 50 (the specimen writ is from *Glanvill*, lib. 1,
c. 6).

One of the features which distinguish a common law writ from the earlier executive writs is the phrase which anticipates non-compliance with the king's command ('if he does not do this. . .'). The party's non-compliance sets in motion the formal procedures for proof of the claim before the king's justices. The proceedings commenced by the above-quoted writ revolved around the question of descent and inheritance. According to the legal language of the time, the demandant is claiming what is his right and his heritage (*son droit et son heritage*). The proof of this claim must be done by tracing the good descent from an ancestor who once had the land rightfully.[6]

In our view, legal consequences of foreign birth must be understood in light of this development of the common law and writ procedures in post-Conquest England. While the parties were allowed to resort to non-judicial, executive means to resolve their land dispute, it would be nonsensical to discuss the 'legal' consequences of foreign birth. The discussion becomes meaningful only when judicial proof of the party's claim was regularly required as a condition for granting an official remedy for private grievances. Birth beyond the sea, however, could not have posed legal difficulties in claiming inheritance while the discovery of judicial truth relied on ordeal (judicial combat) or other supernatural divinatory force.

The brilliant success of inquest, which was welcomed as a new mode of proof, brought an important change. A decisive legal reform, which led to an extensive use of inquest, was accomplished by Henry II when he introduced four petty assizes in the late twelfth century.[7] The question of descent maintained its importance in one of these assizes. The writ for the assize of *mort d'ancestor*, for example, had to specify the location of the land, the command to summon twelve free and lawful men from the vicinity of the land (*duodecim liberos et legales homines de uisneto de illa uilla*), and the following questions to be put to these men: 'Whether O the father of G was seised in his demesne as of his fee

---

[6] S. F. C. Milsom, *Historical foundations of the common law*, 2nd edn (Toronto, 1981) pp. 124–34. Elsie Shanks (ed.), *Novae Narrationes*, 80 Selden Society (1963) pp. xxxi–xxxix (Milsom's introduction).

[7] Development of petty assizes is attributed to the Assize of Clarendon (*c.* 1166) and the Assize of Northampton (1176). Van Caenegem, *The birth of the English common law*, pp. 40–50.

one virgate of land in that vill on the day he died and whether the said G is his next heir'.[8] The remaining three petty assizes were not immediately concerned with the question of descent. But the party who lost in a possessory assize could always bring the matter of right, as opposed to possession, back to the local or the king's court. Then the question would again be discussed in terms of descent and inheritance.

By the end of the twelfth century, it was clear that discovery of judicial truth could no longer rely on ordeal or oath. Already, procedural requirements of oath (wager of law) had become so elaborate that except in some narrowly defined areas, proof by oath had lapsed into virtual disuse by then. Ordeal was definitively abolished in England following the decree of the fourth Lateran Council (1215) which forbade the clerical participation in the ceremony.[9] Judicial combat was still a legitimate method of proving one's right. But in judicial proceedings commenced by a writ of right, the tenant could avoid battle by choosing the grand assize. If, moreover, the demandant started out by putting himself upon the grand assize, the outcome of the case must 'stand or fall by the assize'. Clearly, inquest was the preferred method of proof.[10]

If the inquest (grand assize), rather than battle, was chosen as the method of proving the party's right and inheritance, the proceedings commenced by a writ of right would be stopped upon production of a writ of peace sued out by the tenant. The demandant would have to purchase another writ for summoning four knights from the neighbourhood. These four knights would then elect twelve knights of the same neighbourhood (*duodecim legales milites de eodem visneto qui melius veritatem sciant*) who were to declare on oath which of the parties had the greater right in the

---

[8] *Glanvill*, lib. 13, c. 3 ('Si O pater predicti G fuit saisitus in dominico suo sicut de feodo suo de una uirgata terre in illa villa die qua obiit . . . si ille G propinquior heres eius sit'). For variations, see cc. 4–6.

[9] F. Pollock and F. W. Maitland, *The history of English law before the time of Edward I*, 2nd edn, 2 vols. (Cambridge, 1968), II, p. 601 ('In the twelfth century, such elaborate forms of asserveration had been devised [for oath-taking] that rather than attempt them, men would take their chance at the hot iron'), II, 599 (abolition of ordeal).

[10] *Glanvill*, lib. 2, c. 6. Glanvill extolls the virtues of grand assize and compares them with the drawbacks of judicial combat (lib. 2, c. 7).

land in question.[11] Whether it was a question of right or of possession, therefore, the inquest of the neighbours (the grand assize of knights or the petty assize of free-men) became the most important means of proving the party's claim to the land under dispute. From then on, foreign birth would be problematic.

PROCEDURES OF INQUEST

Real estate management in the Middle Ages required, among other things, a careful surveillance over the tenants' deaths. Upon death of a tenant, the following circumstances had to be investigated before the next legal step could be taken: Were there heirs? Were they legitimate? Were they male or female? How old were they? Various legal consequences (escheat, admittance of the heir to the land, payment of relief, wardship and marriage) depended on the outcome of these investigations.

According to Glanvill, a lord could take the fief of the deceased tenant into his hands if there were uncertainties about who should be admitted as the rightful descendant. The lord might retain the fief until the question of descent was lawfully proved to him. The proof had to be done in adversarial trial proceedings commenced by the party claiming to be the rightful descendant.[12] The king, however, enjoyed a special protection for his feudal interests. Fiefs held in-chief (i.e., directly from him) were automatically taken into the king's hands upon the tenant's death even if there was no doubt as to the rightful heir. Circumstances relevant to inheritance were then investigated by the king's escheators. The popularity of inquest was not limited to adversarial trial procedures. The investigation conducted by the king's escheators also relied on the inquest of the neighbours to resolve doubts relating to the descent and escheat of the land held in-chief.[13]

Whether in adversarial trial proceedings or in the non-

---

[11] *Glanvill*, lib. 2, cc. 7–9. Our explanation assumes the case where the grand assize is chosen by the tenant. Glanvill also gives an explanation of the procedures where the demandant started out by putting on the grand assize.

[12] *Glanvill*, lib. 7, c. 17; lib. 9, c. 6 respectively.

[13] *Glanvill*, lib. 9, c. 6 (Hall, p. 110); *Calendar of inquisitions miscellaneous, passim. Select cases in the court of King's Bench under Edward I*, vol. I, 55 Selden Society (1936) pp. 139–40.

adversarial fact-finding sessions supervised by the king's escheators, the inquest to prove the heir's age and proximity of blood had to rely on personal attestation of the neighbours. Quite often, a person would have been born in the neighbourhood of the land which later involved him in legal disputes. Glanvill revealed this presumption when he explained that a person's age should be proved by 'eight free and lawful men from the neighbourhood of that vill, where the tenement in question lies'.[14] What if, however, the person was born in a county which was different from the county where the judicial proceedings were pending? Could the jury from the vicinity of the land give a verdict on the age of a person born in a different county? The answer was partly provided by Glanvill himself, who stated that the verdict of an inquest ought to be based on the first-hand knowledge of the jurors.[15] An exemplary writ from a fourteenth-century register of writs makes it clear that the age of John 'who was born at L in the county of Leicester and baptized in the church of the said vill' had to be proved by 'the oath of knights as well as of other trustworthy [and lawful] men from that neighbourhood (*de visneto illo*)'. The king's escheator was commissioned to proceed to the county in which the said John was born in order to conduct the inquest. We also have a source which demonstrates that the proof of age of a person claiming the inheritance of lands in Cornwall and Devon was done in Ireland where the person was born. The king's escheator had to cross the sea to conduct the inquest.[16] The same principle was

---

[14] Lib. 13, c. 16 ('octo liberos et legales homines de visneto de illa villa ubi petitum tenementum est').

[15] The only exception, according to Glanvill, was the statement of one's father which was made under exceptionally credible circumstances: 'The knowledge required from the jurors is that they shall know about the matter from what they have personally seen and heard, or from statements which their fathers made to them in such circumstances that they are bound to believe them as if they had seen and heard for themselves' ('Ad scientiam autem eorum qui super hoc iurant inde habendam, exigitur quod per proprium uisum suum et auditum illius rei habuerint noticiam, uel per uerba patrum suorum et per talia quibus fidem habere teneatur ut propriis).' Lib. 2, c. 17. Severe punishment measures awaited those who swore rashly (i.e. without the required first-hand knowledge of the matter) in the grand assize. Lib. 2, c. 19.

[16] *Early thirteenth-century registers of writs*, 87 Selden Society (1970) pp. 244–5 ('qui apud .L. in comitatu Leyc' natus et in ecclesia eiusdem ville baptizatus fuit . . . sacramentum tam militum quam aliorum proborum [et legalium hominum] de visneto illo'). The writ is from a register of writs in the Bodleian Library which G. D. G. Hall dates between 1318 and 1320 (pp. lv–lxi). See also

maintained in adversarial trial procedures as well. The difference was that in the case of a trial it was the jurors who had to travel. The demandant suing for the right or possession of a land took the responsibility to have the original writ directed to the sheriff of the county in which lay the land under dispute. It was an important procedural requirement which facilitated summoning of the competent jury, viewing of the land, and execution of the judgment. The original writ for a possessory assize, for example, contained a clause for summoning the jury from the vicinity of the land under dispute. When the parties met in the courtroom, therefore, the twelve men were expected to be already there, well informed of the case. If, however, the age or proximity of blood of a person who was born in a different county had to be decided, the present assize could not try the issue. The party who was pressed to prove these points ought to obtain the writ *venire facias* which must be directed to the sheriff of the county in which took place the event at issue (birth, for example). Upon receipt of the writ, the sheriff would summon the twelve free-men with the first-hand knowledge of the event and command them to travel to the county in which the case was pending so that they could give their verdict there. Statutes dealing with financial requirements of jurors clearly anticipated the situation where jurors had to travel to a different county to give their verdict. Those who were to be empanelled in such an inquest had to meet higher financial requirements than the jurors who did not have to travel outside the county to give their verdict.[17]

Year book cases confirm our argument. One example should suffice. The demandant in a land dispute stated that when a Joan died without an heir of her body, the manor went to Maunser, her brother. The demandant was a grandson of Maunser. The claim was based on his descent from Maunser. The tenant pleaded that Joan had issue born in Lancashire and that an heir from that issue was still alive in the said county. The tenant offered to prove this

Calendar of Inquisitions miscellaneous, 1–7 Richard II (1377–1384) no. 350 (proof of age done in Ireland).

[17] Fitzherbert's explanation of the writ *venire facias* does not explicitly deal with the situation where the jurors from one county have to travel to another (*Natura brevium*, fo. 206: '[the writ *venire facias*] est briefe direct al vicount q il fac. venir xii loyalx homes et dignes de mesme le pais pur passer et doner lour verdit sur le dit issue pris'). But see Statute of Westminster II (13 Edward I) c. 38 (1284); Statute 21 Edward I (1292) for the differential financial requirement.

by a jury from Lancashire. The demandant responded that Joan died without heir of her body in Berkshire and offered to prove this by a jury from Berkshire. The outcome of the case is not clear from the record. But Bereford J remembered in the case that in an assize of *mort d'ancestor* held in Kent, the jurors responded that they did not know if the demandant was the heir because he was not born among them. The court therefore had to order an inquest to be taken in the place where the demandant was born.[18]

All these are pointing to one thing: unlike in France, the inquest in England persisted as the inquest of the neighbours (*inquisitio patriae*). Jurors were required to have first-hand knowledge of the event about which they were to give a verdict.[19] Belknap CJ explained this as follows: 'In an assize in a county, if the court does not see six or at least five men of the hundred where the tenements are, to inform the others who are further away, the assize will not be taken. *A multo fortiori*, those of one county cannot try a thing which is in another county.'[20] If an inquest assumed to take cognisance of an event transpired in another county, the jurors were liable to be punished by attaint.[21] In a case recorded in *Coram rege roll* (1285), the defendants pointed out that the king's escheator should not have conducted an inquest to prove the age of a foreign-born person: 'Nec videtur eis quod

---

[18] *Year Books of 3–4 Edward II 1309–1311*, 22 Selden Society (1907) p. 151, pl. 46 (writ of cosinage).

[19] The *enquéte* in France took a different course of development under the overwhelming influence of the Canon law. According to Maitland, this divergence is one of the grand problems in the comparative legal history between England and France. Pollock and Maitland, *The history of English law*, II, p. 604. For the expression *inquisitio patriae*, see Statute 12 Edward I (Statute of Wales) c. 8. Statutes repeatedly stress that immediate, first-hand knowledge is required. Statute 28 Edward I, Art. sup. cart. c. 9; Statute 34 Edward III c. 4 (*les plus procheins*); Statute 42 Edward III c. 11 (*q ont meillour conissance de la verite et pluis proscheins*). The terminology was probably derived from *Glanvill*, lib. 2, c. 17 ('duodecim legales milites de eodem visneto qui melius veritatem sciant').

[20] *Le livre des assises et pleas del Corone* (*Liber assisarum*) (London, 1679) 48 Edward III, pl. 5. Quoted from James Thayer, *A preliminary treatise on evidence at the common law* (London, 1898) p. 91. The same principle had already been stated by Justices Malory and Brabazon in 1313. *The eyre of Kent, 6–7 Edward II, 1313–1314*, vol. I, 24 Selden Society (1909) pp. 127–8.

[21] See the cases classified and explained by John Rastell under the heading, 'Ou enquest prend conusance de chose fait en auter counte sur peyn de attaint ou des chose espirituelz et ou de record' in his *Tabula libri magni abbreviamenti librorum legum Anglorum* (London, 1517) 'enquest'.

inquisicio debet fieri de etate alicuius probanda nati in transmarinis partibus.' The jurors were therefore resummoned to certify to the king about 'certain matters touching their original testimony (*de quibusdam articulis inquisiciones illas tangentibus*)'. The record ends there.[22] But if the jurors were found guilty of rashly swearing the foreign-born heir's age without first-hand knowledge, they would face severe punishment.

In my view, a foreign-born person was left with no adequate means to defend himself from allegations regarding under-age or proximity of blood. The inquest, which had to be taken in the birthplace, was impossible because the king's writ could not run beyond the sea. In 1321, for example, we see Herle J confronting a defendant with the following remarks: 'Your father was not from England. How could this court be apprised of whether he was a brother or the uncle or the son since he was not born in this land (*vostre pier ne fut de la ligaunce dengleterre. Coment purra cest court estre apris lequel il fut frer ou uncle ou fuyz, depus qil ne fut pas nee en cest terre*)?'[23] Regarding foreign deaths, Hengham J observed as follows: '[If the ancestor] died out of the kingdom, how could men of this country know whether he died in his demesne or not [i.e., whether he himself was exploiting the land or had granted it to someone else before he died]?'[24] In the case of the foreign death of an ancestor, however, the difficulty of proof could be removed by a special writ of *mort d'ancestor* where the demandant was allowed to state that the ancestor was seised in his demesne 'on the day he embarked his journey abroad' instead of 'on the day he died'.[25] Regarding the foreign birth of an heir, there was no such way out. The obvious result is that a foreign-born heir would be defenceless against a lord who would refuse to allow inheritance. If there is no one else who could claim the inheritance, the fief would fall back on the lord as his escheat.

Certain issues could not be tried by an inquest of the neighbours. The issue of bastardy generally alleged against a party to a lawsuit had to be certified by 'the archbishop or bishop of the

22 *Select cases in the court of King's Bench*, I, p. 139.
23 *The eyre of London, 14 Edward II, 1321*, vol. II, 86 Selden Society (1969) p. 214.
24 *The eyre of Kent, 6–7 Edward II, 1313-1314*, vol. III, 29 Selden Society (1913) p. 48.
25 *Glanvill*, lib. 13, cc. 5–6.

place'.[26] The party applying for a writ for the certification of the
ordinary assumed the responsibility to have the writ directed to
the bishop who had proper ecclesiastical jurisdiction over the
person whose legitimacy was challenged.[27] Under the Canon law,
a person's status as *incola* or *advena* to a parish was determined
mainly by domicile.[28] If the person against whom bastardy was
alleged had no domicile in a diocese whose bishop was bound to
execute the command of the English king, the certification would
be impossible. Even if a person had a domicile in England, it is
unlikely that the bishop would certify legitimacy when no one in
his diocese, except for the immediate family members of the
person, had first-hand knowledge of the circumstances of the birth
and of the parents' marriage. In other words, the bishop's inquest
of bastardy also depended on the common knowledge of the
neighbours.[29] It would follow that those who came over from
beyond the sea – in person or by an attorney – to claim inheritance
had no procedural means to defend themselves from the allegation
of bastardy.[30]

As inquest of the neighbours and certification of the ordinary
became the firmly established means of discovering judicial truth,
the legal difficulty of inheritance confronting a foreign-born
person became insurmountable. For example, Matthew Paris
noted that Henry III was criticised in the Parliament of 1248 for
disinheriting his tenants-in-chief by sending their daughters
abroad for marriage.[31] The point is that if the person thus

---

[26] *Glanvill*, lib. 7, c. 13 (*archiepiscopo uel episcopo loci*). Fitzherbert, *Diversite de
courtz*, fo. C.6v. If bastardy was not generally alleged against a party to the
lawsuit, but against a third party, the issue had to be tried by a jury summoned
from the birthplace of the person. *Year Books of 3–4 Edward II, 1309–1311*, 22
Selden Society (1907) p. 30, pl. 3. *Year Books of 1–2 Edward II, 1307–1309*, 17
Selden Society (1903) p. 95, pl. 42 (the party averred that his father (now
deceased) was not a bastard, and offered to prove this by 'paiys du counte ou il
[the father] fust nee').

[27] William Clerke, *The triall of Bastardie* . . . (London, 1594) fos. 24–38.

[28] W. Onclin, 'Le Statut des étrangers dans la doctrine canonique médiévale' in
L'Etranger, part 2 (Brussels, 1958) pp. 42–7.

[29] R. H. Helmholz, 'Bastardy litigation in medieval England' in his *Canon law and
the law of England* (London, 1987) p. 188. Bishop's certification usually stated
'communis fama laborat quod dicta C. fuerat nata in legitimo matrimonio,' etc.

[30] Quite often, therefore, a wholesale accusation of illegitimacy was thrown against
foreign-born children in general. See Chris Given-Wilson and Alice Curteis,
The royal bastards of medieval England (London, 1984) pp. 138ff.

[31] *Chronica majora*, 7 vols., ed. H. R. Luard, Rolls series (1872–83) V, p. 5

'married off' beyond the sea had all her children over there, then her land would probably fall back into the king's hands when she died. Henry III had to do this because he was in dire need of land due to the vast number of his foreign favourites.[32] That the lands thus removed from *nobiles regni* were given to foreigners from Provence, Savoy and Poitou was noticed, but duly ignored by legal historians as insignificant for the development of the English law of alien status.[33]

By the late thirteenth century, we have clear evidence that foreign birth was treated as fatal to any claim based on inheritance.[34] The expression *alienigena* was often used in this connection. First and foremost, it was a factual description referring to the person's foreign birth or provenance. Now, the question is whether the factual event of foreign birth was linked to the legal status of alien.

LEGAL CONSEQUENCES OF FOREIGN BIRTH

Did foreign birth make a child an alien? The conventional answer given by legal historians is as follows: (1) children born abroad were unable to inherit; (2) the inability to inherit was the proof of their alien status; (3) foreign birth, therefore, makes a person an alien. We began with a simple fact that foreign birth made inheritance impossible. But legal historians have somehow arrived at the twofold conclusion that foreign birth made a person an alien, and that the alien status made inheritance impossible. What was injected in between was their preconceived assumption that aliens, unlike subjects, were under legal disability (i.e. inequality between subjects and aliens), and that no such disability was

('reprehensus est insuper gravissime super . . . [quod] nobiles regni ignobilibus extraneis maritavit').

[32] H. W. Ridgeway, 'Foreign favourites and Henry III's problems of patronage', 104 *English Historical Review* (1989) 590–610. M. Prestwich, *English politics in the thirteenth century* (London, 1990) p. 94.

[33] Pollock and Maitland, *The history of English law*, I, p. 464.

[34] See, for example, a petition filed by Petrus Malore in the Parliament of 1289 (*Rotuli Parliamentorum*, I, p. 44); a charter issued to Elyas Daubeny in 1295 (*Rotuli Parliamentorum*, I, p. 135). These documents, however, have so far been regarded as indicating the legal disability of *aliens* rather than *foreign-born persons*.

applicable to subjects (i.e., equality among subjects). It is an assumption which is not permissible for a historical investigation into the *beginning* of the law of alien status. The assumption defeats the whole purpose of investigation.

Whether children born beyond the sea were regarded as *foreigners* due to their birthplace, I do not propose to investigate. It is a question of ethnicity and group psychology rather than of legal history. Whether they were regarded as *aliens* due to their birthplace, I propose simply to dismiss because the question is grounded upon anachronistic assumptions. All that needs to be said is that foreign-born children could not inherit. They *would* inherit if they *could* prove the descent in spite of their foreign birth. I have already mentioned a case (1285) where a foreign-born heir claimed inheritance in the court of King's Bench arguing that he became full age. In that case, the age of the foreign-born heir was somehow proved by an inquest conducted by the king's escheator. We saw that the legality of such an inquest was challenged. But apart from that, neither the defendants (whom the king had given the land in wardship while the heir was under age) nor the king's justices mentioned a word about the alien or subject status of the heir. All that mattered was whether or not, and how, the proof of the heir's age or the alleged breach of the terms of wardship (the heir was accused of having refused the marriages duly offered to him) could be done.[35] Also, in a *Quo warranto* case brought to the eyre of London (1321), the defendant argued that his foreign-born father (whose inheritance was critically important to the defendant) was 'held and reputed as the son and heir in the city of London'. The court exceptionally allowed an inquest to be

---

[35] Whether the birthplace (Boulogne, in this case) was 'within the king's allegiance' when the heir was born is an anachronistic question. The question assumes that allegiance would determine one's legal status as subject or alien and that allegiance was not a matter of mere geographical location but a matter of subjection to the legitimate political power. It was only in the sixteenth century that common lawyers began to think on this line (ch. 7 below). In the case brought in 1285, the parties disputed whether the Queen consort of Henry III was staying in Boulogne when the heir was born there. This was because the Queen's itinerary was recorded in the Exchequer records, and if the heir was born while the Queen was in Boulogne, his date of birth could be established with greater precision by looking at the Exchequer records showing the Queen's sojourn in Boulogne. All this was aimed at establishing whether the heir had reached full age or not. *Select cases in the court of King's Bench*, I, p. 139.

taken from London ruling that 'if the defendant can prove what he said, it will be very hard (*mult fort*) to exclude him'.[36]

It must be remembered that foreign birth posed no problem, either for an Englishman or for a foreigner, in acquiring or disposing of land by sale or gift. We have already discussed foreign merchants' landholding (in chapter 2). Helen Cam, who edited the manuscripts of the eyre of London (1321), observed as follows: 'The few cases in the Eyre in which aliens are involved show them as fully at home in London, purchasing and owning houses, enjoying legal rights as private persons and making use at will of the legal facilities open to natives.'[37] What she called 'aliens' were, in our view, foreign-born persons, that is, foreign-born Englishmen as well as foreigners who were born abroad. Helen Cam's remark can be understood as a confirmation of our argument that foreign merchants and other foreign-born persons were under no legal disability regarding their *initial* acquisition of houses and land. Also, a number of foreigners were given land and made earls as late as the last quarter of the fourteenth century.[38]

It is worth noting that foreign-born persons were in a better legal position than illegitimate persons. Neither of them could claim inheritance, of course. But, unlike illegitimate persons (whose wealth could only be inherited by the heir(s) of the body), foreign-born persons could count on collateral heirs, as well as the heirs of the body, for transmission of their wealth upon their death. A case brought to the eyre of Northamptonshire (1329–30) offers an example. The jurors stated that the demandant entered the land under dispute as of escheat because his tenant was 'an alien and died without an heir of his body'. Scrope J replied, 'That is not a cause for escheat.' The jurors were instructed to find out whether the 'alien' tenant died 'without an heir'.[39] The same

---

[36] *Eyre of London, 14 Edward II, 1321*, p. 213 (*Rex v. Philip de Beauvais*). We discuss this case in more detail in the following chapter.

[37] *Eyre of London, 14 Edward II, 1321*, p. cxxvii.

[38] For references, see Chris Given-Wilson, *The English nobility in the Middle Ages: the fourteenth-century political community* (London, 1987) p. 42.

[39] *The eyre of Northamptonshire, 1329–1330*, 97, 98 Selden Society (1981–2) p. 501 ('alien et morust saunz heir de son corps . . . Ceo nest pas cause deschete': *Master of Brackley v. Swart*). It is revealed in another case that an 'alien' tenant, Tiedemann Swart, had acquired two messuages of land from the Master of the Hospital of St John and St James of Brackley. See *Eyre of Northamptonshire*, 98 Selden Society, p. 575 (*Holland v. Wollenmongere*).

rule was confirmed in 1349 when one of the king's escheators reported that a manor purchased by Guy Ferre (styled as an 'alien' in the record) was escheated to the earl of Cornwall when Guy Ferre and his wife successively died 'without an heir'.[40] We may assume that the king's escheators were keenly aware of the legal differences between an heir and an heir of one's body.

I cannot find any evidence to suppose that birth beyond the sea made a person an alien. What has so far been treated as the evidence of aliens' legal disability is, in my view, nothing but the evidence of the growing stability and popularity of the judicial procedures of inquest. Foreign-born persons' legal predicament is simply the other side of the brilliant success story of the inquest procedures. Throughout the Middle Ages, foreigners were under no legal disability to acquire land in England. If foreign birth affected them in any way, it affected Englishmen in exactly the same way.

THE STATUTE *DE NATIS ULTRA MARE* (1351)

Foreign-born children's inheritance problem was vociferously raised in Parliament in the middle of the fourteenth century. In those years, a great number of magnates, soldiers, their wives and their retinues had to stay beyond the sea for a long time because of the war. If their wives give birth to children over there, these children would experience serious legal difficulty of inheritance. Indeed, the king himself had foreign-born children then.[41] It is probably wrong to imagine that these children would completely lose everything because of their foreign birth. Although inheritance maintained its importance in real actions, it no longer played a vital role outside the courtroom in the thirteenth and fourteenth centuries. In order to avoid the unfavourable economic consequences likely to be attached to inheritance (wardship, marriage, relief fine), tenants developed a variety of highly sophisticated

---

[40] *Cal. of inquis. misc., 21–25 Edward III*, no. 380.

[41] Ralph A. Griffiths, 'The English realm and dominions and the king's subjects in the later Middle Ages' in *Aspects of late medieval government and society*, ed. J. G. Rowe (Toronto, 1986) pp. 83–105, contains a discussion of the relevant circumstances. I wish to thank Professor Griffiths for his kindness. During the early stage in the preparation of this book, he read some of my writings and made many valuable comments.

methods which brought down the importance of inheritance to the barest minimum.[42] But these methods had to rely on elaborate paperwork. Considering that documents executed beyond the sea had just as much difficulty of legal recognition in England as children born beyond the sea,[43] the evasion methods must have been of little help for those who had to fight across the Channel. In order to avail themselves of these methods, they had to wait until they returned to England. However, this was precisely the question which bothered them most: could they return alive?

The petition (1343)

A suitable legal remedy for foreign-born children was demanded in the Parliament held in 1343. The following questions were posed:

(1) Whether the king's children born beyond the sea could inherit;
(2) Whether the children born abroad 'in the king's service' could inherit; and
(3) Whether foreign-born children in general could inherit.[44]

The answer was easy for the king's children: 'the children of our lord the king shall have inheritance wherever they may be born (*les enfantz nostre seignor le Roi, queu part q'ils soient neez* ...

---

[42] J. M. W. Bean, *The decline of English feudalism 1215–1540* (Manchester, 1968) chs. 3–4; A. W. B. Simpson, *An introduction to the history of the land law* (Oxford, 1961) pp. 163–94; S. F. C. Milsom, *Historical foundations of the common law*, 2nd edn (Toronto, 1981) pp. 200–39.

[43] *Year Books of 1–2 Edward II, 1307–1309*, p. 110, pl. 53 (recognition was denied to a deed 'fait hors du realme' in 'Berwicke ou cest court n'avoit conissance'). *Year Books of 4 Edward II, 1310–1311*, 26 Selden Society (1911) p. 131 (the same for a document executed at Linlithgow, Scotland). *Eyre of London, 14 Edward II, 1321*, p. 347 (a deed of debt drawn in France shall not be enforceable because 'gentz de cest terre ne poet trier le fet'). *Year Book* (Maynard's edn), Trin., 8 Edward III (1334) fo. 51, pl. 38 (a deed executed 'hors de cest Roialme' is challenged). A. N. Sack, 'Conflicts of laws in the history of the English law' in *Law, a century of progress, 1835–1935*, ed. A. Reppy, 3 vols. (New York, 1937) III, pp. 342–454. Regarding an important exception for merchant's deeds, see *Year Books of 4 Edward II, 1310–1311*, p. 153, pl. 10 ('[the plaintiff] est marchaunt, [and] home ne put nynt user en ceo cas lei de terre [on recognition of a deed] en touz poinz ver marchaund, etc.' *per* Bereford J).

[44] *Rotuli Parliamentorum*, II, p. 139.

porteront leritage)'. It is not clear whether the *'heritage'* was
intended to include the crown itself.[45] But, at least, the king's
foreign-born children would have no difficulty from then on in
inheriting royal demesne lands.

The answer also came readily for the children born abroad in
the king's service: 'it is granted in this Parliament that they shall
also be able to inherit wherever they may be born in the king's
service (*accordez est en ce Parlement, q'ils soient aussint enheritez
queu part q'ils soient neez en le service le Roi)'*. This simply
amounted to the king's promise that he would give up his claim of
escheat against his own soldiers who fought and died for him
leaving behind foreign-born children. The reference to 'service'
indicates that the promise applied mainly to tenants-in-chief. The
legal concept of *in seruicio domini regis* was featured already in
Glanvill. King's service in parts beyond the sea was a lawful
ground for allowing at least forty days of delay in lawsuits in the
common law courts.[46] The 'service' referred to the knight service.
Women could not avail themselves of this essoin.[47] It is not clear
whether professional soldiers who followed a captain of their
choice for pay might also have satisfied the requirement *en le
service le Roi* of 1343.[48] However, whether it was rendered as a
fulfilment of feudal legal obligation or as a professional job carried
out under some other covenants, the requirement of 'the king's
service' would probably have to be proved in court by rigorous
documentary evidence.[49]

In the fourteenth century, the king could no longer demand, as
of right, feudal services involving overseas expedition.[50] There is

---

[45] This issue was to be hotly debated by succession tract writers in the reign of
Elizabeth I. See ch. 7 below.

[46] *Glanvill*, lib. 1, c. 27.

[47] *Year Books of 1–2 Edward II, 1307–1309*, p. 142, pl. 71. *Year Books of 3
Edward II, 1309–1310*, 20 Selden Society (1905) p. 158, pl. 8.

[48] On the legal arrangement for professional soldiers, Christopher Allmand, *The
Hundred Years War, England and France at war, c. 1300–c. 1450* (Cambridge,
1989) pp. 40–1.

[49] Regarding the essoin for being in *seruitio domini regis*, Glanvill says: 'whenever
he does appear in court [after an absence of forty days or so], he must have with
him and show immediately a writ of the lord king as his warrant for the essoins
he has cast'. *Glanvill*, lib. 1, c. 27.

[50] F. Stenton, *The first century of English feudalism 1066–1166* (Oxford, 1961)
p. 178; Prestwich, *English politics*, pp. 98–9; A. L. Brown, *The governance of
late medieval England* (London, 1989) p. 87.

ample evidence that Edward III had to give away various favours to his soldiers to coax them to participate in his overseas campaigns. For instance, the king agreed to give up wardships of infant heirs if the 'parent' died during overseas military service. Those who were about to cross the Channel to carry out the king's overseas campaign were exempted from alienation fines. Enfeoffment in use and other arrangements detrimental to the king were generously allowed to tenants-in-chief in the wake of an upcoming overseas military operation.[51] The promise to allow the foreign-born children to inherit if they were born *en le service le Roi*, was just another example of these special deals which were liberally offered during the war.

The implementation of this promise is not likely to have posed serious procedural difficulty. The king, I suggest, could simply order his escheators to refrain from pursuing his claims.[52] If necessary, the foreign-born heir could be provided with the king's special protection in the form of a charter. In the event the heir was impleaded by a third party, the king's protection charter would effectively bar the opponent from raising any issue related to the foreign birth. This kind of protection charter had a long history behind it. Glanvill, for instance, explains that the proceedings of a possessory assize shall stop upon production of 'a royal charter in which the tenement of which seisin is claimed by the assize is specially or expressly confirmed to the tenant [by the king]'.[53] In 1295, Elyas Daubeny was provided with just such a charter. In consideration of his and his ancestors' military services to generations of English kings, Edward I granted the protection as a special favour (*de gratia sua speciali*). According to the charter, Elyas Daubeny could use it in the king's court to suppress any

---

[51] Bean, *The decline of English feudalism*, pp. 144, 146, 241; *Calendar of patent rolls, 1340–1343*, p. 199; *Calendar of patent rolls, 1345–1348*, pp. 223–4, 474, 478 show that Guy Bryane was lavishly provided with numerous royal favours 'for his stay with the king', 'for good service in staying continually by the king's side' or 'for good service in the war of France'. He was one of the captains who carried out Edward III's military operations in Scotland, Flanders and France. I wish to thank Dr Maurice Keen, Balliol College, Oxford, who read an earlier draft of this chapter and made many valuable comments on this point.

[52] In such a case, the king was not giving away the lands after they were vested in him. There was no established law which prevented the king from giving up his claim for *future* escheats.

[53] Lib. 13, c. 11 ('carta . . . regia qua specialiter uel expressim confirmatur ipsi tenenti tenementum cuius saisina petitur per assisam').

plea concerning his foreign birth.[54] Fifty-seven years later, his great-grandson Giles Daubeny was given the same kind of protection by Edward III. Giles Daubeny was born overseas while his father Ralph Daubeny was brilliantly serving the king by carrying out the Crécy-Calais campaign in 1346–7.[55]

However, no answer was given to the third question raised by the petition of 1343, that is, the inheritance of foreign-born children in general. The lawyers (*Gentz de Lei*) pointed out that allowing inheritance for foreign-born children in general was a difficult matter because there were 'various doubts and difficulties which can arise in proving whether such children are true heirs as claimed or dishonestly put in place in order to claim the inheritance (*diverse doutes et difficulteez q purront avenir de prover q tieux soient verrois heirs si debatz ou empeschementz soient mys en lour leritages*)'. The king's special protection, as we saw, resolved the difficulty simply by prohibiting the parties from raising these doubts in legal proceedings. But since it was a 'special' measure, it could not generally be granted to all children born beyond the sea. Only when a person or the ancestors of the person had made specific contributions in the king's benefit could the protection be issued as a *quid pro quo*. Such a measure was consonant with the Classical notion of justice – giving each one his due. Any contrary proposal would have offended medieval lawyers' conception of justice.

Probably, the only legally acceptable way to allow inheritance to foreign-born children *in general* was through a 'legislative' measure,[56] which would require a comprehensive alteration of the

---

[54] *Rotuli Parliamentorum*, I, p. 135. The charter was specifically designed for courtroom use: 'Quod ipse Elias de cetero in quibuscumque Curiis suis Angl' audiatur ut Anglicus . . . et quod non repellatur per illam exceptionem quod alienigena est et natus in partibus transmarinis.' We have already argued that '*alienigena*' was a factual description referring to a person's birthplace. In the absence of the legal category of alien, we doubt whether '*Anglicus*' can be interpreted as referring to the *subject* or *denizen* status. Legal historians, however, have regarded this document as one of the first letters of denization.

[55] Regarding the family of Daubeny, see *Dictionary of national biography*. Ralph Daubeny, whose children were given the king's special protection was one of the three persons specifically named in the statute *De natis ultra mare*. The other two were John de Beaumont and Guy Bryane. We have already seen the king's generosity towards Guy Bryane (note 51, above). John de Beaumont was the uncle of Philippa of Hainault, Queen consort of Edward III.

[56] See in this connection *Renaissance du pouvoir législatif et genèse de l'Etat*, ed. A. Gouron and A. Rigaudière (Montpellier, 1988).

procedures of inquest. Lawyers had to think about the following questions: Where could they direct the writ for summoning the jurors if the opponent of those children took issue with the proximity of blood? If bastardy was generally alleged, which bishop should be commanded to certify the matter? In short, who would dare to give verdict or certification about an event without first-hand knowledge? All they could say in 1343 was that this matter required 'a great deal of advice and good deliberation'.[57]

The statute (1351)

The answer came eight years later. In the Parliament held in 1351, it was enacted as follows:

All children heirs who will from henceforth be born out of the ligeance of the king, provided that, at the time of the birth, their fathers and mothers are, and will be, of the faith and ligeance of the king of England, [shall] have and enjoy the same benefit and advantage of having and carrying the inheritance within the said ligeance . . . in the future.[58]

The result of the great advice and good deliberation is summarised in the phrase 'faith and ligeance'. After eight years of contemplation, lawyers decided that faith and allegiance should override the established legal rules for the proof of descent and inheritance. If the parents were of the faith and allegiance of the king, the children should all be able to inherit in spite of their foreign birth. In order to implement the new rule, the following procedural reform was introduced:

If bastardy is alleged against anyone born beyond the sea, and if it is for a bishop to have the cognisance, then the bishop of the place where the thing demanded is located shall be commanded to certify the king's court where the plea is pending.[59]

The rules regarding certification of the ordinary were thus partly altered so that the ordinary of the place where the land under

---

[57] *Rotuli Parliamentorum*, II, p. 139 ('grant avisement et bone deliberation').

[58] *Statutes of the realm*, Records commission, 9 vols. (1816–28), I, p. 310 ('touz les enfantz heriters, qi serront neez desore dehors la ligeance le Roi, des queux enfantz les piere et miere au temps du nestre sont et serront a la foi et de la ligeance du roi Dengleterre, eient et enjoient meismes les benefice et avantage daver et porter heritage deinz la dite ligeance . . . en temps avenir').

[59] Ibid. ('si alleggee soit, contre nul tiel nee par dela, qil est bastard, en cas ou Levesq doit avoir conissance de bastardie, soit maunde a Levesq du lieu la ou la demande est, de certifier la Court le Roi ou le ple ent pend').

dispute was located could certify the legitimacy of the foreign-born person. In so far as the issue of legitimacy was concerned, foreign-born children would be deemed to have been born in England. The certification procedure should be 'as has been used before in the case of bastardy alleged against those born in England (*sicome auncienement ad este usee en cas de bastardie, alegge contre ceux qi nasquirent en Engleterre)*'.

The statute does not give any procedural solution for inquest which had to be done by a jury. It is therefore not clear how the trial should be conducted if the proximity of blood was challenged. However, it appears that as far as the question of *possession* was concerned, the proximity of blood no longer posed serious threat to foreign-born children in claiming or defending their inheritance. An assize of *mort d'ancestor* brought four years after the statute gives us valuable information.[60] A woman and her two children claimed the possession of inheritance. Their claim was based on the seisin of the woman's father. It was revealed that she had a brother who committed a felony and abjured the realm. The tenant pleaded that since the brother survived his father, the demandants' claim should not be allowed for lack of proximity of blood. An inquest was taken[61] which found as follows: (1) the son abjured the realm ten years before the death of the father; (2) the father died seised; but, (3) it cannot be known whether the demandants were the nearest heirs. The inquest could not find out whether the son survived the father because the son crossed the sea and had not yet come back. Upon this, counsel for the demandants barged in: 'This should be sufficient, no need for further inquiry (*Eux suffre aler sauns pluis enquere*)!' Counsel for the tenant replied with indignation: 'Since when have we stopped inquiring whether the demandants were the nearest heirs or not (*depuis que naver enquere le quel les demaund' sont plus prochien heire ou ne mie*)?' At least from 1227, however, we have clear records

---

[60] Anthony Fitzherbert, *Graunde Abridgement* (*c*. 1514–16), mort d'anc. pl. 28; *Liber assisarum*, 29 Edward III, pl. 11.

[61] It appears that a mixed jury was used. The demandant claimed that the son abjured the realm in the county of C and did not return. The tenant claimed that the son returned and survived his father in the county of W. The demandant's counsel said, 'sur ceo le court fuit en awere le quel le chose serra trie par ass. ou par gentz dauter counte ou par lune counte et lauter.' Thereupon, 'Stouff. [judge] agard' lassise destre pris *en paiis alarg* que fuit issint prise.' (emphasis supplied).

that the proximity of blood ceased to be a critical issue in a possessory assize if its proof involved an examination of circumstances which cannot be tried in England (foreign birth, foreign death of a third party or existence of a potential contestant beyond the sea, etc.).[62] The demandants in our case were therefore awarded the possession without having to prove the proximity of blood. Of course, when the question of right was tried, foreign birth would certainly be fatal to any claim based on inheritance. But the overwhelming popularity and effectiveness of possessory assizes probably dissuaded the drafters of the statute *De natis ultra mare* from making any attempt to fiddle with the well-established jury trial procedures. This, I believe, is why the statute only mentioned the certification of bastardy. In 1368, Parliament had another opportunity to consider and affirm the new rule.[63]

CONCLUSION

Common lawyers and English legal historians have long believed that the statute *De natis ultra mare* is a reliable source of the fourteenth-century English law of alien status. This view, I believe, is wrong. The statute was not about aliens. Nor was it about foreigners. The statute was about foreign-born heirs of the king's soldiers, rich or poor. The question was not their alien or subject status. The question was whether or not they could inherit.

One must not lose sight of the problem situation which the

---

[62] Fitzherbert, *Abridgement*, mort d'anc. pl. 55 (12 Henry III): the demandant's claim was based on the seisin of his brother. The tenant unsuccessfully pleaded that the dead brother had a son who went beyond the sea eighteen years before. The possession, as distinct from the right, of the land was awarded to the demandant, 'salvo predicto W.[the son] iur. suo si redierit ita quod statim habeat ssesiam cum redierit, etc.' Also ibid., mort d'anc. pl. 47 (13 Edward I): the tenant took issue that the demandant had an older brother who was still alive. The plea was ignored by the judges who ruled that the demandant was 'le pluis prochien heire *apparent*' (emphasis supplied). The possession was awarded to the demandant 'et que save soit a f[rere] son poss. quant il vient [from beyond the sea], etc.' If, however, the proximity of blood turned on the circumstances which could be tried by an inquest taken from another county within England, the issue of proximity had to be resolved before the possession could be awarded. See *Year Books of 3–4 Edward II*, p. 151, pl. 46.

[63] Statute 42 Edward III c. 10.

statute purported to resolve. The statute was not dealing with
some conflict between Englishmen and foreigners. The conflict
was between magnates and their tenants. The clash of proprietary
interests between the king and his tenants-in-chief was more or
less resolved in 1343 when children born abroad 'in the king's
service' were allowed to inherit. The question that had to be
resolved in 1351 was whether the less important soldiers who were
not considered to be 'in the *king's* service' should also be able to
provide for their foreign-born children. Until then, their lords had
the law on their side. The tenants did not have a strong case for
their foreign-born children. Lawyers kept referring to *diverse
doutes et difficulteez*. These legal doubts worked in favour of the
lords by increasing their chances of enjoying the escheat. Their
tenants may well have been the beloved subjects of the king. They
might have been faithful enough to die for the king in a foreign
country. But what could lawyers do? Law was law, and faith was
faith. Until 1351, that is.

One may still ask: Granted that the statute was initially enacted
to deal with the problem of inheritance, is it not true that lawyers
immediately used it as a nationality statute? No, not until the first
quarter of the sixteenth century.[64] For the fourteenth-century
common lawyers, foreign-born heirs' inheritance problem was a
legal issue which was equally applicable to foreigners as to
Englishmen. As far as inheritance of English land was concerned,
there was no legal difference between Englishmen and foreigners.

It is, of course, not entirely impossible to insist on the long-
standing interpretative tradition (we will discuss in chapters 7 and
8 how this tradition arose in the sixteenth century), and have the
comfort of affirming that aliens were under legal disability in
medieval England and that birthplace was an important criterion
for determining a person's alien or subject status. In order to do
this, however, one has to pay a price. It must be admitted that
until the last quarter of the fourteenth century, this iron rule was
not applicable to foreign merchants because they were merchants,
nor to foreign clerks because they were clerks, nor to foreign
religious houses because they were religious houses. One has also
to admit that the statute *De natis ultra mare* contains, for some

---

[64] For a detailed discussion, see ch. 7 below.

mysterious reasons, a lengthy clause on bastardy trial procedures which has nothing to do with the law of alien status.

Alternatively, one may wholly dismiss the firmly established tradition, and say that there was no legal rule for the alien or subject status in medieval England. One may then go on to say that there was an unsuccessful attempt in 1383 to deny foreign clerical candidates access to ecclesiastical benefices in England; that the letters patent issued to foreign merchants took an abrupt and enigmatic turn at about the same time; and that the foreign religious houses' lawful claim as tenants of their English lands was finally denied on the basis of an unprecedented argument in 1414. The price for adopting this alternative would be that one will probably have to rewrite considerably the history of the law of personal status in Europe.

6

FAITH AND ALLEGIANCE

In an earlier chapter, I argued that the systematic ban on foreign clerical candidates' access to ecclesiastical benefices had to rely on an argument which has a number of features unprecedented in medieval jurisprudence. Moreover, we have seen that such a ban would actually infringe on the king's and his subjects' well-established patronage rights. This may have been one of the reasons why the attempted ban of 1383 was ineffective and quickly forgotten. Also, when lawful landholding claims of foreign religious houses were ignored and permanent removal of lands from those religious houses was declared in 1414, the ordinance was making an original claim which made reference to the 'relief and support of the communities of the realm'. Some foreign abbots, as we saw, were not impressed by the novel argument, and kept bringing to the king's court their 'lawful' claims as tenants.

It is true, however, that the majority of foreign abbots acquiesced to the new argument and no serious attempt was made to recover their lands. The reason for this is not difficult to understand. Their lands had been in the hands of the English king intermittently for several decades by then. The foreign religious houses concerned most probably had given up the hope of recovering their lands. To hear that their long lost lands would not after all be returned to them was perhaps not painful enough to make them start a lengthy and expensive litigation to recover those lands. Similarly, foreign merchants also appear to have accepted the new argument without much protest. We saw that chancery clerks, from the 1380s onward, kept announcing in the king's letters patent issued to foreign merchants that no one but the king's liege subjects might hold land in England or bring lawsuits in the king's court. The reason why the repeated announcement of the new idea went unchallenged is not difficult to understand either. The announcement was made on the occasion of *granting* some legal benefits to foreigners who successfully applied for an exemption from the higher rate of customs duty. Seizing upon the occasion of foreign merchants' request for tax benefit, chancery clerks began to declare that no one might hold land or bring lawsuits in England except the king's liege-men and that those successful applicants were now exceptionally granted those privileges. The point, however, is that those foreign merchants had already been holding lands and freely using all sorts of legal facilities when they applied for the tax benefit. They were told in a grandiose manner that they could continue to do so (see chapter 2 above).

The fact that the systematic discrimination attempted against foreign clerks was unsuccessful while a similar attempt affecting foreign religious houses and foreign merchants met with little or no resistance can thus be understood with reference to the particular context in which each of these attempts was introduced. When we put aside the *practical* difficulty or ease of implementation and focus instead on the *doctrinal* difficulty posed by the new argument, it must be clear that *all* these attempts were going against the grain of medieval jurisprudence. In the second half of this book, I shall endeavour to show how the overall structure of legal argument was comprehensively recast in the fifteenth and early sixteenth centuries so that the new argument no longer poses any doctrinal difficulty. But before we move on to investigate this remarkable achievement of the early modern jurisprudence, we need to highlight precisely what was new about the argument for systematic discrimination against aliens. In my view, the novelty of the argument consists in the use it makes of the concept of 'public interest'.

The notion of 'common good' or 'common utility' was no doubt thoroughly familiar to all medieval men. That the king and his subjects should all exercise their rights to the common utility of the realm was probably the highest moral political precept which no one ever dreamed of challenging. But how could this noble obligation be enforced when the parties to a litigation could doggedly cling to the adage, *fiat justitia, ruat coelum!* (Heavens might fall, but let justice be done!) and demand that justice – in its narrow individualistic sense – be done at all costs? This is why I believe that the argument for the systematic discrimination against aliens is somewhat significant. It allowed the lofty but hitherto amorphous notion of common utility to be incorporated into the legal language. From then on, disputes involving foreigners were to be resolved on an altogether different platform. The innovation was achieved through the concepts of faith and allegiance. Those who are of the faith and allegiance of the king are subjects and they shall be given legal benefits; those who aren't are aliens and they shall be deprived of legal benefits.

As I emphasised at the beginning, however, faith and allegiance were not new conceptual categories which suddenly occurred to lawyers' minds in the fourteenth century. By that time, these concepts were probably already too old to trace their origin. The novelty of the new argument comes not from the novelty of the concepts of faith and allegiance, but from the innovative way of using these old concepts. Of course, the innovation is no longer new to us. After several centuries of repeated use, we may rightly say that there is nothing new about the 'new' way of using these concepts. Unless we study the old way of using them, we will not be able to appreciate the novelty of the new use. Then, what was the old way of using *fides* and *ligeancia*?

AD FIDEM REGIS

The concept of fidelity to the king, as distinct from the fidelity of a tenant to his lord, is well attested by Glanvill and Bracton. Glanvill, for example, describes the consensual and reciprocal relationship between a tenant and his lord as a bond of mutual confidence (*fidelitatis connexio*) created by homage.[1] The king himself may be a party to such a relationship, which Bracton refers to as *vinculum juris*.[2] But, obviously, the king cannot be a party to every such relationship. According to Glanvill and Bracton, if the king is not personally involved in such a relationship, the parties to it must acknowledge that their mutual bond of confidence would be qualified by fidelity to the king. The homage in this case must be accompanied by a proviso, 'salva fide debita

---

[1] *Glanvill*, lib. 9, c. 4 ('Mutua quidem debet esse dominii et homagii fidelitatis connexio').
[2] *Bracton*, II, p. 228 ('Sciendum quod homagium est iuris vinculum').

domino regi et heredibus suis'.[3] In other words, even though the legal relationship between a lord and his tenant is essentially a relationship of mutual consent, they cannot consent to be unfaithful to the king. The *fides* in this proviso refers to fidelity to the king, which is different from fidelity between parties to the landholding agreement. How was the clause *salva fide debita domino regi . . .* at work? Did it work differently from the *fidelitatis connexio* between a tenant and his lord? Taking of Norman tenants' English land provides a good opportunity to discuss this.

Regarding the legal consequence of a tenant's wrongdoing committed against his lord, Glanvill offers the following explanation:

If anyone does anything to the disinheritance of his lord and is convicted of it, he and his heirs shall by law lose the fee which he holds of him. The same rule will apply if anyone lays violent hands on his lord to hurt him or do him a dreadful injury, and this is lawfully proved against him in the proper court.[4]

The passage may be understood as providing the substantive legal basis for taking the lands of the king's Norman tenants adhering to the French king when John was dispossessed of his inheritance in Normandy. However, as repeatedly stressed by Glanvill and Bracton, definitive removal of lands from a tenant was not permissible until the tenant's breach was duly proven in the lord's court.[5] Therefore, the immediate justification for seizing the Norman tenants' English lands ought to be sought elsewhere. Glanvill further explains that a lord may distrain his tenant in order to compel him to appear in his court (*curia domini*) to answer charges: 'The lord may, of course, lawfully evict his man by the judgment of his court and distrain his man

---

[3] *Glanvill*, lib. 9, c. 1. *Bracton*, II, p. 232.

[4] Lib. 9, c. 1.

[5] See the following phrases from Glanvill's passage quoted above (lib. 9, c. 1): 'si . . . ad exheredationem domini sui fecerit *et super hoc conuictus fuerit*, . . . si manus uiolentas . . . , *et hoc uersus eum legitime in curia fuerit competente probatum*'. *Bracton*, II, p. 236 ('Item si aliquid fecerit contra dominum suum ad exheredationem domini sui: *et quo casu iustum iudicium* quod tenens exheredetur propter obligationem homagii quam infringit'). Regarding the removal of lands from King John in 1202, Ganshof quotes the following text from a contemporary French source: 'Tandem vero curia regis Franciae adunata *adjudicavit* regem Angliae tota terra sua privandum quam hactenus de regibus Franciae ipse et progenitores sui tenuerant' . . . F. L. Ganshof, *Qu'est-ce que la féodalité?* 5th edn (Paris, 1982) p. 251.

to come to his court'.[6] Taking of the king's Norman tenants' lands
was therefore a preliminary procedural measure (distress) which
was intended to be in effect only until the Norman tenants would
appear in the court presided over by the king to clear themselves
or to be lawfully convicted of their wrongdoing.[7] The procedures
for resolving feudal legal disputes between a lord and his free
tenant must be distinguished from the procedures in the king's
court (common law court). For example, trial by inquest was not
available for resolution of a feudal dispute. The matter had to be
judged in the presence of the 'peers' of the accused.[8] For the
resolution of the feudal disputes between him and his Norman
tenants, I suggest, the king could not resort to the procedural rules
regarding essoins and default judgments applicable to common
law trials.[9] In other words, the king's Norman tenants could not
be definitively dispossessed of their lands until they voluntarily
appeared in the court of their lord, and were duly convicted in
accordance with legitimate procedures (*legitime in curia fuerit
competente probatum*). Years after the seizure, therefore, constant
inquiries were still being made about the *terrae Normannorum* to
make sure that they were managed with proper care. The case was
still pending.[10]

But the good news for the king was that his Norman tenants,
like his English tenants, were mortal beings. When they died
without leaving an heir who was legally capable of claiming the

---

[6] Our translation. *Glanvill*, lib. 9, c. 1 ('Et quidem de iure poterit quis hominem
suum per iudicium curie sue deducere et distringere ad curiam suam uenire').

[7] Cf. F. A. Enever, *History of the law of distress* (London, 1931) p. 69.

[8] *Select pleas in manorial and other seignorial courts*, vol. I, 2 Selden Society (1988)
pp. lxvi–lxvii. The *judicium parium suorum*, which was demanded and promised
in Magna Carta (1215), had nothing to do with the verdict of a jury (*inquisitio
patriae*) in common law trials. See also *Glanvill*, lib. 9, c. 1 for procedures for
resolving feudal disputes in the lord's court.

[9] Essoins and default judgments in the common law trials are explained in
Glanvill, lib. 1, cc. 11–33.

[10] J. H. Le Patourel, *The medieval administration of the Channel Islands,
1199–1399* (London, 1937) p. 28. Sir Maurice Powicke, however, asserts that
'the disposal of lands *doubtless* became permanent' as the hope of an amicable
settlement dissipated (*The loss of Normandy, 1189–1204* (Manchester, 1913)
p. 423, emphasis supplied). I nevertheless believe that there is considerable
room for doubt. The tentative nature of the seizure of the Normans' lands was
noted, and described by Maitland as 'that curious dislike of perpetual dish-
erison'. F. Pollock and F. W. Maitland, *The history of English law before the time
of Edward I*, 2nd edn, 2 vols. (Cambridge, 1968), I, p. 461.

inheritance, the king would have the escheat of their land and the case would be closed. The king must have particularly appreciated the common law rule that children born beyond the sea could not inherit. It would not be unreasonable to suppose that the king's Norman tenants would often have their children born in Normandy or in other parts beyond the sea. What if, however, some of the heirs were born in England and were not personally responsible for the wrongdoing (*exheredatio, atroci iniuria*, etc.)? It is not clear whether the king could lawfully prevent the heir from doing the homage and claim the lands. We have not been able to find actual cases where this issue was squarely posed for decision. But this should not affect our argument. Regardless of whether the king could claim the land or not, the legal relationship between the king and his Norman tenants (including their heirs) must be understood wholly within the context of the consensual and reciprocal agreement between them. It is a question of *viculum iuris* created by homage. There is, in these cases, no room, nor any need, to discuss the concept of fidelity to the king as the ruler. The issue was about the *fidelitatis connexio* between *a* lord and his tenant. The king happened to be the lord here.

But, not all Normans were tenants-in-chief. What about the Normans who held their English lands from a mesne lord? Could the king seize their lands as well? When they died leaving no heir who could successfully claim the inheritance, could the king ignore their immediate lord and claim the escheat? The answer seems to have been in doubt to say the least. In a case brought to the King's Council in 1243, we see a mesne lord – not the king – taking seisin of the land which would have descended on a person staying in Normandy (*Boistard* v. *Cumbwell*). The mesne lord justified this measure by arguing that the person in Normandy did homage to the bishop of Bayeux, who was a homager (tenant-in-chief) of the king of France, the enemy of the king of England. This argument is interesting for two reasons. First, no claim was made as to whether the person staying in Normandy was the *only* remaining heir. Granted that that person was somehow unable to inherit, if there was a brother or sister, the inheritance would descend on the next available heir (no felony on the part of the ancestor was alleged in the case). But the point was not raised at all by the parties. Second, no claim was made that a wrongdoing or injury was done to the mesne lord himself. If, for example, the tenant had failed to render the service due or to provide a suitable substitute, or had otherwise breached the contractual fidelity to the lord, the latter could have justified his repossession of lands relying on these grounds. But what the mesne lord said in this case was that the heir of his tenant was unfaithful to the king. In all likelihood, the heir appears to have argued that neither his ancestor nor he himself did anything to breach their contractual obligation owed to the lord. The heir must have wanted the land and asked the lord to accept his homage. Otherwise, the dispute would not have arisen in the first place. Now, the lord, unable to allege a breach of contractual *fidelitas*, seems to have resorted to the *fides* directly owed to the king ('salva fide debita domino regi') as mentioned in the proviso of the homage. Have not they (the tenant, now deceased, and the lord) agreed that their feudal relationship should always be qualified by the saving clause about *fide debita domino regi*? As the heir has violated this promise by doing homage to the king's enemy, thus the mesne lord seems to have argued, the heir must not be allowed to do the homage and take the land.[11] The case came before the King's Council. The land was provisionally taken into the king's hands until the king could decide this matter. As a compensation for the temporary loss of the seisin of the land, the mesne lord was given 15 marks. On the day assigned for the definitive judgment on this matter, the king's chief justiciar failed to show up. We do not know the outcome.[12]

The absence of the chief justiciar must have been particularly disappointing for the mesne lord if we are to suppose that he was aware of an Exchequer record of 1239 where another mesne lord in a similar position was allowed to keep his Norman tenants' lands when they fell back on him as his escheats: 'It is granted that the Earl of Leicester shall have the Normans' lands which are of his fee when they fall back on him as his escheat.'[13] The record

---

[11] The heir, of course, was not party to the agreement between the lord and the deceased tenant. But the feudal legal obligation did not evaporate upon the death of the tenant or the lord, but descended on their respective heir. See *Fleta*, vol. III, 89 Selden Society (1972) p. 38.

[12] *Select cases before the King's Council, 1243–1482*, 35 Selden Society (1918) pp. 1–2 (*Boistard* v. *Cumbwell*).

[13] Public Record Office, King's Remembrancer, Memoranda rolls, 18 m. 12d ('sciatis quod concessimus dilecto . . . comes Laycester quod per omnes terras suas habeat et teneat terras Normannorum que sunt de feodo suo cum exciderint

appears after the lapse of about thirty years from the initial seizure of *terrae Normannorum*. Norman tenants were beginning to die.

In 1245, two years after *Boistard* v. *Cumbwell*, we find a case where a Norman abbot's lands, which were taken into the king's hands as *terrae Normannorum* in 1244, were restored to the abbot. The reason was that the abbot held the lands of a mesne lord and, therefore, was not a tenant-in-chief: 'the abbot holds all his lands in England of the Earl, and with respect to his lands, he did homage to the Earl as the lord of the fiefs'.[14] One may, of course, entertain the possibility that not all Norman tenants were adhering to the French king; that this particular abbot was faithful to the English king; and that this was the reason why he could recover the lands. But the point we are making is that, whether or not this was the case, the record of the Close roll keeps entirely silent about the question of being faithful to the king. All it says is that the abbot did homage to his lord, who was not the king. The king had to return the lands because the abbot maintained the *fidelitatis connexio* with his lord, not because the abbot was *ad fidem regis*.

However, a Latin treatise of the late thirteenth century, commonly known as *Prerogativa regis*, contains the following clause which indicates that a significant change was introduced in the meantime:

The king shall have escheats of the lands of Normans, of whose fee soever they may be, saving the service belonging to the immediate lords of the same fee.[15]

This statement is designed to eliminate the doubt about whether the king could claim the escheat of *terrae Normannorum* not held

---

tanquam escaeta sua'). See *Dictionary of medieval Latin from British sources*, fasc. III (London, 1986), 'escaèta'.

[14] *Close rolls 1242–1247*, p. 337 ('idem abbas, qui omnes terras quas habet in Anglia tenet de eodem comite, . . . et de terris ipsis fidelitatem fecit eidem comiti tanquam domino feodi').

[15] Our translation. *Statutes of the realm*, I, p. 226 ('Rex habebit escaetas de terris Normannorum, cujuscunque feodi fuerint, salvo servitio, quod pertinet ad capitales dominos feodi illius'). We follow Maitland in rendering *capitalis dominus* as the 'immediate lord' rather than the chief lord or the liege lord. Pollock and Maitland, *The History of the English law*, II, p. 234. The treatise was probably written in the reign of Edward I. The king's special rights as the feudal lord are discussed. The text sets forth various exceptional measures regarding wardship, marriage, primer seisin, homage, escheat, alienation of fief, exercise of advowson, etc. which became applicable when the king was involved in these feudal legal relationships. It is often regarded as a statute.

directly from him. If the king's justiciar who did not show up in the case of 1243 could have relied upon this clause, he would have gladly announced that the land should remain with the king and that the mesne lord should be content to receive the compensation for the loss of the feudal service.

One must ask, however, on what ground could the king intervene in a legal relationship between a lord and a tenant created by homage? On what legal basis could the king claim the escheat which would normally go to the lord? This is not to suggest that the king could under no circumstances interfere with the relationship between a lord and his tenant. If the tenant was lawfully convicted of certain serious wrongdoing, the king would intervene and take the lands whether or not they had been held directly from him. But this intervention occurred only *after* the *fidelitatis connexio* between a lord and his tenant had been formally severed by a judicial sentence. Moreover, the dissolution of the contractual bond in such a case was amply publicised by pulling down the houses and rooting up the trees of the wrongdoer.[16] In this sense, the king could not be said to temper with the *vinculum iuris* between a lord and tenant since the bond had already been dissolved. Obviously, the king's claim to have the escheats of the Normans' lands was not based on a formal judicial sentence convicting the Norman tenants. Otherwise, it would be rather difficult to explain why the clause of *Prerogativa regis* proposed a compensation for the mesne lord. We are inclined to believe that the king's claim to have the escheats of the Normans' lands *cujuscunque feodi fuerint* could not be justified by the established rules of felony. Instead, the rather daring claim of the king was based on the notion of 'Prerogative'. In other words, the claim had no known legal ground for justification. It is precisely at this point that faith to the king, as distinct from the *fidelitatis connexio* between a lord and his tenant, is mentioned in the text. The above-quoted clause of *Prerogativa regis* is followed by this passage:

And this also is to be understood where any inheritance descendeth to any that is born in the parts beyond the sea, whose ancestors were from the time of king John under the allegiance of the kings of France (*ad fidem regis Franciae*), and not of the kings of England (*ad fidem regis Angliae*).[17]

---

[16] See, for example, *Glanvill*, lib. 7, c. 17.

[17] *Statutes of the realm*, I, p. 226 ('et hoc similiter intelligendum est, si aliqua haereditas descendat alicui nato in partibus transmarinis, et cujus antecessores

We assume that this passage is not about escheats because the question of escheat has already been dealt with in the clause that precedes this. Escheat normally happened when a tenant died without *any* legally recognisable heir. If the eldest son of a tenant was illegitimate, for example, the inheritance would go to the next legally recognisable heir(s), if any. In this case, the lord could not claim escheat. The above-quoted passage is dealing with the case where the closest heir(s) happened to be born beyond the sea. In normal circumstances, the inheritance would go to the next available heir(s).[18] If, however, the deceased had been *ad fidem regis Franciae*, the above-quoted passage provides that the king should immediately intervene and snatch away the opportunity of inheritance from the next available heir(s). The passage applies whether or not the lands were held directly from the king. If the lands were held from mesne lords, the king's interception would have had to have been accompanied by a compensation for the feudal service belonging to the mesne lord (*capitalis dominus*). This, we believe, is the full meaning of *hoc similiter intelligendum est*.[19]

The fidelity in *ad fidem regis* appearing in the above-quoted passage cannot have meant the mutual bond of confidence (*fidelitatis connexio*) arising from homage. The argument contained in the passage turns on the non-contractual bond of faith between the king (the ruler) and his subjects (the ruled). But the bond of faith was mentioned with regard to the deceased only. The living heir's faith to the king was entirely irrelevant. The deceased ancestor's faith to the king was mentioned not to discriminate against the dead tenant or his foreign-born heir, but to determine the question of 'prerogative' escheat which operated to the detriment of mesne lords or of the next available heir(s) of the deceased tenant. The above-quoted passage allows us to conclude that if the deceased ancestors were *ad fidem regis Angliae*, the inheritance

fuerunt ad fidem regis Franciae, ut tempore regis Johannis, et non ad fidem regis Angliae').

[18] See R. Brook, *Graunde Abridgement* (London, 1573) denizen & alien, pl.7, pl. 14.

[19] It is further explained in *Prerogativa regis* that upon the death of John of Monmouth, Henry III obtained many escheats of the Normans' lands held of others (*de feodi aliorum*). Henry III's claim to the escheats was, of course, qualified by the compensation of the due and customary service for the mesne lords. Ibid.

would take its normal course. That is, if the closest heir was born abroad, the inheritance would go to the next available heir(s). If all the heirs were born abroad, the lord, not necessarily the king, would have the escheat.

One further point worthy of note is that the above-quoted text of *Prerogativa regis* shows no interest in specifying whether it was the father or the mother who was *ad fidem regis*. Since the text was dealing with the questions of inheritance and escheat, it was appropriate and accurate to use the legal category of 'ancestors (*antecessores*)'. It did not matter whether it was the father or an aunt who chose to adhere to the French king. All that mattered was that they should *die* seised of inheritable fiefs. As long as they remained alive, they could not be *antecessores* and, therefore, the question of inheritance would not arise. It is unlikely that this text had anything to do with the subject or alien status of the heir. However, lawyers and scholars were to rely on this text to develop fantastic theories about paternal or parental descent of English nationality.[20]

Whether or not the document *Prerogativa regis* was actually enforced as a statute is beside the point.[21] As a contemporary legal text (I assume that it was composed between 1243 and 1343), it poses a problem of interpretation. So far, it has been interpreted as suggesting the birth of nationalistic jurisprudence in England. I hope that I have demonstrated some possibility of a different interpretation. I believe that the text should, as any historical text would, throw light on the circumstances in which it was composed. The question which the text purported to resolve was not at all 'nationalistic'. The focal point of contention was whether the escheats of the Normans' lands held of mesne lords should go to the king or to the mesne lords. The question could not be resolved unequivocally by relying on Glanvill or Bracton. The ambiguity could, and in fact did, work in favour of mesne lords. This was the moment when the document was composed. The text took a clear

---

[20] See chs. 7 and 8 below.

[21] We note, nevertheless, that justices of eyre in the early fourteenth century routinely made the following inquiries: 'de *eschaetis* domini regis, que sunt & qui illas tenent . . . tam de terris Normannorum quam de aliis' and 'de hiis qui tenent terras Normannorum, Flandrensium, Britannorum vel aliorum extraneum *cujuscunque feoda sint*' (emphasis supplied). *The eyre of Kent, 6–7 Edward II, 1313–1314*, Vol. I, 24 Selden Society (1909) pp. 29, 31 (Articles of the eyre, nos. 7, 34).

stance in favour of the king, and attempted to provide a ground for prerogative escheat. The text was not expressing a nationalistic or xenophobic sentiment. The struggle was between the king and the mesne lords. The text was not inventing a hitherto unknown idea, either. It was using the notion of fidelity (*fides*) to the king which was basic to Glanvill and Bracton (*salva fide debita domino regi et heredibus suis*).

In order to take the lands of his Norman tenants-in-chief, the king had no need to invoke the notion of *ad fidem regis*. The consensual and reciprocal agreement which bound the parties (*vinculum iuris*) provided sufficient legal means for the king to cope with the situation after the loss of Normandy. In order to take the Normans' lands held of mesne lords, however, the king had to rely on the concept of *ad fidem regis*, as distinct from *fidelitatis connexio* between a lord and a tenant. But the text of *Prerogativa regis* shows that when the lawyers thus relied on the concept of *ad fidem regis*, they did so in a way which did not at all affect the legal position of foreign-born heirs. If the ancestors were *ad fidem regis Franciae*, prerogative escheat would take place. If the ancestors were *ad fidem regis Angliae*, ordinary escheat would take place. In either case, the foreign-born heir was denied inheritance regardless of his or his ancestor's fidelity or infidelity to the king. Now, the statute *De natis ultra mare* was making an entirely different use of fidelity to the king. According to the statute, the parents' fidelity to the king would have the power to *enable* their foreign-born heirs to inherit. Previously, the notion of *ad fidem regis* was not capable of doing this. As far as the concept of *fides* is concerned, this is an innovative change of *mode d'emploi*. Then, what about *ligeance*?

LIGEANCE

Professor Maitland suggested that *ligeance* originally referred to a geographical tract before it took up the meaning of allegiance.[22] This may be true, but not entirely true. Before *ligeance* was employed to refer to a tract of land, the term had already been used to refer to a certain quality of interpersonal relationship.

---

[22] Pollock and Maitland, *The history of English law*, I, p. 459.

Glanvill, for instance, used the term to explain the pre-eminent relationship between a tenant and his 'liege' lord.[23] Also, the treaty between Henry II and William, king of Scots (the Treaty of Falaise, 1174) contains the following passage which indicates that the term was used to refer to the relationship of fidelity rather than a piece of land: *Similiter heredes regis Scottorum et baronum et hominum suorum homagium et liganciam facient heredibus domini regis contra omnem hominem.*[24] Bracton also uses the term to refer to something other than a geographical tract. He remarks that during the military conflict between John and Philippe Auguste, William Marshal, Michael de Fiennes and many others were 'faithful to both kings (*ad fidem utriusque*)'. He continues as follows: 'if war occurs between the kings, each of them remains personally with the king to whom he has done liege homage (*ligeantiam*) and has his *servitium debitum* done to him with whom he does not stand in person'.[25]

In any forms of human association, the relationship of power, subjection and solidarity is bound to be expressed in one way or another. Whether it is called *ligeancia*, *fidelitas* or allegiance is of secondary importance. For Glanvill and Bracton, however, it seems that the notions of power and subjection did not play a vital role in expressing the spatial perception of geographical expanse. Land was land, and *ligeance* was *ligeance*. But in the late thirteenth century, we begin to see that the territorial extent of the king's legitimate power is also called *ligeance*. According to the early fourteenth-century legal terminology, out of the *ligeance* (*hors de la ligeance*) could often mean 'out of England'. Likewise, within

---

[23] Lib. 9, c. 1 ('Potest autem quis plura homagia diversis dominis facere de feodis diversorum dominorum, sed unum eorum oportet esser precipuum et cum ligeancia factum').

[24] E. L. G. Stones, *Anglo-Scottish relations 1174–1328*, 2nd edn (Oxford, 1970) p. 4 ('Likewise the heirs of the king of Scots, and of the barons, and of their men, shall do homage and swear allegiance to the heirs of the king [of England] against all men'). The contemporary materials put together by Stones show that *homo ligius* and *dominus ligius* formed part of the common legal terminology of the time. Various spellings were used: *homo ligeus* (pp. 78, 126); *leggius homo* (p. 16). The Treaty of Falaise also mentions *ligiam fidelitatem* (p. 4).

[25] Our translation is based on *Bracton*, IV, p. 329 (f. 427 b): 'et ita tamen si contigat querram moveri inter reges, remaneat personaliter quilibet eorum cum eo cui fecerit ligeantiam, et faciat servitium debitum ei cum quo non steterit [or *fecerit*] in persona'. See also George Duby, *Guillaume le Maréchal* (Paris, 1984) pp. 178–89.

the *ligeance* (*deinz la ligeance*) often meant 'within England'.[26] Was the old usage of the term *ligeance* completely outdated by then? We do not suppose so. It appears that the term was used in an ambivalent manner by the early fourteenth century. In other words, the term carried a certain amount of ambiguity with it. We shall investigate how common lawyers made use of this semantic ambiguity.

I have already mentioned a case brought to the eyre of London in 1321 (*Rex* v. *Philip de Beauvais*).[27] The case was about inheritance of a franchise. The defendant (the grandson of the recipient of the franchise) was having difficulty because his father, through whom the defendant's entitlement to the franchise must be traced, was born beyond the sea, and foreign birth was nearly fatal to a good descent. However, the king's serjeant Geoffrey Scrope made a big mistake when he began the argument as follows: 'From your grand-father you cannot establish the descent because your father was not of the *ligaunce* of England (*vostre piere ne fut nient de la ligaunce dengleterre*).' Herle J immediately intervened with a subtle suggestion that Scrope used *ligaunce* to refer to the geographical location of the father's birth: 'Scrope tells you that your father was not of the *ligaunce* of England. How can this court know whether he was brother, uncle or son, as he was not born in this land (*depus qil ne fut pas nee en cest terre*)?' But the defendant's counsel, Shardlow, saw the opportunity. He maximised the ambiguity of the term *ligaunce* by pushing the case towards the question of homage: 'we pray that the grandfather was married to his wife in London, and the father was held and reputed as their son, and did homage to the king of England and died in his homage, and therefore the father was of the *ligaunce* of the king of England'.

In fact, whether or not the father did homage to the king was irrelevant to the focal question of the case. The father must have done homage to the king with regard to the house which his father

---

[26] For example, Anthony Fitzherbert, *Graunde Abridgement* (*c.* 1514–16) Aiell, pl. 8 (1312): 'le demaundant fut nees hors de ligeans de roi dengleterre'; *Year Book 13 Edward III, 1339*, Rolls series (1883–1911) pp. 76–8: 'aiel ne murrust seisi deins le legians le roy dengleterre'. In addition to these references given by Maitland, see also *Calendar of inquisitions miscellaneous, 21–25 Edward III*, no. 415; *Calendar of patent rolls, 1348–1350*, p. 191.

[27] *The eyre of London, 14 Edward II, 1321*, vol. I, 86 Selden Society (1969) pp. 213ff.

(the defendant's grandfather) conveyed to him during his (the defendant's grandfather's) lifetime.[28] No challenge was therefore made with regard to the house itself. After all, the case was not about the house, but about whether the father inherited the franchise (the immunity from certain tallages and subsidies to be levied upon the house) so that it could be, upon his death, transmitted to the defendant. The fact that the father acquired the house as the *assignee* adds nothing to his legal position as the *heir* for the immunity granted to his ancestor, who failed to mention it specifically in the deed of assignment of the house. Clearly, Shardlow was responding to his opponent's use of the term *ligaunce*. Scrope realised the consequence and rephrased his argument in extremely dry, spatial terms: 'Then, admit that he was born over there (*la outre*).' Shardlow would not budge: 'the father did his homage to the king'. Scrope was indignant, but confident of his victory: 'You cannot deny then; judgment for the king!' Surprisingly, Scrope's request was refused. Somehow, the court was persuaded that if a person was of the king's *ligaunce*, it would be harsh to exclude the person ('Il serra mult fort en tiel cas destrangere le'). The judges who had initially been rather cynical about the defendant's claim were now inclined to allow the defendant to prove what he said. At the beginning of the case, for example, Stanton J threw the following remark at the defendant: 'you cannot show that you are the heir without showing that your father was heir, and that you cannot do.' Stanton J was now full of sympathy.[29] He asked Shardlow, 'Then, do you want to aver what you said and demur for judgment for the rest?' 'Yes, sir' said Shardlow.[30]

Shardlow must have been happy – not because he changed the whole course of European legal development, but because his argument was accepted. Perhaps it verges on a truism to say that changes of legal rules are introduced to meet the exigencies of the circumstances. Herle J made it clear that the change was introduced because of practical considerations ('il serra 'mult fort' . . .'). But we must ask why the judges *began to* think that it would be 'very hard' on the defendant to apply the established proce-

---

[28] *Calendar of close rolls, 1279–1288*, p. 110 gives the record of conveyance.
[29] *Eyre of London, 14 Edward II, 1321*, pp. 213ff.
[30] An inquest was allowed to be taken from London. Ibid.

dures of inquest. If judges and lawyers had always felt the same way, then why would they have developed and maintained until the early fourteenth century an elaborate body of legal rules offensive to their sense of justice? I contend that before any proposal for a major legal change could be made, the conception of justice had to change. The case of *Rex* v. *Philip de Beauvais* shows that what used to be regarded as justice from the earliest days of the common law (i.e., excluding foreign-born persons from inheritance because of the difficulty of proof) had now begun to offend the changed conception of justice.

However, Shardlow's victory in this case was incomplete. Even though he succeeded in having an inquest taken from London, he certainly was not in a position to offer immunity to jurors. It must have been difficult to find jurors who would ignore the threat of attaint and give a verdict in favour of the defendant without first-hand knowledge of the circumstances of his father's foreign birth. On the day assigned for the judgment, Shardlow failed to show up. The franchise was taken into the king's hands and the defendant was fined. Shardlow's feat of manipulating the ambiguity of *ligeance* was remarkable. But he could not offer an entirely satisfactory solution for foreign-born persons' inheritance problem. This is why a petition had to be made in Parliament in 1343.

For Geoffrey Scrope and many previous generations of lawyers, the Channel was an undeniable geographical and legal barrier. *Ligeance* was then used to describe the legal disability of a person born *hors la ligeance*. But the ambiguity of *ligeance* opened up a possibility of using it to *overcome* such legal disability. We saw Shardlow tenaciously repeating with unswerving determination, 'the father did homage to the king and, therefore, was of the *ligaunce*'. His remarkable technique of blurring the term was to be adopted by the drafters of the statute *De natis ultra mare*. According to the statute, if both parents are 'de la ligeance du Roi' when their children are born 'dehors la ligeance le Roi', those children shall henceforth have the inheritance 'deinz la dite ligeance'. It is quite amazing to see that a woman giving birth to a child *dehors la ligeance* of the king can be, at that selfsame moment, *de la ligeance* of the same king.

As a result of the ambiguous use of *ligeance*, the basic terms of spatial perception, such as 'in (*deinz*)' and 'out (*dehors*)', have become impregnated with sophisticated ideological significance. 'Within the *ligeance*' is no longer an expression which simply describes the geographic location of an object or an event. The realm has ceased to be a mere *locus* which is populated by people whose personal legal status is widely but justly different. The mysterious power of *ligeance* would *homogenise* the legal status of people 'within' it. Already, the kingdom had long been conceived as a quasi-spiritual union of people miraculously bound together by the bond of faith and alliance (sometimes spelled as *lyance*) to form a mystic body (*corpus mysticum*). At the same time, everyone of the medieval Christendom was thoroughly familiar with a parallel claim that the membership of the mystic body of Church was the key to obtaining the salvation (ultimate liberty) through Our Lord, of whom 'our lord the king' was the earthly deputy.[31] Some lawyers, however, discovered that a tactful manipulation of terminology could demolish the thin dividing line between spiritual and temporal liberty. With the new use of *ligeance*, our lord the king could truly fulfil his mission in this earthly kingdom by graciously (*gratiis*) dispensing liberty, temporal as well as spiritual, to all those who are 'within' his *ligeance*, 'within' the mystic body of which he is the head. From then on, by engaging oneself within the bond and bounds of faith and allegiance of our lord the king, one would obtain liberty, spiritual and temporal.

In 1368, the English Parliament had another opportunity to consider and affirm the new way of legal reasoning. A petition was made that children born in Calais, Guines, Gascony and elsewhere in the overseas lands and seignories that pertained to our lord the king should be able to inherit just like children born within England. The argument was that one's legal condition 'within' the *ligeance* should not be affected by a geographical barrier. Whether one was 'in' or 'out' was no longer a spatial question. Lawyers seemed to have already completely forgotten about the legal problems of jury trial and certification of bastardy. As long as one was 'within' the bond of *ligeance*, one was 'within' the realm, and therefore equal legal rights should be extended. The petition was

---

[31] There is a considerable amount of literature on this point. For a short bibliography, see J. L. Harouel, J. Barbey, E. Bournazel et al., *Histoire des institutions: de l'époque franque à la Révolution*, 2nd edn (Paris, 1989) pp. 87, 301–2. One may also consult the works of G. Duby, M. Bloch, W. Ullmann, J. Le Goff, E. Kantorowicz, J. Krynen, etc. See pp. 189ff. below.

granted.[32] It was a small step from there to the ruthless legal discrimination against aliens who were 'without' the bond of *ligeance*. Lawyers were all ready. They were waiting for the death of the old king.

CONCLUSION

In the preceding chapter, I argued that the statute *De natis ultra mare* was not about foreigners, nor about the law of alien status. It is now time to complement that argument. It was an argument which was made to meet the pressing need to be rid of the unfortunate interpretative tradition regarding the statute. I wished to stay away from the wasteful – from a historical viewpoint – discussion about whether the statute introduced the rule of *ius sanguinis* into the so-called 'common law rule' of *ius soli*. By arguing that the statute had nothing to do with the law of alien status, I hoped that we could prepare the way for assigning an even greater significance to the statute.

We must now stress that the statute was indeed one of the most prominent landmarks in the history of the law of personal status in Europe. The statute was the pithy summary of the new way of using the old concepts of faith and allegiance. The statute was not *immediately* concerned with foreigners or aliens. But, before any proposal for legal discrimination against aliens could be made, faith and allegiance must first of all be introduced into the law of personal status. Before legal inequality between subjects and aliens could be discussed, legal and moral equality among subjects had first to be proclaimed as the norm.

Medieval lawyers were probably all too familiar with the notions of faith and allegiance. But no one seems to have used them in the way the statute *De natis ultra mare* did. The statute ushered in a completely different approach to the law of personal status. From then on, faith and allegiance would first and foremost be used to determine whether a person was 'within' or 'without' the mystic body politic, which became the sole vehicle leading to salvation, temporal as well as spiritual. From then on too, it would be unthinkable that the insider status is not necessarily connected

---

[32] Statute 42 Edward III c. 10.

to a promise of legal benefit and advantage. This was going to be, as it were, a 'gospel' for villeins and other natural-born Englishmen whose insider status had long been useless in promoting their legal position. A new dividing line was to be drawn in the law of personal status. Those who had faith and allegiance in our lord the king would be the insiders. They should all be given legal benefits and advantages. Those who lacked faith and allegiance were outsiders. No legal benefit should be given to them. The mystic body politic was thus given a new life as the pivotal concept in the law of personal status. A very long chapter in the history of the law of personal status which lasted from the Antiquity to the later Middle Ages was about to be over.

Under the old regime, men were divided primarily between the free (*liberi*) and the unfree (*servi*). Under the new regime, men are divided between insiders and outsiders. What was for Roman jurists an intuitively obvious division was to be condemned as an absurd and reprehensible vestige of a bygone era by the fifteenth century. It was to become increasingly difficult to believe that the notion of mystic body politic did not play any part in the ancient and medieval legal analysis of personal status. Sooner rather than later, a comprehensive reinterpretation of all earlier sources was to be undertaken. This was done by some of the ablest renaissance jurists who could not but believe that what was an intuitively obvious and natural division for them (the division between insiders and outsiders) must also be so for others. The fascinating details of this marvellous interpretative feat are mostly beyond the scope of this book even though they are important in understanding why not only in England but all over Europe the history of the law of alien and subject status could not be written so far. In the remaining part of this book, we shall focus instead on how the fifteenth- and sixteenth-century common lawyers interpreted some of the late medieval sources and thereby laid the foundation for a new era of the law of personal status which revolves around the concepts of faith, allegiance and mystic body politic.

Part II

HISTORIOGRAPHY

7

THOMAS LITTLETON, JOHN RASTELL AND EDMUND PLOWDEN

For a long time in Europe, inequality was the moral and legal ideal. The fundamental division in the law of personal status was between the free and the unfree. All other divisions were subordinate to this *summa divisio*. In the preceding chapters, we have examined an important change which was introduced in England in the fourteenth century. First came the remarkable shift of outlook: faith and allegiance should guarantee the enjoyment of legal benefit within the realm (1351). Then came, as a corollary, the idea that a lack of faith and allegiance should disqualify a person from the enjoyment of legal benefit and advantage within the realm. A new approach to the law of personal status was being introduced. The new *summa divisio personarum* was to be drawn between those who were within (having faith and allegiance to the king) and those who were without. All other categorical divisions among persons would be given secondary importance. It was, in my view, a revolutionary change in the law of personal status in Europe.

However, a change of legal outlook does not automatically introduce new legal terms and definitions. Change of law entails change of resource distribution patterns. To reduce the resistance of adversely affected groups, it is preferable that the change should be introduced with minimum visibility. The inherent ambiguity of language will provide the key to a discreet, but successful legal change. In this chapter, we shall examine how the fifteenth- and sixteenth-century common lawyers manipulated legal terminology and accomplished a silent revolution in the law of personal status. In particular, we shall discuss the process through which the old expression 'alien ne hors la ligeance' was charged with new meanings.

LITTLETON'S DEFINITION OF ALIEN

The term 'alien' or 'alienigena' had long been used as a factual description which made reference to a person's overseas birth or foreign provenance. There is a good example which demonstrates this point. The king's writs and charters issued in post-Conquest England were often directed to 'omnibus fidelibus suis, Francigenis et Angligenis'.[1] We therefore know that the new French settlers in England (*Franci*) were incorporated into the (English) king's *fideles*. However, these new *fideles* were also described as *alienigena* in contemporary legal texts: 'It is held to be a case of *murdum* if an *alienigena* is killed and it is not known who committed this offence, or the slayer is not handed over by the appointed day.' The identity of 'alienigena' is further clarified by the following clause: 'If any Frenchman or Norman or any person from across the see is slain, and . . .' Also, these 'alien' *fideles* were given a special privilege in oath-taking. They were not bound to swear strictly according to the forms of oath.[2] There was no inconsistency or confusion. In these texts, *fidelis* was used as a legal category, whereas *alienigena* was a factual description of ethnic provenance. The king's *fideles* comprised men of various ethnic origins.[3]

In other texts, however, we see that 'alien' or 'alienigena' was used to refer to the birthplace, rather than ethnic origin, of the person thus described. In the early fourteenth century, for example, foreign-born persons were referred to in judicial proceedings as 'alien' or 'alien nee hors la ligeance'. Since place of birth does not necessarily determine a person's ethnic identity, an 'alien nee hors, etc.' could either be an Englishman or a foreigner. The situation was potentially problematic. In the political context, 'alien' was clearly carrying a stigma by then. The term had been repeatedly used throughout the thirteenth and fourteenth centu-

---

[1] See p. 14 above.

[2] *Leges Henrici primi*, ed. L. J. Downer (Oxford, 1972) p. 289 (c. 92, 9b: 'Murdum enim habetur si alienigena occidatur, et quis hoc fecerit ignoretur uel ad diem non reddatur'); p. 285 (c. 91, 1: 'Si quis Francigena uel Normannus uel denique transmarinus occidatur, et . . .'); and p. 205 (c. 64, 3a: 'Francigene quoque vel alienigene in verborum observantiis non fragunt').

[3] Of course, the English were the principal ethnic group. Hence, the use of the epithet 'alienigena' for the Normans in England. After all, England was the kingdom of 'rex Anglorum'.

ries in launching vehement political attacks on foreigners.[4] The technical, courtroom use of 'alien nee, etc.' did not take full account of this political situation. In fact, the problem was squarely posed when the question of foreign-born children's inheritance was discussed in 1343 and 1351. The petition (1343) and the statute (1351) carefully avoided the term 'alien'. Instead, the expression 'infant heirs (*enfantz heritiers*)' was used throughout. Even though it was a judicially accepted practice to use the term 'alien' to refer to a foreign-born person (whether ethnically English or not), it was politically incorrect to describe the children of the king's beloved soldiers as 'aliens'.

By the fifteenth century, the legal ideal was clearly that those who lack faith and allegiance to the king shall not be given legal benefit. The old meanings of *alienigena* or *alien nee hors, etc.* obviously could not give adequate expression to this new ideal because they were not at all touching on the question of faith and allegiance. What was the solution, then?

Instead of inventing new terminology corresponding to the new *divisio personarum*, common lawyers in the fifteenth century continued to use the old expression 'alien nee hors, etc.' as if nothing had happened.[5] Thomas Littleton was following this tradition. In his *Tenures* (*c.* 1450–60), he defined aliens as those 'born out of the *liegance* of our lord the king (*ne hors de la liegance nostre seignr le roy*)'. He further elaborated that 'born out of the *liegance*' meant 'born in such country as is out of the king's *liegeaunce* (*nee en tiel pays q est hors de la liegeaunce le roy*)'.[6] Statutes enacted in Tudor years were in complete agreement with Littleton's definition in that alien status was defined by birthplace only. Alien merchants were described as 'dyvers Merchaunts straungers born owt of this realme'. Aliens were those 'borne in other Realmes' or 'borne out of this realme of England or other our said lorde the kinges obeisaunce'.[7]

However, the apparent continuity of terminology is concealing

---

[4] D. A. Carpenter, 'King Henry III's "statute" against aliens, July 1263', 107 *English Historical Review* (1992) 925–43. Professor J. H. Baker kindly drew my attention to this article. During the centuries immediately following the Norman Conquest, the term *'alienigena'* was not carrying the stigma. See note 2 above.

[5] For example, *Year Book*, Hil. 14 Henry IV, fos. 19–20, pl. 23 (1413), *Year Book*, Hil. 7 Edward IV, pl. 17 (1467), *Year Book*, Trin. 9 Edward IV, pl. 3 (1469).

[6] T. Littleton, *Tenures*, printed by R. Pynson (London, *c.* 1510) fo. xiv (r).

[7] Statute 1 Henry VII c. 2 (1485); Statute 4 Henry VII c. 23 (1488): 'any

an important legal change. Until Serjeant Shardlow's remarkable pleading strategy was accepted by the court (1321), to be born 'within' or 'without' the *ligeance* was a spatial question; that is, whether a person was born 'in this land (*en cest terre*)' or 'over there (*la outre*)'. Without altering *any* of these terms, English lawyers achieved one of the most significant changes in the law of personal status. By the time of Littleton, few, if any, doubted that to be born 'within' or 'without' the *ligeance* was a question of faith and allegiance. Hardly anyone could remember that the question of overseas birth originally arose in connection with the procedures of inquest, which had little to do with faith and allegiance of the heir or the deceased.

How did common lawyers manage to do this? The word *ligeance* holds the secret. The double meaning of *ligeance* provided the ideal means to reify the bond of faith and allegiance. The infiltration of faith and allegiance into the law of personal status was discreetly done because the entry was gained through their reified substitute: birthplace. The ambiguity of the word *ligeance* allowed new ideas to be discussed in old terminology. Lawyers did not have to reveal the identity of their novel claim that the bond of faith and allegiance should override the established law and legal procedures. Common lawyers kept talking about *ligeance*, and stuck to the old-fashioned cliché 'nee hors la ligeance' or 'nee deinz la ligeance'. But the art of double-talk afforded by *ligeance* guaranteed that birthplace itself was already sufficiently imbued with faith and allegiance to our lord the king.

Reification of faith and allegiance was complete when not only alien status, but also subject status was defined in terms of birthplace only. By the sixteenth century, statutes usually defined subjects as those 'borne within this Realme of England, Wales or Irlond' or 'Englishemen naturally borne within the kinges Graces Dominions and obeisaunce'.[8] Lawyers no longer needed to mention faith and allegiance in defining subject or alien status. It sufficed to mention birthplace only. Faith and allegiance used to be rhetorical elements of political and theological discourse. They have now turned into pivotal concepts of the law of personal status

---

merchaunt or other persone straunge borne oute of your obeisaunce'. Statute 32 Henry VIII c. 14, § 7 (1540).

[8] Statutes 6 Henry VIII c. 11 (1514), and 32 Henry VIII c. 16 (1540) respectively.

which can be suitably discussed in the courtroom using the technical 'legal' term of birthplace. Sooner or later, even lawyers themselves would forget why they picked up place of birth as the legal criterion of subject and alien status.[9]

By arguing that the new legal ideal was expressed by the old terminology 'alien nee hors, etc.' and that alien and subject status was defined in terms of birthplace only, we are in fact flatly rejecting the canonical position. Legal historians, of course, have unanimously treated the statute *De natis ultra mare* as introducing or confirming the rule of parental descent of alien and subject status (the so-called *ius sanguinis*). Since the statute requires parents' faith and allegiance as a condition for the children's inheritance, historians have believed that parentage, as well as birthplace, contributed to the determination of a person's alien or subject status. We saw, however, that neither Littleton, nor any of the statutes enacted in those years, treated parentage as relevant to alien or subject status. In the following pages, we shall discuss how the statute *De natis ultra mare* was interpreted by the sixteenth-century lawyers. There, we shall have an opportunity to see how parentage was introduced in the English law of alien status.

EARLY STATUTE-BOOKS

Littleton was probably the last English jurist who could comfortably write a treatise on the common law relying on his own authority. He did not feel obliged to crowd his pages with citations of precedents or authorities handed down from the past.[10] Therefore, we may not interpret his or his contemporaries' silence on the statute *De natis ultra mare* as conclusive evidence that the statute was regarded as irrelevant to the definition of alien status. After Littleton's death, however, statutes and judicial decisions began to be viewed from a different perspective. The earliest extant edition of an abridgement of statutes seems to have been printed in *c*. 1481.[11] The earliest edition of a chronological

---

[9] See p.174 below.

[10] John H. Baker, *An introduction to English legal history*, 3rd edn (London, 1990) pp. 225–8.

[11] *Statutes of the realm*, Records Commission, 9 vols. (1816–28), I, p. xxi. The

compilation of statutes was printed shortly thereafter.[12] From the reign of Henry VIII, statutes appear to have been regularly published at the end of each session of Parliament.[13] The appearance of printed statute-books suggests that members of the legal profession treated statutes with new reverence. Statutes were no longer regarded merely as decisions of Parliament upon complaints about matters of private interest. We see a statute-book being advertised by its editor who proudly claimed that 'for as muche as statutes be one of the pryncypall groundes of the lawe, so that yf the statute be unknowen, the lawe is unknowen in the poynt'.[14]

Littleton could expound the law as he 'knew' it from his practice, rather than as he 'found' it in some written texts of the past. But such a manner of discourse was soon to be regarded as unacceptable for presentation of legal argument. The style of legal argument began to show a growing dependence on the written texts from the past. Students of the common law were now urged to search for ancient statutes because 'the moste part of them retayne theyr force, and bynde the kyngs subiectes unto this day'.[15]

Exhortations to look to the past could be heard with regard to year book cases as well. The first printed abridgement of year book cases appeared in c. 1490.[16] The larger and more widely used abridgement of Sir Anthony Fitzherbert was first published in c. 1514–16. Appearance of commonplace books and widespread

---

copy is kept in the Harvard Law Library. *Short-title catalogue of English books 1475–1640* (STC) No. 9513. It contains an abridgement of statutes up to 1455.

[12] *Nova statuta* (printed by W. de Machlinia c. 1482). The Bodleian Library has a copy probably printed in 1484 (Arch. G. d. 28). It contains statutes from 1 Edward III to 22 Edward IV (1481).

[13] The first contemporaneous sessional publication of statutes seems to have been carried out by Machlinia or Caxton in the reign of Richard III (1484). *Statutes of the realm*, I, p. xxi.

[14] *The greate abbrydgement of all the statutes of Englande untyll the xxx yere of the reygne of our moste drad souerayne lorde kynge Henry the eyght . . .*, printed by W. Rastell (London, c. 1538). It is an enlarged and updated edition of John Rastell's abridgement of statutes printed in 1527. The quoted passage is from the preamble to the table of the newly abridged statutes inserted towards the end of the book.

[15] From the preface of *The great charter called in latyn Magna Carta with divers olde statutes*, printed by R. Redman (London, c. 1540s).

[16] The compilation is attributed to Nicolas Statham (d. 1472). Baker, *Introduction*, p. 212.

circulation of printed abridgements clearly suggest that judicial decisions began to be viewed from a different perspective. As oral pleadings gradually lost importance and gave way to new ways of raising questions of law in legal proceedings, the nature and purpose of case reporting changed. Year book cases were now treated as 'sources' of the common law. In the prologue of *Les comentaries ou les reportes de dyvers cases* (1571), Edmund Plowden made it clear that his objective was to provide judges and lawyers with the judicial decisions of the past 'most firm to trust unto'.[17] Now, the common law had to be 'found' in earlier decisions of the court and in statutes previously made in Parliament. I propose to examine how the statute *De natis ultra mare* and other related medieval legal texts were classified and presented in early statute-books. It will provide valuable information about the late fifteenth- and early sixteenth-century understanding of these texts.

The statute *De natis ultra mare* was featured from the very beginning. In the earliest extant copy of the abridgement of statutes (*c.* 1481), the statute was digested under the heading 'those born beyond the sea (*Nati in partibus transmarinis*)'. However, it was given a very cursory treatment. The statute was not mentioned again anywhere in the book. There was a separate heading, 'Aliens'. But it only listed a statute on jury *de medietate linguae* and a statute on alien priors' ability to hold benefices.[18] A cross-reference at the end of the section on 'Aliens' refers the reader to the section on trial. Under the heading 'Triall', we again find a statute on the mixed jury. With this amount of information, it is difficult to know why the statute *De natis ultra mare* was maintained separately from the heading 'Aliens'.

The first chronological compilation of statutes (*c.* 1482) offers a more revealing treatment of our statute.[19] The same heading 'Nati in partibus transmarinis' was used again. But the editor gave the following description of the statute: 'How man from beyond the sea shall inherit in England (*Coment home de ouster le meer serra enherite en Engleterre*)'. This time, the statute 42 Edward III c. 10 was newly indexed as a related statute. Interestingly enough, the

---

[17] John H. Baker, 'Records, reports and the origins of case-law in England' in his (ed.) *Judicial records, law reports, and the growth of case law* (Berlin, 1989) pp. 41–2.

[18] Statute 28 Edward III st. 3; Statute 1 Henry V c. 7, respectively.

[19] *Nova statuta* (printed by W. de Machlinia).

statute *De natis ultra mare* was indexed under the headings 'Bastardie' and 'Trialle' as well. The editor gives the following description regarding the statute: 'Bastardy shall be tried by the ordinary of the place where the writ is brought (*Bastardie serra trie par lordinar del lieu ou le bre est porte*).' Like the 1481 abridgement, there is a heading 'Aliens' which keeps silent about the statute *De natis ultra mare* and the statute 42 Edward III c. 10.

In 1499, Richard Pynson printed an enlarged edition of the 1481 abridgement.[20] The arrangement of 1481 was largely retained. However, there was one important change which reflected the arrangement of the chronological compilation of *c.* 1482. That is, the statute *De natis ultra mare* was abridged under the heading 'Triall' as well. Pynson explained that the statute dealt with the bastardy trial procedures applicable to a person born beyond the sea.[21] The section on bastardy, however, does not contain a cross-reference to the statute *De natis ultra mare*. But the copy kept at the Harvard Law Library shows that this oversight was corrected by a contemporary hand who added the cross-reference to this statute at the end of the section on bastardy. Pynson newly inserted a heading 'Estraungers'. But, neither this nor the heading 'Aliens' contained any mention of the statute *De natis ultra mare*. Pynson's 1499 abridgement was frequently re-edited in the sixteenth century. The statute *De natis ultra mare* and the statute 42 Edward III c. 10 received the same treatment in all these editions.[22]

From *c.* 1500, Pynson began to print chronological compilations of statutes as well. His *Nova statuta* (STC No. 9265) was an enlarged version of Machlinia's edition of *c.* 1482. A number of statute-books known as *The great boke of statutes* were subsequently printed and updated based on this edition.[23] In all these editions which follow the arrangement of Machlinia and Pynson, the statute *De natis ultra mare* and the statute 42 Edward III c. 10

---

[20] The volume has no title page. It begins 'Incipit Tabula huius libri' and ends 'Explicit abbreuiamentum statutorum . . .' STC No. 9514.

[21] 'Bastrdie allege en cely que fuit ne doust le mere serra trie p lordinar del lieu ou le bre est pt come ad ee. use de bastardie all. contre ceux que nasqrent en engle'.

[22] For example, *Abbreuiamentum statutorum . . .* (printed by Pynson in 1521) STC No. 9516; *Le breggement de touts les estatuts . . .*, printed by R. Pynson (London, 1528) STC No. 9517; *Abridgement of statutes*, printed by R. Redman (London, 1539) STC No. 9542.

[23] For example, *The great boke of statutes*, printed by R. Redman, T. Berthelet and J. Rastell (London, *c.* 1533).

were indexed as dealing with inheritance and bastardy trial procedures applicable to a person born beyond the sea. The heading 'Aliens' makes no reference to these statutes.

In light of the foregoing, we may conclude that lawyers in the fifteenth and early sixteenth centuries were well aware of the statute *De natis ultra mare*, but they did not treat it as relevant to alien or subject status. By that time, there was no doubt that foreign birth made a person an alien; and that an alien was often portrayed as banned from all types of common law transactions as well as inheritance.[24] However, a great deal of imagination would be necessary to say that since the statute *De natis ultra mare* enabled certain children to inherit, it was therefore about those children's subject status. Sooner or later, however, someone would nevertheless make such a bold move.

JOHN RASTELL AND ELIZABETHAN SUCCESSION TRACTS

In 1519, John Rastell printed the first English abridgement of statutes. It appears that he had planned an improvement of Pynson's 1499 abridgement by taking 'this lytell payne to translate out of the frenche into englysshe'. However, the 1519 edition was incomplete. Many statutes, including *De natis ultra mare*, were omitted.[25] A fuller edition was printed in 1527.[26] Our statute was now translated into English. But when Rastell replaced the usual heading 'Nati in partibus transmarinis' with a new heading 'Englisshemen', he was doing much more than translation.[27] In the following year, he printed an abridgement of statutes in their original language. The heading 'Englisshemen' was deleted accordingly, and the old heading 'Nati in partibus transmarinis' reappeared. But the meaning of the heading could never be the same again. The section ends with a cross-reference to the clause

---

[24] See p. 158 below (Littleton's explanation of an alien's *complete* legal disability). Whether or not and how thoroughly this principle was actually put into practice in the fifteenth century is not our topic.

[25] See the copy kept in the British Library (B. E. 11/1).

[26] Like the previous edition, this copy has no title page. It begins 'The statutes. Prohemium Johannis Rastell . . .' and ends 'Emprynted in the chepesyde in the xix yere of the reygne of . . . Kinges Henry the viii.' The British Library has a copy (C. 65. aa. 13).

[27] Ibid., fo. 69.

on prerogative escheats of the Normans' lands. This is where John
Rastell differed most from his contemporaries. And this, of
course, is where he is closest to modern British legal historians'
understanding of the beginning of the law of alien status.[28]

In fact, John Rastell's originality was already revealed in a
glossary of legal terms which he printed in those years. There, he
gave the following definition of alien status:

Alyon is he of whome the fader is born and he hymselfe also borne out of
the elegiaunce of our lord the kyng, but yf an alyon come and dwell in
englond whyche is not of the kynges enemyes and here ad issu this issu is
not alion but englysh, also if an englysh man go over the see with the
kyngs lycence and ther ad issu this issu is not alyon.[29]

He claimed that his expositions were 'as well out of the bokis of
mayster littelton as of other bokis of the law'. As far as the above-
quoted definition is concerned, however, his claim was a gross
misrepresentation. Littleton never mentioned the parents' allegiance in defining alien status. The statute *De natis ultra mare* never
mentioned the children's subject status in enabling them to inherit.
Rastell somehow believed that these two could be combined. In
fact, his crude combination was full of errors. He ignored that the
statute *De natis ultra mare* required *both* parents' allegiance as a
condition for the children's inheritance. Also, he invented the
king's licence for crossing the sea. The statute only mentioned that,
for the purpose of the children's inheritance, the mothers should
have crossed the sea by permission and wilful consent of their
husbands.[30] Most of all, he interpreted that allowing inheritance
was equivalent to, or based on, the recognition of the children's

---

[28] See *Magnum abbreuiamentum statutorum Anglie usqz ad annum xv H. viii
inclusiue*, printed by J. Rastell (London, 1528).

[29] *The exposicions of the termys of the law of england and the nature of the writt . . .
gaderyd and brevely compylyd for yong men very necessarye* (London, *c.* 1525–7).
It was repeatedly printed in the following decades and is better known as
Expositiones terminorum.

[30] See, however, *Year Book*, Hil. 22 Henry VI, pl. 5. The ancestor crossed the sea
without the king's licence, took a wife there and had an issue. The issue shall not
inherit and the land shall be escheated. The king's licence was mentioned here as
a justification for escheat, not as a condition for the issue's subject status. The
ancestor was probably regarded as treasonous for having violated the ban against
defection. That is why the inheritance did not descend on the next available
heir. Brook explains this point and indicates that under normal circumstances
(i.e., not involving the violation of the royal ban against crossing the sea), if the
eldest son is an alien, the inheritance will go to the next available heir. R. Brook,
Grande Abridgement (London, 1573) denizen & alien, pl. 14 and pl. 7 (when the

subject status. This interpretation was not only a non sequitur, but also against the year book cases of 1413 and 1474. The case of 1474, for example, allows the possibility to interpret that a foreign-born child who has successfully claimed the inheritance relying on the statute *De natis ultra mare* would still need the king's letters patent in order to be engaged in other common law transactions such as purchase or gift of land. In spite of the statute which allowed inheritance, foreign-born children seem to have remained aliens unless and until they specifically obtained the king's letters patent enabling them to operate like subjects.[31]

The impact of John Rastell

John Rastell died in 1536. Until 1563, he only had one disciple for his innovative, but faulty interpretation: his son William Rastell.[32] Even though the Rastells maintained a near monopoly in printing and marketing subsequent editions of statute-books, none of the statutes in the early sixteenth century adopted their definition of alien status. The hugely successful editions of their *Expositiones terminorum* did not change the law either. In 1537, for example, an attorney and fellow of Gray's Inn, Robert Aske, was interrogated in connection with an insurrection called the 'Pilgrimage of Grace'.[33] He had proposed the repeal of a statute empowering Henry VIII to dispose of the crown to a person of his choice.[34]

---

eldest son is an alien, this does not lead to escheat because alienage, unlike attaint, is not corruption of blood).

[31] Anthony Fitzherbert, *Grande Abridgement* (*c.* 1514–16) deinzin, pl. 3 ('Mesqz un alien soit jure en un lete de succession destre loial et foyal al roy unc. il nest enable de purchas terre ou tenementz si non que il soit fait able par letter le roy, et ceo en un chall., etc.'). Fitzherbert wrongly attributed this case to Mich. 14 Edward III. We believe that the case was decided in Mich. 14 Edward IV, (1474). See *Year Book*, Mich. 14 Edward IV, pl. 6. The copy of the *Abridgement* kept in Cambridge University Library shows that the mistake was corrected by a contemporary hand. For the year book case of 1413, see *Year Book*, Hil. 14 Henry IV, fos. 19–20, pl. 23 as well as Brook, *Abridgement*, denizen & alien, pl. 11. Professor Baker kindly drew my attention to this case.

[32] See *The greate abbrydgement of all the statutes of Englande* . . ., printed by W. Rastell (London, *c.* 1538). It was enlarged and printed again in 1542. See also *A collection of all the statutes* . . ., printed by W. Rastell (London, 1557, 1559). It was frequently re-edited during 1559–1620. In all these editions, W. Rastell faithfully followed his father's interpretation.

[33] *Dictionary of national biography*, under 'Robert Aske'.

[34] Statute 28 Henry VIII c. 7 (1536).

When he was forced to defend himself for 'grudging against the actes of the kinges Parliament', he explained as follows:

[Anyone] borne vnder the crown of this realme may clame . . . the law of this realme as ther inheritance [and this law enables them] frely to by & sell landes & goodes & take by descent, and so cannot an alien do nor clame. [I]f the crown wer giffyn by the kinges highnes to an alian . . . how should this alien by reason haue it . . . because he is not born vnder the allegiance of this crown.[35]

Robert Aske discusses alien status without any reference to parentage. Aliens are portrayed as incapable of all types of common law transactions, personal as well as real. We see the triumph of Littleton, who explained in the previous century that 'if an alien wants to bring a *real or personal* action, the tenant or defendant can say that he is born out of the ligeance of our lord the king and demand judgment whether he shall be answered'.[36]

In 1541, however, an important change was introduced. A naturalisation act was passed which provided that children of an English father who were born abroad shall be 'from henceforth reputed & taken kinges natural subject as lawfull persons borne within this Realme of England'.[37] Just as much as it reveals the growing influence of the Rastells' new interpretation, so much does it show that until that very moment, the law of subject and alien status was based exclusively on birthplace. Birth out of the realm makes a person an alien as explained by Littleton. Both parents' allegiance exceptionally enabled inheritance as provided by the statute *De natis ultra mare*. However, whether such a person could be engaged in other common law transactions, such as sale or gift, was a widely open question. As indicated by the

---

[35] Mary Bateson, 'Aske's answer regarding the illegitimacy of Lady Mary', 5 *English Historical Review* (1890) 562–4.

[36] *Leteltun teners newe correcte*, fo. xiv (r). Emphasis supplied. Coke, of course, attempted to qualify Littleton's sweeping statement. Coke suggested that an alien's legal disability should be applicable to real actions only. Coke was apparently relying on the authority of Plowden who made this argument in his succession treatise which we discuss shortly. Plowden's view is supported by Brook, *Abridgement*, denizen & alien, pl. 10 (38 Henry VIII, 1546): 'alien nee poet porter action personell et serra repond sans este dishable . . . et econtre in action real et idem videtur in action mixte'. See also ibid., pl. 16 (1479: an alien can bring a personal action in the common law and the plea of alien born is applicable only to real actions and mixed actions; in the business world of merchants, aliens can buy and sell and their deals are valid, hence, *ex equitate*, they must have actions for debts and their assets).

[37] Statute 33 Henry VIII c. 25.

year book cases of 1413 and 1474, the prevalent opinion was probably that the person would still need the king's letters patent to be engaged in such transactions. To be allowed to inherit was not enough to alter the person's alien status. These were the circumstances under which the statute 33 Henry VIII c. 25 was introduced. The statute provides that the father's subject status would remove the children's alien status.[38] For the first time, therefore, (paternal) lineage was partially introduced into the law of subject and alien status. In our view, it was not based on any precedent. If anything, it was based on the faulty interpretation of the family of Rastells.

John Hales' tract (1563)

However, a decisive victory was assured for the Rastells when their interpretation was adopted by John Hales in 1563. This outspoken tract-writer was deeply involved in the Elizabethan politics which revolved around the question of succession to the crown. As a Protestant supporter of Catherine Grey (a descendant of Mary Tudor, the younger sister of Henry VIII), John Hales' mission was to exclude Mary Stuart and Margaret of Lennox (both of whom were descendants of Margaret Tudor, the elder sister of Henry VIII). To this end, he wrote a tract entitled 'A Declaration of the Succession of the Crown Imperiall of Ingland'.[39] His strategy was obvious from the outset. '[B]y Nature', he argued, 'there ought to be great Difference betweene English Men and Straungers.' But the situation was complicated because one of the two ladies to be branded as 'straungers' was in fact born in England (Margaret of Lennox). Established law was of no use to John Hales because it took no account of parentage in conferring the subject status on children who were born in England.[40] Even the statute 33 Henry VIII c. 25 was not very helpful because all it said was that foreign-born children of an

---

[38] See, in this connection, Brook, *Abridgement*, denizen & alien, pl. 21 (of uncertain date; Brook simply notes that the case is from the printed abridgement of assize reports). The father's subject status appears to have passed not only to the children, but to his wife as well ('Engloys passa le méere et mary feme alyen, per ceo le feme est dallegeans le roy et son issu enheritera').

[39] Printed in George Harbin, *The hereditary right of the crown of England asserted* (London, 1713) appendix, pp. xx–xlii.

[40] See Brook, *Abridgement*, denizen & alien, pl. 9 (1544): an alien's son born in

English father should no longer be aliens. What John Hales
needed was an argument that English-born children of an alien
father should not be English subjects.

Under these circumstances, John Hales adopted Rastell's innovative interpretation because it allowed scope for an argument for
paternal descent of alien status. John Hales' politically charged
argument was therefore based on the assumption that the statute
De natis ultra mare was 'expoundinge the Law in this Case'.
Accordingly, the legal disability of Mary Stuart was derived from
the following arguments: (1) she was not the king's child; (2) she
was not born within the king's ligeance; and (3) her parents were
not at the faith and allegiance of the king. The first and the third
arguments were utterly superfluous. The second argument alone
would have been necessary and sufficient to explain the legal
disability of Mary Stuart. But John Hales was deploying the two
other arguments as a preface to the fantastic theory of paternal
descent of alien status which he was about to unfold with regard to
Margaret of Lennox.

It is according to 'God's plan', claimed John Hales, that men
are 'the more worthy' than women. Children should therefore
follow the condition and estate of their fathers. To some extent,
this theory was supported by the statute of 1541 which introduced
the paternal descent of *subject* status. John Hales wanted to add a
new claim (paternal descent of *alien* status) which no one had ever
made. He speculated that the 'proposition (that every Person
borne in Ingland, of what Nation soever his Parents were, shold
be free in Ingland) can[not] be justified by any reason'. Since
'customs not grounded upon reason cannot prescribe', he concluded that Margaret of Lennox – her father was a Scot – should
not be a free-woman even though she was born in England.[41]
What is being attacked here as 'customs not grounded upon
reason' were in fact the definitions of alien and subject status
unanimously upheld during the fifteenth and early sixteenth
centuries. The time had changed enough and Littleton's unequi-

England is English, not an alien ('Et le fits de alien quel fits est nee in Angleterre
il est Angloys et non alien').

[41] Harbin, *The heriditary right*, pp. xxxiv, xxxvii. The father of Margaret of
Lennox was Archibald Douglas, the sixth earl of Angus. He was married to
Margaret Tudor after the death of her first husband.

vocal definition of alien status was now disgracefully castigated by an unworthy pamphleteer as an 'unreasonable custom'.[42]

Throughout his tract, John Hales frequently referred to 'Praesident and Example' which included historical events, narrative passages from chronicles, legal texts on dilatory exception against French enemies (Bracton), on the king's escheat of the Normans' lands (*Prerogativa regis*), and even Littleton's definition of alien status. None of these, however, were used accurately. In fact, he misquoted Littleton, misunderstood the important year book case of 1474, misinterpreted the naturalisation statute of 1541 and kept silent about Tudor statutes which were immediately relevant to the alien and subject status. Superficial as his legal learning was, he was an immensely influential advocate of the Puritan cause in Elizabethan succession politics. The family of Rastells finally found an indiscreet, but vociferous follower.[43]

The succession tracts

John Hales' tract provoked vehement and voluminous responses.[44] However, all subsequent debates were conducted within the framework laid out by his tract. No one raised any doubt about Hales' assumption that the statute *De natis ultra mare* was about subject and alien status. The statute was unanimously regarded as removing the 'disabilitie of foreyne birthe'.[45] Removal of disability, it certainly was. But what did they mean by 'foreyne birthe'?

To answer this question, we must first understand that birth 'within the ligeance', on the other hand, was viewed by then as guaranteeing the 'liberty of England'. John Hales' following remark is revealing: 'For if you will put Straungers and right Englishe Men in one case, what avaylesth the liberty of Ingland?

---

[42] 'He [John Hales] evidently picked up a smattering of law while working for his uncle, Sir Christopher Hales, who had been Solicitor General and Attorney General under Henry VIII. His was probably the superficial learning that makes for a good pamphleteer.' Mortimer Levine, *The early Elizabethan succession question, 1558–1568* (Stanford, Calif., 1966) pp. 62–3.

[43] See George T. Peck, 'John Hales and the Puritans during the Marian exile', 10 *Church History* (1941) 159–77 for a more favourable portrayal of Hales and his role as the Elizabethan Puritan parliamentarian.

[44] See the appendix at the end of this chapter.

[45] BL Harleian MS 849 (Plowden's treatise, 1567) fo. 14r.

What profits it to be an English Man borne?'[46] The same attitude
was shared by all lawyers of the sixteenth century. We have
already quoted a statute of 1541 where the king's subjects were
described as *'lawfull* persons borne within this Realme of
England'. None of those who were involved in the succession
debate realised that they were dealing with a statute (*De natis ultra
mare*) which was enacted when a large number of people born
within the realm were still unable to claim the status of lawful
persons (*legales homines*). That anyone born within the king's
ligeance could be legally disabled within his kingdom was no
longer an acceptable ideal although probably it was still the
reality. At least in theory, lawyers all agreed that faith and
allegiance to our lord the king should make one free. Birth within
the 'obeisaunce of our lord the king' was indeed the key to
'liberty'.[47]

Now, legal disability (deprivation of liberty) was only for those
who failed to be born under the 'obeisance of our lord the king'. It
was beyond the pious imagination of the sixteenth-century
lawyers that not only foreigners, but also Englishmen, were
suffering from the so-called 'disabilitie of foreyne birthe' until the
early fourteenth century. They did not recognise that there was a
time when the 'disabilitie of foreyne birthe' arose because of law
(procedures of inquest), not because of faith and allegiance. This
very statement would appear to them as a contradiction in terms.
For, by that time, faith and allegiance had long been the axiomatic
premises of the law.

John Hales' succession tract was circulated in these years. The
moment the statute *De natis ultra mare* was presented as removing
the 'disabilitie of foreyne birthe', none of the sixteenth-century

---

[46] Harbin, *The hereditary right*, p. xxx.
[47] This is the essential structure of the monotheistic ideology shared by Judaism,
Christianity and Islamism. See, for example, the meaning of 'Islam' and
'Muslim' explained in Mohammed Arkoun, *L'Islam*, 2nd edn (Paris, 1992)
pp. 34–8: 'obéissance amoureuse' is the key to the ultimate liberation. See also
Faouzi Skali, *La Voie Soufie* (Paris, 1985) pp. 33–4: 'La relation d'un individu
avec l'archétype divin dont il est l'expression est la relation d'un serviteur ('Abd)
avec son Seigneur (Rabb).' This is how the ultimate liberator is identified with
the ultimate master (*Dominus*) and how the 'subject' status was the key to the
'liberty of Englishman born'. What distinguishes Christianity from Judaism and
Islamism, however, is the concept of the 'mystic body of Christ' which is unique
to the Christian ecclesiology and which provides the ideological foundation of
the law of alien and subject status.

lawyers could escape from the potent grip of their own assumptions, that is: (1) foreign birth meant alien status; (2) alien status meant legal disability; and (3) no such disability should affect the king's subjects because they were guaranteed equal liberty through 'obeisaunce'. According to the sixteenth-century legal vocabulary, 'foreyne birthe' could not by any means be a factual description. It signified a category of personal legal status characterised by the lack of faith, allegiance and obedience. Little did it matter that the statute *De natis ultra mare* carefully avoided the terms 'alien' and 'liege' which were in common use in the fourteenth century. Nor were they troubled by the statute's lengthy clause on bastardy trial procedures which did not make much sense to them. No one found it odd that neither Littleton, nor year book cases, nor any of the Tudor statutes mentioned this statute in connection with alien or subject status. They also put away a number of early statute-books where this statute was presented as irrelevant to the alien or subject status. Finally, no one cared to remember that as late as 1541, Parliament enacted a statute based on the assumption that the statute *De natis ultra mare* was irrelevant to the alien or subject status of foreign-born children.

This, in my view, is how the statute *De natis ultra mare* began its career as *the* nationality statute of England. Also, this is how parental descent was partially introduced into the English nationality law.[48] In the remaining pages, we shall discuss two manuscript tracts. They form part of the Elizabethan succession tracts. But their importance merits a separate treatment.

PLOWDEN'S MANUSCRIPT (1567)

As a devout Catholic lawyer, Sir Edmund Plowden felt obliged to refute the widespread Protestant propaganda against Mary Stuart. After spending the Christmas of 1566 'serch[ing] reasons and groundes of the lawe', he wrote in 1567 a tract entitled 'A treatise proving that if our Soveraigne Lady quene Elizabeth (whom god blesse with long lyffe and many children) should dye without

---

[48] France has a rather different history regarding the introduction of the parental descent of nationality. See Anne Lefebvre-Teillard, '*Ius sanguinis*: l'émergence d'un principe (éléments d'histoire de la nationalité française)', 82 *Revue critique de droit international privé* (1993) 223–50.

issue, that the Quene of Scotte by her birth in Scotlande is not
disabled by the lawe of England to receive the crown of Ingland
by discent.'[49] Knowing the numerous obstacles which lay in the
area of inheritance law, he greatly appreciated the merit of an
argument that the 'crown being a thing incorporate, the right
thereof does not descend like the case of private inheritance, but
goes by succession as other corporations do'.[50] Accordingly,
Plowden developed a sophisticated argument about 'the two
bodies of the king'. That, of course, was to argue that legal
disabilities of foreign birth 'extende but to bodies naturall only[;
they] can not be applyed to bodies politicke'. Although a person
may not herself or himself be a body politic, 'the body naturall is
extolled by the conjunction with the body politicke and altered in
qualitie'. Therefore, he concluded, foreign birth is 'non impedi-
ment from receipte of *that that maketh a body politicke* and so not
from receipt of the crowne'.[51]

Plowden was counting on year book cases where the plea of
'alien nee, etc.' was held inadmissible with regard to the head of
English daughter-houses of foreign religious orders. Plowden
claimed that these cases 'declared the lawe truely that an alien
might be a Bishopp, Abbot or parson within this realme' (fo. 17r).
As we saw, however, the question of foreign birth arose only in
connection with the proof of descent. The plea of 'alien nee, etc.'
was inapplicable to the religious houses because they do not have
children. Plowden did not recognise that the plea of 'alien nee, etc.'
in the fourteenth century had nothing to do with the alien or
subject status. Although the effectiveness of the plea did depend on

---

[49] BL Harleian MS 849.

[50] On this point, Plowden was in complete agreement with his friend, justice of the
Common Pleas, Anthony Brown (d. 1567). The same argument was repeated by
J. Leslie, *A defence of the honor of Mary* . . . (London, 1569) fo. 68r. Regarding
the dating of the manuscript treatise of Anthony Brown, see Marie Axton, 'The
influence of Edmund Plowden's succession treatise', 37 *Huntington Library
Quarterly* (1974) 209–26.

[51] Emphasis supplied. Our quotations are from the first part of his treatise (fos.
1r–18v), which is entirely devoted to this argument. The theory of the 'king's
two bodies' had already appeared in *Willion* v. *Berkeley* (75 Eng. Rep. 380; also
printed in his *Les Comentaries ou les reportes de dyvers cases* (London, 1571) 248).
The prologue to his *Comentaries* also contains a lengthy discussion on this
theory and it attracted the attention of Maitland and Kantorowicz. Neither of
these authors, however, seems to have been aware of Plowden's manuscript
treatise on the succession question.

the distinction between corporate body and natural body, the plea was applicable to Englishmen as well as to foreigners. After all, if foreigners became bishops, abbots or parsons in England, that was not because they formed corporations conjoining their body natural with the body politic of bishopric, abbacy or parsonry,[52] but because *anyone* could be presented, collated, provided or elected to these posts as long as the relevant procedures of the laws of the Church and of the realm were duly observed.

But why should the sixteenth-century lawyers waste any time trying to understand the past when they found 'valuable' texts which – if appropriately interpreted – could put them in good stead in the polemic exchanges in which they were deeply involved? Plowden's treatise goes one step further and shows that even if they were forced to remember the past, they would rather avoid doing so if the past should be damaging to their present argument. Already in December 1565, one of the anti-Stuart authors clearly suggested that Mary Stuart's claim could be effectively denied without having recourse to her alien status. According to this anonymous author, an elder brother born in France, for example, would be denied inheritance 'for our law medilith not with' a person born out of the realm. Instead, the inheritance should go to the younger brother born within the realm because 'th'one [the younger brother] is known unto the lawe and not the other'. The author left no doubt that it was a question of law (cognisance of jury) rather than one of faith and allegiance: 'for if the Law could take notice of the elder brother in France, surely the younger Brother should never inherit'.[53]

Plowden must have realised that such an argument would be fatal to Mary Stuart's claim. Since the argument allowed virtually no room for manoeuvring, the best way out of it was to dismiss it altogether. Plowden began his argument by setting forth two possible causes for the disability of a French-born heir. First, he gave a full statement of his adversary's argument:

[A] French borne can not be knowne or tryed within Inglande to be discended of the [father] for that he and his father were borne out of the

---

[52] See *Maitland – selected essays*, ed. H. D. Hazeltine et al. (Cambridge, 1936) p. 87 ('On the whole it seems to me that a church is no [corporate] person in the English temporal law of the later Middle Ages').

[53] 'Allegations against the Surmised Title of the Quene of Scotts . . .' BL Harleian MS 4627, fo. 18r.

Realme, and of thinge chaunced out of the realme our lawe takethe no
knowledge, for tryalls by our lawe are by twelve men and these men are
not bounde to enqwyre of any thinge beyond the seas.

In other words, a foreign-born heir was unable to inherit, not
because he (she) was an alien, but because 'no Jury of this realm is
bound to take knowledge, nor non otherwais there is by the lawe
to trye or knowe that the french borne is descended of the
[ancestor]'.

The second possible reason, according to Plowden, is based on
faith and allegiance. It is supposed that the hereditary descent of a
French-born child could be tried in England without any legal
difficulty, and

yet the frencheman shoulde be disabled for that he was borne in the
allegiance of another prynce to whom he is subject, not to the king of
Inglande, and if he is subjecte to an other to whom he oweth faith and
ligeance, then the lawe accounteth him a straunger to the realm, and
therefore disableth him to take by discent any inheritance.

Having thus defined the two possible causes (fo. 9v), Plowden
embarked on an examination of a number of precedents to 'prove'
which of the two was the true cause of the 'disabilitie of foreyne
birthe'. He took notice of year book cases where an ecclesiastical
benefice became vacant because the incumbent was made bishop of
a diocese beyond the sea, or because the incumbent was stripped of
all his temporalities upon conviction of heresy in papal curia. How
could a jury in England try the issue of vacancy, asks Plowden (fo.
10), if the jurors were unable to inquire into the matters transpired
beyond the sea? It is true that the jury did try the issue of whether
the benefice was vacant; but jurors were not concerned with the
reasons for the vacancy. Indeed, the detailed reasons of vacancy
were matters of the Canon law which could not have been tried by
a common law jury even if they had taken place in England.
Precisely because of this jurisdictional problem, common law
judges took great pains to instruct the jury that 'voidaunce serra
generalment trie [i.e., whether vacant or not], et noun pas certein
voidaunce especialment [i.e., how it became vacant]'.[54]

---

[54] *Year Book*, Pas. 19 Edward III, pl. 27 (Fitzherbert, *Abridgement*, triall, pl. 57).
See Cheyette, 'Kings, courts, cures, and sinecures: the statute of provisors and
the common law', 19 *Traditio* (1963) 295–349 for a detailed discussion of this
topic. Also see *Year Book*, 21 Edward III, fos. 6b–7; *Year Book*, 5 Edward III,
fo. 9. The early stage in the development of this technique with which the king's

Plowden also claimed that death abroad was triable by a jury in England. The writ for the assize of *mort d'ancestor*, so he argues, required that jurors should inquire whether the demandant was the closest heir even if the ancestor died abroad while on a pilgrimage. How could they do this, asks Plowden (fo. 10v), 'unles they mighte take knowledge that he were dead'? Plowden did not note that this was indeed the reason why a special type of writ had to be devised where the demandant was allowed to state that the ancestor was in possession of the land in his demesne 'on the day he embarked his journey abroad' instead of 'on the day he died'.[55] Plowden went on to argue that promises made abroad by merchants, bills drawn abroad and obligations undertaken abroad were all recognised in England (fo. 10r). We wonder how Plowden could say this. As we saw, documents executed beyond the sea had just as much difficulty of legal recognition in England as foreign-born heirs.[56] We also know that deeds of merchants were given an exceptional treatment. Probably, Plowden did not fully appreciate the following remark of Justice Bereford: 'because he is a merchant . . . a man cannot use the law of the land [regarding the recognition of a deed] in all its points against a merchant'.[57]

Furthermore, Plowden seemed to have relied on the faulty interpretation of John Rastell on more than one occasion. In his *Tabula libri magni abbreviamenti librorum legum Anglorum* (1517), Rastell listed several year book cases under the heading 'where the inquest took notice of things transpired beyond the sea (*Ou les enquest prend notices de chose oust la mer*)'.[58] Plowden accordingly argued that the jury was 'bound to . . . take knowledge of the circumstances pertaining to the tytle of the land and the clayme of

court asserted the jurisdiction in matters of ecclesiastical benefices is demonstrated in *Select cases in the court of King's Bench under Edward I*, vol. I, 55 Selden Society (1936) p. 42. Plowden cites and relies on these cases without adequately discussing their full significance (fo. 10r).

[55] *Glanvill*, lib. 13, cc. 5–6. Furthermore, Plowden wrongly suggested that the proximity of blood was somehow connected to the death of the ancestor. Whether a person was the closest heir was usually determined by the birth of the heir rather than by the death of the ancestor.

[56] See p. 117 above.

[57] *Year Books of 4 Edward II, 1310–1311*, 26 Selden Society (1911) p. 154 ('pur ceo q'il est marchaunt . . . home ne put nynt user en ceo cas lei de terre en touz poinz ver marchaund, etc.').

[58] *Tabula libri magni abbreviamenti librorum legum Anglorum* (London, 1517), 'enquest'.

the partie, and if parte of the circumstance chaunced beyond the sea, they are bound to take knowledge of it, or else the lawe shoulde be unperfecte and wante tryall in many cases' (fo. 10r). If, however, Plowden had taken a little pain to peruse the actual cases thus indexed by Rastell, he would have immediately realised that in all those cases, the possession, as distinct from right, was *provisionally* awarded because of the impossibility of proving the circumstances beyond the sea (foreign birth, foreign death, existence of a person beyond the sea, etc.).[59]

At any rate, Plowden was convinced of the accuracy of his interpretation when he observed as follows: 'Of those precedents we maie see that mariage beyond the sea, contracte beyond the sea, death beyond the sea, lyffe beyond the sea, birthe beyond the sea and any other things innumerable chansing beyond the sea maie be tryed and understode in Ingland.' He further explained that such trials caused 'no inconvenience sithence witnesses that were present at the birthe[, etc.] may be brought to instruct the Jurye which Jury are bounden to harken to witnesses upon payne of Atteinte' (fo. 11r). Plowden did not take into account that he was dealing with cases which had been decided when the jurors themselves were required to have the first-hand knowledge of the matter. If they should 'harken to' someone else to base their verdict, that was the very ground for punishing them by attaint.[60] Plowden's explanation only shows how much the law had changed in the meantime, not how the law *was* when those precedents actually appeared.

After what he regarded as a thorough examination of relevant year book cases, Plowden concluded that the 'disabilitie of foreyne birthe' was not 'in any case . . . grounded upon the reason that it [foreign birth] cannot be tryed or understode in England, but it is upon an other reason [i.e., faith and allegiance]' (fo. 11r). This is a solemn statement by the devout Catholic lawyer renowned for his erudition that faith and allegiance must be the foundations of the law of personal status. Plowden was squarely confronted with an accurate interpretation of the lawful, as opposed to faithful, past. As far as we know, this was the last time that the historically accurate understanding of 'foreyne birthe' was ever discussed. But

[59] For detailed discussion of the relevant cases, see pp. 122–3 above.
[60] See pp. 108–11 above.

it was discussed only to be hastily dismissed by Plowden. By doing so, he could drive the succession issue into the arena of faith and allegiance, and exploit the ambiguity of the term *'ligeance'*. We shall see how confident he was in arguing that Mary Stuart was not out of the *ligeance*.

'CERTAINE ERROURS UPPON THE STATUTE . . .'

Having rejected probably the most dangerous argument against Mary Stuart's succession claim, Plowden put forward a pro-Stuart argument based on the ambiguous notion of *ligeance*. He claimed, together with other pro-Stuart authors such as Anthony Brown and John Leslie, that Scotland was not 'out of the ligeance' because the kingdom of Scotland was 'holden of the kyng of England . . . and homage hathe ben don by the king of Scotts to the kings of Englande'.[61] Birth in Scotland, according to them, was therefore birth 'within the ligeance'.

However, the weakness of this argument must have been glaring. It was tantamount to an insult to the numerous Scotsmen in those years who were paying dearly for the letters of denization or acts of naturalisation to be rid of their 'disabilitie of foreyne birthe'.[62] It was also against many year book cases where Scotsmen were excepted as 'alien born out of the ligeance'.[63] An

---

[61] BL Harleian MS 849, fo. 18v. The same argument was made by Anthony Brown. BM Harleian MS 555, fos. 23v–24. Bishop Leslie reproduced most of Anthony Brown's arguments including this one. *A defence of the honor*, fo. 66r.

[62] There are at least 272 known examples of Scotsmen who obtained denization or naturalisation during the years 1510–1601. See *Letters of denization and acts of naturalization for aliens in England, 1509–1603*, ed. William Page (Lymington, 1893) introduction. Our calculation is based on the table attached to the introduction.

[63] *Year Book*, Ames Foundation, Mich. 8 Richard II, p. 141; Fitzherbert, *Abridgement*, continuall claime, pl. 13. See also Dyer's summary of the case of Mary, Queen of Scots (110CP 40/495, m. 334) in *Reports from the lost notebooks of Sir James Dyer*, 110 Selden Society (1993–4) p. 256. In *Southwell* v. *Fysshe* (1453), the defendant put forward an *exceptio* arguing that the plaintiff was born out of the ligeance in Scotland. A further allegation, however, was made that the plaintiff's parents were also born out of the ligeance. In our view, this was an unnecessary allegation which was added in anticipation of the plaintiff's possible *replicatio* which would be based on the parents' allegiance. As far as we know, there is no evidence that this case played any role in the fifteenth-century definition of alien status. Three years later, in another case, we see an *exceptio* against the plaintiff who was born in Scotland. Parents' birthplace was not

alternative argument was therefore prepared. Accordingly, Plowden opined that 'the quene of Scotts is not out of ligeance of the Crowne of England albeit it were graunted that the subjects of Scotland were'. He was counting on the feudal legal relationship which existed, at least in theory, between the queen of Scotland and the king of England. Plowden was very emphatic: 'Shall we saie the chiffe homager [tenant-in-chief] of the crowne of England hath no societie nor affinitie with England, but is a mere stranger? Phye, phye, that is to ffar oute of the way. The subjeccion by homage counter pleadeth it.'[64]

These were the circumstances under which a Protestant author wrote a treatise entitled 'Certaine errours uppon the statute made the xxv th yere of Kinge Edward the third, of children borne beyonde the sea, conceyved by Serjaunt Browne and confuted by Serjaunt Ferfax in manner of a dialogue'.[65] The author was probably overwhelmed by Plowden's impressive display of 'aucthorities and boke cases' relating to the 'true' cause of the 'disabilitie of foreyne birthe'. Accordingly, the cognisance of jury was never mentioned again. Instead, the author concentrated his efforts on clarifying the meaning of _ligeance_. Since Plowden's emphatic argument that Scotland was 'within the ligeance' was based on an artful confusion of homage and allegiance ('subjeccion by homage'), a sharp distinction between these two concepts was imperative.

Our Protestant author began as follows: '[h]omage is nothing ells but a lawfull tenure and service instituted by the mutuall

---

mentioned at all. _Holburn_ v. _Wartre_ (1456). _Reports . . . of Sir James Dyer_, p. 257. Professor Baker kindly drew my attention to these references. The cases on mixed jury, however, treated Scotsmen as no different from Englishmen for the purpose of determining the need for a mixed jury. See John Harington, _A tract on the succession to the crown_ (written in 1602), ed. Clements Markham (London, 1880) p. 24 for references. For legal treatment of Scotsmen in criminal cases in border counties, see Cynthia Nevill, 'Border law in late medieval England', 9 _Journal of Legal History_ (1988) 335–56.

64 BL Harleian MS 849, fos. 26v, 29r.
65 Cambridge University Library MS, Mm. 6. 70. What appears to be the author's autographical copy has recently been acquired by Cambridge University Library (Add. 9212). The treatise, probably written by Serjeant William Fleetwood in _c_. 1580–8, is in the form of a dialogue. But both Serjeant Fairfax and Serjeant Brown are fictitious. The manuscript was widely circulated. Edward Coke had a copy (Holkham Hall MS 678, fo. 17). His argument in _Calvin's case_ clearly indicates that he consulted this treatise closely. See ch. 8 below. Professor Baker kindly brought this treatise to my attention.

agreement of the giver and taker in respect of some tenemente given'. By stressing that the relationship of homage is a reciprocal contractual legal relationship, the author attempted to bring out the contrast between homage and *ligeance*, which is a non-contractual relationship of political power and subjection. According to him, homage is, 'as it were, more of good Neighbourehod then of subjection'. This explanation can certainly enjoy the support of Bracton and most of his contemporaries in medieval Europe, who would have agreed that homage institutes a reciprocal legal relationship (*vinculum iuris*) between the lord and the tenant.[66] However, the problem is not as simple as this. Like any contractual legal relationships, homage creates a bond of mutual confidence between the parties. As Glanvill makes clear, this bond had all along been understood as the bond of fidelity (*fidelitatis connexio*).[67] *Ligeance*, too, had long been understood as a bond of faith and loyalty (*fides*) between the king and his subjects; so much so that the king's subjects were for many centuries known as his faithfuls (*fideles*). The sublime ideal repeatedly professed by Christian kings of medieval Europe was that their authority did not come from the sword, nor from the law, but from *the* faith. Ideally, their subjects should obey them not out of fear, nor out of harsh legal constraints, but out of faith. Precisely, it was this bond of faith which bound together the ruler and the ruled in a mystic body (*corpus mysticum*) within which subjection and liberty were curiously intermingled.

Had political subjection been explained in terms of violence, *auctoritas, potestas, imperium* or *ius*, things would have been different. But ever since the conversion of Constantine, the political authority and subjection in Europe have been discussed in terms of faith, alliance and 'promise', if not contract. By the time Plowden was writing his succession tract, no one would have accepted that true subjection – which leads to true liberty – could possibly be based on anything but true faith. As far as any sixteenth-century lawyers could remember, subjection to the king was, and had always been, grounded upon the bond of faith. Plowden, therefore, had no reason to distinguish between the bond of *ligeance* and the bond of homage, for both of them were

---

[66] See pp. 128–9 above.   [67] *Glanvill*, lib. 9, c. 4.

grounded upon the bond of faith; both of them were grounded upon a trustful 'promise'.[68]

All promises bind the parties. But the author of 'Certaine errours . . .' sees that there is an important difference in their binding power. The author explains that 'one tenaunt maie be of divers Lordes fees and homage'.[69] In other words, the bond of fidelity created by homage does not prevent the parties from engaging themselves in other similar bonds of fidelity with third parties. But,

legiaunce . . . is the bonde of faith swallowinge up all others, and the greatest among creatures, religion to the Creator reserved, due by the lawe of god and nacions from the subject to the prince. . . . [A] tenure or oath of homage ableth not an aliann to be a subject of the legiaunce of England nor to be a person capable of inheritance like an English mann.[70]

According to the Protestant author, nationality is a question of this 'bonde of faith swallowinge up all others'. Even if Mary Stuart was the chief homager of the king of England and, therefore, could rely on the bond of trust created by the homage, that would not make her any less alien. The contractual bond of trust (*fidelitatis connexio*) is 'instituted' by the parties in accordance with the (positive) law of the kingdom. It arises and disappears as a result of the parties' own doing. The bond of *legiaunce*, on the other hand, transcends the parties' will or action. It is 'ordained' by 'the lawe of god and nacions'. Once homage and allegiance are defined in these terms, the conclusion is obvious. What has been

---

[68] Plowden was not alone in his confusion of allegiance and homage. Many sixteenth-century jurists shared the same outlook. As a result, the question of allegiance and alien status was often approached from the feudal law. See Polly Price, 'Natural law and birthright citizenship in *Calvin's case* (1608)', 9 *Yale Journal of Law and the Humanities* (1997) 73–145 for a discussion of Craig's *Jus feudale* and his understanding of the law of alien status. The confusion lingered on into the twentieth century. See John Salmond, 'Citizenship and allegiance', 17, 18 *Law Quarterly Review* (1901, 1902) 270–82, 49–63. In the latter half of his article, Salmond attempts to explain allegiance in terms of the feudal bond of fealty. The confusion, of course, was in full swing among medieval historians who put forward the thesis of 'feudal anarchy'. For a brief account of recent historical studies which distance themselves from this long-lived confusion, see Keechang Kim, 'Etre fidèle au roi: XIIe–XIVe siècles', 293 *Revue Historique* (1995) 225–50.

[69] Cambridge University Library MS, Mm. 6. 70, fo. 3v. See also *Glanvill*, lib. 9, c. 1 ('Potest autem quis plura homagia diversis dominis facere de feodis diversorum dominorum').

[70] Cambridge University Library MS, Mm. 6. 70, fos. 3v, 4v.

ordained by the natural law (Mary Stuart's lack of *legiaunce*) cannot be overridden by the human law (homage). The subject's allegiance to the king is not a matter for the mortals. Our author concludes his argument with the following remark: 'One God, one king, one legiaunce.'[71] This is the most revealing explanation of the meaning of allegiance understood by the sixteenth-century lawyers. Common lawyers have come a long way. Neither Glanvill nor Bracton would have easily imagined that the meaning of *ligeancia* could be stretched this far. The rest of the Elizabethan succession debates were not immediately relevant to the development of the English nationality law.[72]

CONCLUSION

Legal vocabulary usually survives revolutionary legal changes. However, it is the morphology of vocabulary which survives, and conceals the radical semantic change. No revolution can be accomplished without a fundamental semantic change. The unchanging continuity of terminology is therefore deceptive. Deception arises from ambiguity. But it is the inherent ambiguity of language which guarantees its unending utility. For example, 'liberty' and 'subjection' used to be regarded in law as mutually exclusive categories. We are now entirely familiar with the mystic fusion of 'subjection' and 'liberty'. As we have seen, even the most basic terms of spatial perception such as 'in' and 'out' could also be loaded with highly charged ideological significance. The surprising durability of legal terms such as obligation, action, person, citizen, liberty, *ligeance*, etc. only shows their remarkable versatility and ambiguity.

In this chapter, I have argued that the development of the English law of alien status must be studied by examining how the

---

[71] Ibid., fo. 4v. See also a case of 13 Eliz., fo. 38 reported by Johaniis Page, 'De personis', BL Hargrave MS. 379 (not earlier than 1653) Liber primus, fo. 202 (an English born cannot claim to be a subject of the Spanish king; one cannot waive the allegiance one has by virtue of one's birth). Professor Baker kindly drew my attention to Page's manuscript. See, in this connection, Thomas Martin, '*Nemo potest exuere patriam*: indelibility of allegiance and the American revolution', 35 *American Journal of Legal History* (1991) 205–18.

[72] For an overview of various other issues raised during the succession debates, see Levine, *The early Elizabethan succession question*.

fifteenth- and sixteenth-century lawyers manipulated the old expression 'alien nee hors la ligeance'. It was essentially a process of semantic change of legal terminology such as 'alien', 'in', 'out' and 'ligeance'. A historical investigation into legal changes is, in a sense, a linguistic exercise designed to enhance the investigator's sensitivity to diachronic changes of the meanings of legal terms. Pursuit of precedents, done without paying due attention to semantic changes of legal terminology, must remain a lawyer's occupation rather than a historian's task.

In the preceding pages, we have focused particularly on the changing meanings of *ligeance*. *Ligeance* was, as it were, the two-faced Janus which opened up the gate so that faith could enter into the law of personal status. Once the entry was made, the bond of faith would eventually demolish the bond of law, which had been the guiding principle of the law of personal status. Once the 'spinal cord' was thus destroyed, what used to be a coherent body of legal rules for personal status would then be viewed as an incoherent heap of often incomprehensible rules and maxims which stand in need of a 'reasonable' explanation. Elizabethan succession tract writers, for example, did not have the faintest idea why birthplace became the decisive criterion for a person's legal status. They were seriously debating how it was possible that the 'place of birth, being an accidently and externall thing, should sever such a natural conjunction as proximity of blood'. They could think of anything but the bond of faith: 'beholde how brute beast driven from the place of birth . . . tries to return to the birth place'.[73] Faith became thoroughly natural. Nature was by then thoroughly impregnated with faith.

[73] Cambridge University Library MS, Mm. 6. 70, fos. 5v–8v.

SUCCESSION TRACTS

Anti-Stuart	Pro-Stuart

1563 John Hales, 'A Declaration of the succession of the Crown . . .'
BL Harl. MS, 550; printed in G. Harbin, *The hereditary right of the crown of England . . .* (London, 1713)

1565(?) by Anthony Browne (d.1567)
BL Harl. MS, 555, fos. 11r–47v. Regarding the dating of this treatise, see M. Axton's article in 37 *Huntington Library Quarterly* (1974) 209–226

1565 Anon., 'Allegations against the surmised title of the Queen of Scotland . . .'
BL Harl. MS, 4627 fos. 10r–26v; printed, see BL ref. C. 55. c. 3

1566 An answer to the 'Allegations against . . .'
CUL MS Gg. iii. 34, fos. 107–17

1566 'A "Letter" on the Elizabethan succession question 1566' ed. by M. Levine in 19 *Huntington Library Quarterly*, no. 1 (1955)

1566 An anti-Suffolk tract printed in W. Atwood, *The fundamental constitution of the English government* (London, 1690)

1567 Edmund Plowden, 'A treatise proving that . . .'
BL Harl. MS, 849, fos. 1–38

1569 J. Leslie, *A defence of the honor of Mary . . .*
facsimile reproduction in 1970

1584 Anon., *The copy of a letter written by a Master of Arte of Cambridge . . .*
reprinted in 1641 under the title 'Leycesters Commonwealth'. Reprinted again in 1904 by F. Burgoyne

***c.* 1580–1588** Anon., 'Certaine errours uppon the statute made xxvth yere of Kinge Edward the third, of children born beyond the sea . . .'
CUL MS, Mm. 6. 70, fos. 1–30; CUL MS Add. 9212

1602 John Harington, 'A Tract on the Succession to the Crown'
printed in 1880 by C. Markham

Note: See also Robert Aske's 'Examination' (1537) printed by M. Bateson, 5 *English Historical Review* (1890) 562–4

8

CALVIN'S CASE (1608)

Queen Elizabeth I outlived all the heated debates arising from the succession question and died in 1603. The accession of James VI of Scotland to the crown of England marks the beginning of a long and tortuous process through which 'British' political and legal discourse has been created and recreated until this date.[1] Regarding the political union of the peoples, the claims of James VI and I found an excellent means of expression in the concept of the 'mystic body politic'. The following passage from his speech in the English Parliament seems to reveal the basic framework of his thought:

What God hath conioyned then, let no man separate. I am the Husband, and all the whole Isle is my lawfull Wife; I am the Head, and it is my Body; I am the Shepard, and it is my flocke: I hope therefore no man will be so vnreasonable as to thinke that . . . I being the Head, should haue a divided and monstrous Body.[2]

Lawyers, however, were encountering difficulties in giving legal effect to his enthusiastic claims about Great Britain. In an effort to draw up a scheme of 'real and effectual' union of the two

---

[1] See J. G. A. Pocock, 'Two kingdoms and three histories? Political thought in British context' in *Scots and Britons, Scottish political thought and the union of 1603*, ed. Roger Mason (Cambridge, 1994) pp. 293–312; Jenny Wormald, 'James VI and I: two kings or one ?', 68 *History* (1983) 187–209; Jenny Wormald, 'The creation of Britain: multiple kingdoms or core and colonies?', 2 *Royal Historical Society Transactions*, 6th series (1992) 175–94; Brian Levack, *The formation of the British State: England, Scotland and the Union, 1603–1707* (Oxford, 1987) chs. 2 and 3. For a more recent and comprehensive treatment of the topic, see now *The British Problem, 1534–1707: State formation in the Atlantic Archipelago*, ed. Brendan Bradshaw and John Morrill (Basingstoke, 1996) ch. 6.

[2] King James VI and I, *Political writings*, ed. Johann P. Sommerville (Cambridge, 1994) p. 136. On the notion of the mystic body in general, see Ernst Kantorowicz, *The king's two bodies: a study in mediaeval political theology* (Princeton, N.J., 1957).

176

kingdoms, Commissioners of Union were appointed in 1604 by the Parliaments of England and Scotland respectively. Also, a number of learned tracts dealing with the question of legal union were written and circulated during this period. But the English Parliament of 1606 showed a strong resistance to the proposal for further union, especially to the proposed naturalisation of James VI and I's subjects in both kingdoms.[3]

Under these circumstances, *Calvin's case* was brought to the Court of King's Bench and to Chancery. The facts were simple. Plaintiff Robert Calvin, a child born in Scotland after the accession of James Stuart, claimed some land in England. The defendant pleaded that the plaintiff ought not to be answered because he was an alien born in Edinburgh, out of the allegiance of the king of England. The plaintiff demurred to this plea. The demurrer provided the opportunity to discuss and settle the question of the legal status of Scotsmen in England after the accession of James I.[4]

ALLEGIANCE: BY LAW OR BY NATURE?

All parties to *Calvin's case* agreed that those who were born in Scotland before the accession were aliens in England. The focal

---

[3] For the act of Parliament appointing the Commissioners, see *Constitutional documents of the reign of James I, 1603–1625*, ed. J. R. Tanner (Cambridge, 1930) pp. 31–2. Questions relating to the legal union are discussed in detail by Bruce Galloway, *The union of England and Scotland, 1603–1608* (Edinburgh, 1986) and Brian Levack, *The formation of the British State*, ch. 3. For some of the union tracts, see *The Jacobean union: six tracts of 1604*, ed. B. Galloway and B. Levack (Edinburgh, 1985).

[4] The political importance of the case made it one of the most elaborately argued cases in the common law history. All justices of the King's Bench and Common Pleas, barons of the Exchequer, Lord Chancellor Ellesmere and Sir Francis Bacon, the king's counsel, participated in the argument. According to Sir Edward Coke, 'never any case in man's memory was argued by so many judges'. 7 *Coke's Reports*, 'The preface'. Some of the arguments advanced in *Calvin's case* and Serjeant Moore's account of the Parliamentary proceedings of 1606, where a number of lawyers and judges were invited to offer their views on Scotsmen's legal status in England, are collected in *Complete collection of state trials*, ed. W. Cobbett et al., vol. II (London, 1809) cols. 599ff. Our quotations are from this volume. For a modern assessment of the views put forward in this case, see Polly Price, 'Natural law and birthright citizenship in *Calvin's case* (1608)', 9 *Yale Journal of Law and the Humanities* (1997) 73–145.

issue of *Calvin's case* was therefore whether the children born in Scotland *after* the accession (*postnati*) were to be treated as subjects or aliens in England. It was a question of law, that is, whether James Stuart's accession to the English crown altered the scope of allegiance so that birth in Scotland became from then on birth 'within the allegiance'.[5]

By the time of *Calvin's case*, it was no longer sensible to doubt that allegiance was the decisive criterion of a person's legal status. In fact, all through the fifteenth and sixteenth centuries, allegiance had been discussed in legal proceedings whenever the geographical location of an event was mentioned. A person may be born, a document may be executed, a couple may be married, an uncle may die *hors la ligeance* or *deinz la ligeance*. This *ligeance*, of course, also meant the bond of faith linking the king and his beloved subjects. Without saying it, lawyers had all along been talking about faith each time they mentioned *ligeance*. The bond of faith thus became the pivotal element of legal reasoning. By the time of Sir John Fortescue, there was no point in distinguishing the bond of faith from the bond of law. According to him, it is the bond of law (*lex* a ligando *dicitur*) which has the power to unite a multitude of individuals; to efface somehow their individuality; and to form an elevated, mystic body (*corpus mysticum*).[6] Thomas Littleton was closely following the same line of ideas. The kingdom was envisaged as a network of law. Birth out of this network − birth out of the *ligeance* − resulted in complete denial of the 'help and protection by the king's law or by the king's writ': in short, out of *ligeance*, out of legal protection. Since *ligeance* was the judicial equivalent of the bond of faith, we may also say: no faith, no legal protection. A complete fusion of law and faith has been achieved in the name of *ligeance*. In *Calvin's case*, Edward Coke accordingly observed: 'Ligeantia est quasi legis essentia.'[7]

---

[5] In his *Exposicions of the termys of the law* . . ., John Rastell transliterated 'ligeance' into 'elegiaunce'. During the reign of Elizabeth I, succession tract writers repeatedly used the spelling 'allegiance', which became the standard English rendering of the term. Various spellings were used in the fourteenth century: *ligance*, *lyance*, *ligeaunce*, etc. Etymologically, allegiance means a 'bond' (from '*ligare*' in Latin). The French and English words 'alliance' and 'lien' have the same origin.

[6] See ch. 1 above.

[7] See 7 *Coke's Reports*, 4v.

Basing themselves firmly on this tradition, those who were against Calvin's claim argued that the subjection to the king was a legally defined relationship rather than a manifestation of undefined extra-legal power. According to them, 'allegiance [was] tied to laws'. Stressing that the bond of allegiance between the king and his subjects was a bond of law, they specifically referred to Fortescue's formula, '*lex* a ligando *dicitur*'. They further explained that 'every nation hath a precinct wherein the laws have operation'. It was also pointed out that the English law did not extend to Scotland. As long as the laws of two kingdoms remained separate and distinct, 'naturalization, being measured by allegiance, must still remain several and distinct in either nations'. Since allegiance was subjection, they also said that *postnati* in Scotland 'are not *subject* to the laws of England, and therefore should not have the benefits of the laws of England' (col. 567, emphasis supplied).

However, a new generation of lawyers such as Francis Bacon looked upon this argument as unsuitable for 'a warlike and magnanimous nation fit for empire' (col. 595). They needed a conclusion that 'the king's power, command and protection extendeth out of England'. Sir Edward Coke wanted the same conclusion. He hoped that the king's 'subjects in all places may be protected from violence, and that justice may equally be administered to all his subjects' (cols. 621, 623). In fact, they were advocating James I's imperial claim that all the peoples under his subjection – in and out of England – should be united in one political and legal unit. In order to achieve such a union, it was necessary to have the notion of allegiance liberated from the confines of the kingdom and its law. This, however, was impossible as long as one remained faithful to the legal structure of kingdom envisaged by Fortescue and Littleton. When Francis Bacon posed the question, 'shall it be said that all allegiance is by law?', he was pointing the knife at the heart of the problem. A full-scale operation was launched against Fortescue's view, '*lex* a ligando *dicitur*'. Bacon did this by introducing the notion of 'original submission' which was supposed to be 'natural and more ancient than law'. He postulated a period when the king was presumed to have governed the people without law, but by 'natural equity' only. He argued that since original submission could be observed during this period as well, people's subjection to the prince must be 'the work of the law of nature' (cols. 579–81). Fortescue understood allegiance in terms of *lex* ('*lex* a ligando *dicitur*'). Bacon now corrects it and says that it is the law of nature, not the law of the kingdom, which binds the prince and his subjects.

Edward Coke and Chief Baron Fleming had already advanced a similar opinion in the Parliament held in 1606. Serjeant Moore summarises their arguments under the following headings: '1. Allegiance was before laws; 2. Allegiance is after laws; . . . 5. Allegiance extends . . . beyond the circuit of laws' (cols. 569ff.). Coke repeated the same argument two years later in *Calvin's case*. Francis Bacon's rather philosophical discussion about 'original submission' was now given a more juristic appearance by Coke, who introduced the fourfold division of allegiance: (1) natural allegiance; (2) acquired allegiance; (3) local allegiance; and (4) legal allegiance (homage).[8] He then concluded that 'the ligeance or faith of the subjects is due unto the king by the law of nature' (cols. 615, 629). Coke's argument that people's subjection to the prince was based not on the law of the kingdom but on 'ligeantia naturalis, absoluta, pura, et indefinita' (col. 615) was not compatible with Littleton's ideas about the king's law and the king's legal protection. Littleton, therefore, had to go. As we saw, Littleton explained that a person under outlawry, or without the king's protection because of his violation of *praemunire*, was 'out of the help and protection by the king's law or by the king's writ'. But Coke argued that such a person was still under the 'natural law' protection of the king because the king may, for example, pardon him one day and protect him again (cols. 631–2). The bond of obedience and protection between the king and his people was no longer grounded simply upon law as Littleton and Fortescue understood it. According to Coke and Bacon, it was grounded upon the law of nature. Nature will certainly liberate allegiance from the confines of the kingdom.

This was the focal issue of *Calvin's case* (i.e., whether allegiance was a bond of subjection institutionalised by the law of the

---

[8] Coke admitted that this division was not based on the existing law: '[In discussing several kinds of allegiance], we need to be very wary, for this caveat the law giveth, "ubi lex non distinguit, nec nos distinguere debemus;" and certainly "lex non distinguit"' (col. 615).

kingdom or archetypal submission grounded upon the law of nature). The issue can, no doubt, be described using the distinction between the king's body politic and body natural. The question then would be whether allegiance is due to the king's body politic or his body natural. Approached from this angle, *Calvin's case* featured prominently in the well-known study of E. Kantorowicz.[9] But our aim here is to bring out the dynamic of legal change which is observable in the tension between the positive law and the law of nature. For the common lawyers of the time, the distinction between the king's body politic and body natural was important mainly because it allowed the possibility of arguing beyond the constraints of the existing law of the kingdom and put forward new ideas in the name of the law of nature. The appeal to the supposedly 'unchanging' law of nature was indeed the commonest technique of disguising bold proposals to change the existing law.[10] At any rate, the overwhelming majority of the judges (twelve out of fourteen) and Lord Chancellor Ellesmere concurred in the opinion that allegiance was grounded upon the law of nature; and, therefore, it ought not to be confined within the kingdom of England. Accordingly, it was decided that the plaintiff Robert Calvin – even though he was born out of the kingdom of England – must not be regarded as an alien in England. A founding stone of the British Empire was now

---

[9] Kantorowicz, *The king's two bodies*, pp. 4, 7, 14–16, 364–72, 408.

[10] This point was noticed by Gierke. See Otto von Gierke, *Natural law and the theory of society, 1500 to 1800*, 2 vols., trans. E. Barker (Cambridge, 1934) I, pp. 35–6 ('In opposition to positive jurisprudence, which still continued to show a Conservative trend, the natural-law theory of the State was Radical to the very core of its being. Unhistorical in the foundations on which it was built, it was also directed, in its efforts and its results, not to the purpose of scientific explanation of the past, but to that of the exposition and justification of a new future which was to be called into existence'). The distinction between the king's body politic and body natural provided a means of getting around the common law rules of inheritance applicable to foreign-born persons, of which Mary Stuart was one. Freed from the strait-jacket of the positive law of the kingdom, the supporters of Mary Stuart's claim could develop their argument relying on the law of nature and the theory of corporation. See p. 164 above. On the importance of natural law in seventeenth-century European legal development in general, see Alan Watson, *The making of the Civil Law* (Cambridge, Mass., 1981) pp. 83–98. A concise discussion of the role of natural law in the Stuart political discourse can be found in J. Sommerville, *Politics and ideology in England, 1603–1640* (London, 1986) pp. 12–17.

securely laid upon the law of nature. As we shall see, however, this
would be a major stumbling block for legal historians.

TRANSCENDENTAL CONCEPTION OF THE COMMON LAW

Calvin's case was a showcase of opposing methods of legal
reasoning. These methods need to be discussed separately from
the conclusions at which one may arrive through them. A method
of reasoning does not necessarily dictate any particular conclusion.
Different persons may reach different conclusions using the same
method of reasoning. Also, the same conclusion may be reached
through different methods of reasoning. It is therefore not surprising that those who were opposed to Calvin's claim shared the
same method of legal reasoning with some of those who were
favourable to Calvin's claim. Also, we shall see that those who
allowed Calvin's claim did not always share the same method of
legal reasoning.

Edwyn Sandys, who was actively involved in the Parliamentary
debate concerning the question of legal union, and was opposed to
the naturalisation of *postnati*, opined that the issue posed by
Calvin had not been dealt with by any law or custom. Since
'deficiente lege recurritur ad consuetudinem' and 'deficiente con-
suetudine recurritur ad rationem naturalem', he argued, the issue
must be decided according to '*ratio naturalis* [which] is the law of
nations called "ius gentium"' (col. 563).[11] Lord Chancellor
Ellesmere, who concurred in the majority opinion, developed this
point further. He observed that '[t]here is no direct law for him
[Calvin] in precise and expresse tearmes; there was neuer iudge-
ment before touching any borne in Scotland since king Iames
beganne his happie raigne in England; hee is the first that is
brought in question' (col. 677). He argued that 'when there is no
direct lawe, nor precise example, we must "recurrere ad rationem,
et ad responsa prudentium"'; for, 'otherwise much mischiefe and
great inconuenience will ensue. For new cases happen euery day:
no lawe euer was, or euer can be made, that can prouide remedie

---

[11] On the Parliamentary career of Edwyn Sandys, see Willard M. Wallace, 'Sir
Edwin Sandys and the first Parliament of James I', PhD thesis, Univ. of
Pennsylvania (1940) ch. 2.

for all the future cases, or comprehend all circumstances of humane actions which judges are to determine' (col. 676).

The emphasis on 'responsa prudentium' – i.e., reasoned opinions of leading jurists – led him to a lucid discussion of the mechanism of legal change. He observed that 'auncient lawes are changed by interpretation of the judges'. The change of law was depicted as a process of adaptation to the changed circumstances: 'the wisedome of the iudges found them [ancient laws] to bee vnmeete for the time they liued in, although very good and necessarie for the time wherein they were made'. Inevitably, therefore, 'some lawes, as well statute lawe as common law, are obsolete and worne out of vse: for, all humane lawes are but *leges temporis* [laws of the time]' (col. 674).[12] Since he saw that *Calvin's case* was 'the first precedent, which . . . had no precedent when it began', he refrained from relying on the authority of past legal texts. Instead, the remedy was sought in the law-making power of judges. Accordingly, his argument was based on what the law should be, rather than what the law had been. No doubt, however, in their quest for the new *leges temporis*, judges would be guided by *prudentia*: the eternally valid *ratio*.

Sir Edward Coke had different ideas. He claimed that 'the laws of England are so copious in this point' (col. 612). The same view was shared by Francis Bacon. In his speech delivered to the Parliamentary Committee on *postnati*, Bacon asserted that the Committee's task was 'not to consult of a law to be made, but to declare the law already planted' (col. 563). We do not know whether they would have unreservedly approved of Chief Justice Popham's claim that the laws of England 'had continued as a rock without alteration in all the varieties of people that had possessed

---

[12] He discussed several instances of legal change which were effected by judicial interpretation. For example, '[i]n aucient time, one present, aiding, comforting, and assisting to a murder, was taken to bee no principall, but an accessorie, as it appeareth M. 40 Edw. 3, fol. 42 et 40 . . . But now in that case he is iudged a principall' (col. 675). Professor Knafla thinks that Baron Ellesmere's understanding of the historicity of law might have come from the works of the Dutch jurist Joachim Hopper, whom Ellesmere regarded as 'one of the gravest and best learned lawyers of our age'. Louis Knafla, 'The "country" Chancellor: the patronage of Sir Thomas Egerton, Baron Ellesmere' in *Patronage in late Renaissance England, papers read at a Clark Library Seminar, 14 May 1977*, ed. French Fogle and Louis Knafla (Los Angeles, 1983) p. 64. On Lord Chancellor Ellesmere's career and thoughts, see Louis Knafla, *Law and politics in Jacobean England* (Cambridge, 1977).

this land, namely the Romans, Brittons, Danes, Saxons, Normans and English' (col. 569).[13] But Coke certainly believed that the law had already reached the stage of *optima regula* after having been 'in many successions of ages . . . fined and refined'. It is therefore unlikely that he would deem it liable to further historical changes. He clearly disagreed with Lord Chancellor Ellesmere's view that laws may, or rather must, be changed by judicial interpretation. Coke argued that 'no man ought to take upon him to be wiser than the laws'. Lord Chancellor Ellesmere saw that human laws were constantly in the making at present. Coke, on the other hand, believed that 'our days upon the earth are but as a shadow' which would be condemned to complete darkness without the brilliance of the *optima regula* of the past (col. 612). Law – as *optima regula* – was therefore given an unassailable and transcendental existence which is entirely removed from the actual workings of the judiciary.

The conception of law which does not allow for historical changes will bless the search for precedents with the logical certainty of finding them. As the law is viewed as perfect and immutable, it would be inherently impossible not to have precedents or settled law for any issue. All that has to be done is to 'find' the right text and 'correctly' interpret it as the precedent in point. The only reason why a vast number of legal texts dating from the biblical era were plundered was because those texts were believed to embody the everlasting and unchanging *optima regula*, and therefore were thought to be still effective and immediately applicable. Coke could hold such a belief because he did not recognise the difference between the law of the past and the law of the present. Law, understood as *optima regula*, does not change. It is neither possible nor desirable to discuss the 'historical' circumstances under which a legal text was composed. Ironically, it was this transcendental conception of law which led him 'diligently [to] search out the judgments of our forefathers'. All his discussions about the 'judgments, resolutions, and rules . . . in our

---

[13] Popham was repeating Fortescue's view. According to Fortescue, 'The kingdom of England was first inhabited by Britons; [then by Romans, Saxons, Danes, but finally by Normans,] whose posterity hold the realm at the present time. And throughout the period of these nations and their kings, the realm has been continuously ruled by the same customs as it is now.' Sir John Fortescue, *De laudibus legum Anglie*, ed. and trans. S. B. Chrimes (Cambridge, 1942) pp. 39–40 (ch. 17).

books in all ages concerning this case' were therefore pseudo-historical. We saw that Lord Chancellor Ellesmere's penetrating understanding of the mechanism of legal change actually prevented him from relying on legal texts of the past. As law would change constantly at the hands of succeeding generations of judges, the legal texts of the past obviously could not be a trustworthy guide to the law of the present.

Lord Chancellor Ellesmere's approach is based on a historically sound assumption that law and legal text are not disengaged from the circumstances of 'the time they were made'. He clearly saw that judges, on the other hand, had to deal with the changed circumstances 'for the time they liued in'. It is indeed tempting to speculate that this keen awareness of the tension between the past and the present in legal reasoning could have promoted a meaningful dialogue between lawyers and historians. As it turned out, however, this type of lawyers has failed to attract the attention of historians simply because they seldom mention or rely on past legal texts in their legal argument. Lawyers like Coke, on the other hand, have attracted a great number of historians because of their impressive parading of past texts. As we pointed out, however, their dependence on past texts is due to their transcendental conception of the common law. Their conviction that the common law has remained unaltered from time immemorial (or from the moment it reached the status of *optima regula*) is obviously unhistorical. The mutual attraction between these lawyers and legal historians, which is generated by the concurrence of their interests in past texts, is therefore hiding a seed of disappointment. But amidst the heady chase for 'precedents', the widening gap between lawyers' and historians' understanding of the past is often forgotten.[14]

THE NEW *SUMMA DIVISIO PERSONARUM*

No one in *Calvin's case* doubted that the division between subjects and aliens was fundamental to the law of personal status. Francis

---

[14] On the shaping of the concept of 'precedent', see John H. Baker, 'Records, reports and the origins of case-law in England' in his (ed.) *Judicial records, law reports, and the growth of case law* (Berlin, 1989) pp. 15–46.

Bacon, who was counsel for the plaintiff Calvin, stated that 'there be but two conditions by birth, either alien or natural born' (col. 583). Edward Coke repeated the same idea: '[e]very man is either *alienigena*, an alien born, or *subditus*, a subject born' (col. 637). The modernity of their legal outlook has not been adequately appreciated so far. Unless, however, the legal condition of the persons belonging to the category of aliens or subjects is respectively postulated as sufficiently uniform within the chosen category, the division – or the contrast between the two categories thus divided – would not make much sense. Accordingly, Bacon stressed that a natural-born subject is 'complete and entire' and therefore 'hath a capacity or ability to all benefits whatsoever'. He admired the 'wisdom of the law of England . . . both because it distinguisheth so far [i.e., between subjects and aliens] and because it doth not distinguish farther [i.e., among natural-born subjects themselves]' (cols. 582–3). Lord Chancellor Ellesmere also argued that 'he that is born an intire and perfect subject ought, by reason and lawe, to have all the freedomes, privileges and benefits pertaining to his birth-right' (col. 691). Edwyn Sandys, who was opposed to the naturalisation of *postnati*, also understood that the subject status would confer 'the full rights of Englishmen born among us' (col. 564).

Coke, it is true, defended nobility – the inequality among the subjects – as the 'king's creation' (col. 634). Since he reasoned that allegiance and subject status were matters of the 'law of nature', his argument that Scotsmen should equally be treated as subjects had no effect on the existence of nobility, which was viewed as instituted by the 'law of man'. But the trend was irreversibly set for equality. Bacon's explanation, for example, contains the essential features of the modern notion of legal equality: 'I say capacity or ability [to all benefits whatsoever]; but to reduce *potentiam in actum*, is another case. For an earl of Ireland, though he be naturalized in England, yet hath no voice in the parliament of England, except he have either a call by writ, or creation by patent; but he is capable of either.' 'The law is equal, and favoureth not' (cols. 582–3, 595).

As subjects were deemed equal in their capacity to enjoy legal rights, so were aliens deemed equally deprived of the 'full rights of Englishmen born'. Coke, for example, averred that '[t]he question of this case . . . was, whether Robert Calvin . . . be an alien born, *and consequently* disabled to bring any real or personal action for any lands' (col. 609, emphasis supplied). The disabilities were indiscriminate, that is, they affected *all* aliens without any further distinction. This allows us to conclude that the division between subjects and aliens has now become the *summa divisio* of the law of personal status. Sooner or later, it would override all other formerly recognised legal distinctions among persons. Blackstone's remark which we quoted at the beginning of this book is a masterly summary of this trend of legal development: 'The first and most obvious division of the people is into aliens and natural-born subjects.'[15]

THE BEGINNING OF A HISTORIOGRAPHICAL TRADITION

We saw that the argument against the naturalisation of *postnati* could enjoy the formidable support of Littleton and Fortescue. The proponents of this argument (Edwyn Sandys, Roger Owen, John Bennet, John Dodderidge, etc.) were therefore in a better position to claim that they were merely following the opinion of their predecessors, hence, closer to the truth. Indeed, they appear to have criticised Coke and Bacon's idea as a 'novelty', an unprecedented opinion. The attack must have been especially hurtful for Coke. Probably out of indignation, Coke made a colossal effort to amass a vast number of passages from the past. He then asserted that his argument was 'rather a renovation of the judgments and censures of the reverend judges and sages of the law in so many ages past, than any innovation' (col. 656). Bacon went one step further. He launched a counter-attack against his opponents. He branded his opponents' argument as 'this new opinion, whereof there is *altum silentium* in our books of law' (col. 584).

Coke and Bacon's indignation when faced with the allegation of novelty of their argument may be appreciated in light of the fact that they were actually closely following the opinions of the Elizabethan succession tract writers. For example, Coke was repeating Plowden's claim that 'jurors may take knowledge of

[15] William Blackstone, *Commentaries on the laws of England*, 4 vols. (Oxford, 1765–9) I, p. 354.

things done out of the realm' (col. 655).[16] Bacon was faithfully
following Rastell's faulty interpretation of the statute *De natis
ultra mare* and asserted with confidence that '[b]y the statute of 25
Ed. 3, all children in any parts of the world, if they be of English
parents . . . are *ipso facto* naturalised' (col. 585).[17] We have also
seen that the Protestant author of 'Certaine errours uppon the
statute [25 Edw. III st. 1]' put forward an argument that
'legiaunce . . . is the bonde of faith . . . due by the lawe of god and
nacions'.[18] Coke and Bacon were relying on it almost word for
word. The fact that such an idea could not expect much support
from Littleton or Fortescue was no obstacle for Coke and Bacon
to treat the passage they found in the above-mentioned treatise as
a 'precedent'. Other precedents which fall foul of their argument
need simply to be ignored or reinterpreted. We saw how the
statements of Littleton and Fortescue regarding the bond of law
and allegiance were modified by Coke and Bacon. The task of
lawyers is to win the case they are arguing at present. Past texts
(precedents) are invoked to add judicial authority to the party's
present argument, not to elucidate the historical accuracy of the
party's understanding of the past.

At any rate, the views expressed by Coke and Bacon were
largely accepted in the following century by Sir Matthew Hale.[19]
For example, Coke and Bacon have argued that the clause of
Prerogativa regis concerning the *terrae Normannorum* and Bracton's explanation of dilatory exceptions against French enemies
were the evidence that Normans and other Frenchmen who were
born outside of the kingdom of England – like the plaintiff Calvin
– *could* hold English lands and therefore were the king's subjects.
This, of course, was to argue that subject status and allegiance
must not be limited to the confines of the kingdom. The seizures
of the Normans' lands and dilatory exceptions against the French
were regarded as temporary interruptions during the war (cols.
603–4, 644). Hale accepted this; but with some revision based on
his own conjecture. The following is his explanation, and I believe
that this marked the beginning of the historiographical tradition

---

[16] Bacon made the same claim (col. 589).
[17] Coke also believed without a shadow of doubt that the statute was about the
alien and subject status of foreign-born children (col. 628).
[18] See p. 172 above.
[19] *Hale's prerogative of the king*, 92 Selden Society (1975) pp. 260–1.

which has enjoyed an unchallenged acceptance until today: '[The seizure of the Normans' lands] at first was but in nature of a sequestration *donec terrae fuerint communes* yet when the hope of the recovery of Normandy grew desperate, grew a settled and fixed estate in the crown.'[20]

SEMANTIC STRUCTURE OF EARLY MODERN LEGAL DISCOURSE

We have argued that by the end of the fifteenth century, common lawyers began to show a growing dependence on written texts of the past.[21] By the time of the Elizabethan succession debate, no legal argument could be taken seriously unless it was accompanied by some mention of 'aucthorities and boke cases' or the 'old laws and customs of our own country . . . by use and longe continewance of time observed'.[22] When *Calvin's case* was brought, it already had long been a standard practice of presenting legal argument to speak from books and rolls. Edward Coke, for example, proudly noted that *Calvin's case* was argued by those who 'spake not out of their own head and invention', but 'diligently search[ed] out the judgments of our forefathers' (col. 612). A vast amount of Roman and medieval legal texts was cited and incorporated in the sixteenth-century legal discourse. *All* these texts, however, were approached and interpreted from a new vantage point. We will discuss a few examples.

Lawyers of the sixteenth century did not refrain from drawing a parallel between the law of their kingdom and the Roman law concept of *ius ciuile*. In Justinian's *Digest*, *ius ciuile* was explained as 'our law *(ius nostrum)*'. It was a law which could be obtained by adding something to, and deducting something from, the law which was common to all *(ius commune)*. It was a law which was proper to us *(ius proprium)*.[23] Gaius had explained *ius ciuile* in a

---

[20] *Hale's prerogative of the king*, p. 58. See Maitland's explanation of the beginning of the English law of alien status which we quoted on pp. 12 and 17 above.

[21] See pp. 151–3 above.

[22] J. Leslie, *A defence of the honor of Mary* . . . (London, 1569) fo. 55v; E. Plowden, 'A treatise proving that . . .', BL Harl. MS, 849, fo. 18v, respectively.

[23] *D.* 1. 1. 6 ('itaque cum aliquid addimus uel detrahimus iuri communi, ius proprium, id est ciuile efficimus. Hoc igitur ius nostrum constat aut ex scripto aut sine scripto').

similar manner: 'All peoples governed by [statute] laws and customs observe partly their own peculiar law and partly the common law of all mankind. That law which a people establishes for itself, as a law peculiar to it, is called *ius ciuile*, that is, the special law of that *ciuitas*.'[24] *Nos* in '*ius nostrum*' of Justinian's *Digest* must originally have meant the *populus* of a *civitas*. But what is *populus*? How many of the sixteenth-century lawyers would have refrained from understanding the word *populus* as Fortescue understood it; that is, a multitude of individuals bound together by the bond of law and faith to form a mystic body (*corpus mysticum*)?[25] Classical Roman jurists probably did not have a clear idea about how the mystic body of *populus* could be used in explaining the law of personal status.[26] Their law of personal status was grounded upon the division between free-men and slaves. This division did not turn on an argument as to whether a person was within or without the mystic body of *populus*. Whether one is an insider or an outsider is presumably a question which human beings constantly ask of themselves and of others. It would surely be senseless to doubt that the notions of 'insiders' and 'outsiders' are the fundamental categories of human psychology which have repeatedly been exploited in political and theological discourse. But whether legal vocabulary was capable of giving expression to these psychological categories in the context of the law of personal status is an entirely different matter. The term *persona* in the Classical Roman legal texts invariably referred to a human being (*homo*).[27] Whilst this vocabulary is maintained, a

---

[24] Gaius, *Institutes*, 1. 1 ('Omnes populi qui legibus et moribus reguntur partim suo proprio, partim communi omnium hominum iure utuntur. nam quod quisque populus ipse sibi ius constituit, id ipsius proprium ciuitatis, est uocaturque ius ciuile, quasi ius proprium ipsius ciuitatis'). Also *D*. 1. 1. 9.

[25] See pp. 5–6 above. Of course, Fortescue's conception of *populus* was firmly rooted in the Thomist tradition which approximated *populus* to *ecclesia* and *civitas*. See Yves Congar, ' "Ecclesia" et "populus (fidelis)" ' dans l'ecclésiologie de S. Thomas' in *St Thomas Aquinas 1274–1974*, ed. Armand Maurer (Toronto, 1974) pp. 159–73.

[26] On the concept of *corpus mysticum* in the later Roman law jurisprudence, see Arnold Ehrhardt, 'Das Corpus Christi und die Korporationen im spät-römischen Recht', 70, 71 *Zeitschrift der Savigny-Stiftung für Rechtsgeschichte*, Rom. Abt. (1953, 1954) 299–347; 25–40.

[27] Basile Eliachevitch, *La Personnalité juridique en droit privé romain* (Paris, 1942) p. 353 ('Les Romains ne connaissaient pas les personnes juridiques. Pour eux n'existait qu'un seul sujet de droit, l'individu. Quand ils parlaient de la *persona*, ils n'avaient jamais en vue autre chose que l'individu'). See also Alexander

persona cannot normally contain several *personae* 'within' it except for the case of pregnant women, perhaps. By the same logic, whether or not one is a free-man is not a question which can be answered by looking at whether one is 'within' a mystic, corporate *persona*. The very concept of the mystic corporate body was something which the Classical Roman jurists could not capture or express with their legal vocabulary. Likewise, until the first half of the fourteenth century, children born 'out of the *ligeance*' were not 'outsiders' of the English kingdom or the common law. Those born 'within the *ligeance*' were not 'insiders' either. They were neither outsiders nor insiders. As far as medieval common lawyers were concerned, they were 'persons' whose legal claim must be judged by law (procedures of inquest) rather than by faith, allegiance and the mystic body politic. The sixteenth-century law of personal status, on the other hand, seemed wholly to revolve around the concepts of 'insiders' and 'outsiders' of the mystic body of *populus*.

To be a *civis* in the Roman law of personal status meant to have *libertas*.[28] The continuity was maintained in medieval legal terminology where *civis* was often identified with *liber homo*. But how far can we stretch the continuity? The sixteenth-century common lawyers might well have claimed that the king's subjects within his kingdom — which was understood by an analogy to *civitas* in Roman law — were enjoying the 'liberty of Englishmen born'. Even better, aliens were subjected to legal disability just as non-citizens in Roman law were experiencing varying degrees of legal

Philipsborn, 'Der Begriff der Juristischen Person im römischen Recht', 71 *Zeitschrift der Savigny-Stiftung für Rechtsgeschichte*, Rom. Abt. (1954) 41–70. Similar remarks can be made with regard to the Greek legal vocabulary of the same period. See F. Devisscher, 'La dualité des droits de cité dans le monde romain, d'après une nouvelle interprétation de l'édit III d'Auguste découvert à Cyrène' in his *Nouvelles études de droit romain public et privé* (Milan, 1949) p. 111.

28 See, in general, A. N. Sherwin-White, *The Roman citizenship* (Oxford, 1965). See also François Jacques and John Scheid, *Rome et l'intégration de l'empire, 44 av. J. C. – 260 ap. J. C.*, vol. I, (Paris, 1990) *Les Structures de l'empire Romain* ch. 6; Claude Nicolet, *Le Métier de citoyen dans la Rome républicaine*, 2nd edn (Paris, 1976) pp. 31–70; François Jacques, ed., *Les cités de l'occident Romain* (Paris, 1992) *passim*. The same approach was taken in the Ancient Greek world. For a brief introduction and bibliography, see Raoul Lonis, *La Cité dans le monde grec: structure, fonctionnement, contradiction* (Paris, 1994); Claude Mossé, *Le Citoyen dans la Grèce antique* (Paris, 1993).

incapacity. Citizenship comes with liberty, just like before. What is the difference, then?

What the sixteenth-century lawyers did not recognise was that personal liberty in Roman law did not flow from political subjection. Personal liberty in Roman law may be obtained, not through political subjection, but by removal of personal subjection. The Roman law of personal status constituted a self-sufficient logical structure which was severed from the question of submission to political authority. Their *ius personarum* remained within the sphere of *ius privatum*, which was distinguished from *ius publicum*. Roman jurist Florentinus' well-known definitions of liberty and slavery are particularly revealing because he managed to explain the two key concepts of the law of personal status without any reference to the question of political subjection: 'Liberty is one's natural faculty to do what is not prohibited by law or by force. Slavery is an institution of *ius gentium* whereby one is, against nature, subjected to the ownership of another.'[29] For the jurists who were living under the *Pax Romana*, the question of political subjection could not have been a useful criterion for personal legal status. For all practical purposes, disputes concerning personal legal status arose among those who were already *sub imperio poluli Romani*. Numerous *divisiones personarum* which the jurists employed to distinguish first of all between *liberi* and *serui* and then among *cives, latini, latini Iuniani, peregrini, peregrini dediticii*, etc. were indeed ways of dividing those who were already subjugated to the Roman imperial power. Not surprisingly, Roman jurists steered clean away from the question of political subjection in discussing the law of personal status. The sixteenth-century lawyers, however, were no longer capable of discussing the law of personal status without mentioning allegiance and obedience. By then, personal liberty was inseparably bound up with political subjection.

The strange union of personal liberty and political subjection is in fact full of surprises. The judges and lawyers in *Calvin's case* were assuming that birth within the allegiance would guarantee 'a capacity or ability to *all benefits whatsoever*' (emphasis supplied).

---

[29] 'Libertas est naturalis facultas eius quod cuique facere libet nisi si quid ui aut iure prohibetur; seruitus est constitutio iuris gentium, qua quis dominio alieno contra naturam subicitur'. *D.* 1. 5. 4.

Here, we must note that personal liberty was no longer regarded as requiring distribution among subjects (each subject is given *all* liberty). Medieval lawyers, on the other hand, understood *libertas* as something which requires distribution. Since liberty was thought to involve disposition of material resources (for example, if I am free to eat a loaf of bread, that particular loaf will become unavailable for other people's consumption), the value of liberty was also deemed as essentially material. Notwithstanding all rhetorical claims to the contrary, *libertates* were therefore regarded, in practice, as marketable commodities which were sold, inherited, granted and leased with or without various conditions attached to the transaction. The existence of the market and the pricing system for *libertates* indicates that a distribution mechanism was at work. Liberties, therefore, were *distributed*. *Ius* was essentially the mechanism of just distribution of personal *libertates*.[30] As in the case of any commodities whose allocation is largely entrusted to the functioning of a market and its pricing mechanism, some managed to acquire them, and some did not. In other words, liberties belonged only to those who had *acquired* them – in the name of justice, of course. This is why legal inequality was the essential attribute of the Classical notion of justice.[31]

Sixteenth-century lawyers no longer subscribed to this idea because they understood personal liberty by close analogy to spiritual liberation. The spiritual dimension of liberty was certainly not new. But, in so far as the law of personal status was concerned, it was not known or, at least, not incorporated into the legal argument until the mid-fourteenth century. Spiritual liberty requires a peculiar distribution pattern because it involves disposi-

---

[30] *D*. 1. 1. 10 ('Iustitia est constans et perpetua uoluntas ius suum cuique tribuendi').

[31] It is beyond the scope of this book to attempt to provide a bibliography of general works on liberty and justice. We may only mention specific works such as *La notion de liberté au moyen âge, Islam, Byzance, Occident*, ed. A. Gouron and M. Boulet-Sautel (Paris, 1985); Jean-François Poudret and Danielle Anex-Cabanis, 'L'Individu face au pouvoir seigneurial d'après chartes de franchises de suisse romande au moyen âge' in *L'Individu face au pouvoir*, vol. III, *Europe occidentale XIIe–XVIIIe siècles* (Brussels, 1989) p. 177; Paul Ourliac and Jean-Louis Gazzaniga, *Histoire du droit privé français – de l'an mil au Code civil* (Paris, 1985) p. 173. The importance of the pricing mechanism in the Aristotelian notion of justice is stressed by Peter Stein and John Shand, *Legal values in Western society* (Edinburgh, 1974) pp. 59–62.

tion of spiritual resource, which is inexhaustible.[32] Because of its
unlimited availability, every one *could* have unlimited supply of
spiritual resource. If, however, this is allowed, spiritual liberty
would be valueless. It is therefore necessary to maintain a distribution pattern where certain individuals shall be prevented from
enjoying it in spite of its inexhaustible supply. According to the
medieval Christian theology, the distribution of spiritual liberty
(salvation) turns on faith. The resulting distribution pattern is 'all'
or 'nothing' because faith was understood as a question of 'yes' or
'no'.

Francis Bacon's argument in *Calvin's case* suggests that the
distribution pattern of personal liberty is closely copied from the
medieval Christian soteriology. According to him, allegiance to
our lord the king shall guarantee the capacity to take 'all benefits
whatsoever'. Lord Chancellor Ellesmere also argued that the
subjection to the king would make a person 'intire and perfect'.
The reason a subject can take 'all the freedomes, priviliges and
benefits' is because he is 'complete and entire'. An alien cannot be
an 'intire and perfect' person in law because he lacks faith and
allegiance to our lord the king.

From then on, legal debate on liberty would shift its focus from
the question of 'doing' to the question of 'being'. Florentinus'
definition which we quoted earlier has another merit of demonstrating that *libertas* was understood as a person's faculty 'to do'
something.[33] But the fifteenth- and sixteenth-century lawyers
were in complete agreement that personal liberty was an 'ontolo-
gical' question which must be answered either 'yes' or 'no'. The
question was no longer '*what* is one free to do?'. The new question
persistently to be asked is *whether or not* one *is* free, that is,
whether one's existence is judicially 'perfect'. We have already
seen that faith in our lord the king holds the key to the perfection
of one's 'being', legal as well as spiritual. Among the 'entire and
perfect' beings who have thus obtained freedom, the question of
liberty can no longer be discussed in positive terms of 'faculty to
do' this or that. As *all* entire and perfect beings must be allowed

---

[32] See, in this connection, John 4: 13, 14 where Jesus claims that '[e]veryone who
drinks this water will be thirsty again, but whoever drinks the water I give him
will never thirst. Indeed the water I give him will become in him a spring of
water welling up to eternal life.'

[33] See his definition of liberty (*D*. 1. 5. 4) quoted in note 29 above.

all benefits whatsoever, liberty becomes a negative question of 'toleration'.

For the same reason, the modern legal concept of equality must not be confused with the equal distribution of *libertates.* The equality in the modern legal argument is a notion which entirely does away with the very concept of distribution. Each subject's share ought to be 'full and entire'. In fact, the concept of 'share' is in itself inappropriate to the discussion of equality in modern jurisprudence. *Each* subject takes *the entirety*; and still, there are plenty of leftovers. It is inexplicable because it is a miracle. What distinguishes the equality of subjects from the equality of *cives* in Roman law is that the former is based on faith, obedience and the mystic body politic whereas the latter is based on *ius* and *iustitia.* Those who are under the 'obeisaunce of our lord the king' are given liberty. In their 'plenitude' of liberty, they are equal; equally 'perfect'.[34] It is an equality which becomes possible only when liberty is seriously confused with spiritual liberation.

According to Bacon, it is the 'law' which has the power to deliver this kind of equality: 'The law is equal, and favoureth not.' Obviously, he was not talking about the *ius* to which Gaius or Bracton referred. For the Roman and medieval jurists, *ius personarum* was the very mechanism of unequal distribution of *libertas.* Their law (*ius*) was unequal, but it was grounded upon 'justice'. The point is that as long as justice is the basis of law, law cannot deliver liberty to all. Invariably, some will have it, some will not. Only when law is truly grounded upon faith, can liberty be freely (*gratiis*) delivered to everybody in the name of law. Of course, 'everybody' here means an exclusive category of those 'within' the bond of faith: that is, everybody within the mystic body.

These, in our view, are the semantic assumptions of the sixteenth-century lawyers when they put forward their legal argument about individuals and society. All past texts were to be approached and interpreted from this point of view. Whenever they saw the word *alienigena,* they would treat it as a legal status characterised by the lack of faith and the resultant position as an 'outsider' to the mystic body they read into the contemporary

---

[34] The king's letters patent issued to John Swart in 1397 seem to express this idea. John Swart was portrayed as *adeo libere et integre sicut unus de ligeis nostris* (as free and entire as one of the king's liege-men). See p. 57 above.

texts. Documents which contain any mention of 'alien' merchants, 'alien' clergy, 'alien' priories or 'alien-born' children were interpreted as either confirming the legal predicament of aliens or – when the texts do not show a discriminatory legal treatment – as forming an exception to the law of alien status. Conversely also, whenever they saw some legal disabilities affecting certain individuals, they did not hesitate to conclude that the legal disabilities were the evidence of their alien status. We have seen how the legal disabilities of foreign-born persons were interpreted. The legal status of *peregrini* in Roman law, Jews and Lombards (money-changers) in medieval European kingdoms were examples to which the sixteenth-century lawyers frequently referred.[35] Finally, whenever they came across a topographical name (*Anglia, Francia, Hispania, Roma*, etc.), they would understand it as a territorial embodiment of allegiance. Whenever they encountered an appellation of a group of individuals (*Franci, Angli, barbari, serui, ciues*, Jews, Christians, etc.), they would see a *populus* bound up by the bond of faith to form a mystic body. 'Insiders' of such a mystic body are to be saved because they remain 'within' the bond of faith and obedience. 'Outsiders' are damned because they have no faith, they show no subjection. This is how the sixteenth-century lawyers interpreted and understood legal texts of the past. Must we not admit that anachronistic exploitation of terminology is the very basis of the progress of jurisprudence?

CONCLUSION

That the proposal for mutual naturalisation was made upon the accession of James I is significant in itself. When William of

---

[35] This is why the legal treatment of Jews in medieval Europe is sometimes thought relevant to the development of the law of alien status. This book does not discuss the legal treatment of Jews not merely because they were expelled from England in 1290, but more significantly because their history is largely irrelevant to our topic. Whether or not Jews were legally discriminated against is entirely beside the point because *most* people in medieval Europe were under *some* kind of legal disability. The legal distinction between aliens and subjects, on the other hand, is grounded upon the assumption that faith and allegiance to the political ruler will guarantee the full enjoyment of legal liberty. Jews in medieval England, however, knew no kings other than the king of England. Whatever might have been the reason for the discrimination and their eventual expulsion, it cannot be associated with the law of alien and subject status.

Normandy was enthroned as the king of the English in the eleventh century, no one thought it necessary to discuss the alien or subject status of *Franci* in England and *Angli* in Normandy. This was because personal legal status did not depend on political subjection. A serf was a serf regardless of who happened to come to the throne. Whether in England or in Normandy, a free-man was a free-man as long as he could prove his free status. Regardless of whether the king of the English happened to have an additional title as the duke of Normandy, a foreign-born heir could not inherit land in England if he could not prove his good descent. The Conquest did not bring any change to this fundamental structure of legal analysis.

Of course, legal historians have long held the view that *Franci* and *Angli* became somehow incapable of distinguishing each other after the Conquest, thus achieving some sort of political and legal fusion due to a grand scale confusion of ethnic identity. We have already argued at some length that this view stands on no historical basis.[36] For the sake of argument, however, let us for the moment not question the validity of such an explanation. Still, it does not seem to provide a satisfactory explanation about the beginning – or the lack until the beginning – of the law of alien status. It can only explain a *temporary* lack of the law of alien status. We are still left with no explanation about the beginning which, according to this scheme of explanation, must lie before the introduction of the temporary lack. Rather, legal historians seem to regard what Maitland has called 'the two great classes of men' as inescapable categories.[37] The division may temporarily disappear or reappear. But these fluctuations are understood as resulting from external circumstances such as feudalism, Norman Conquest and the loss of Normandy. Whenever the circumstances are right, the division will reappear then. The explanation, therefore, is about the beginning of these circumstances, rather than the beginning of the division itself. This is where the influence of *Calvin's case* proves most enduring. We explain why we think so.

As we saw, the majority in *Calvin's case* held that allegiance or the division between subjects and aliens was the work of the law of

---

[36] See pp. 14–15 above.

[37] F. Pollock and F. W. Maitland, *The history of English law before the time of Edward I*, 2nd edn, 2 vols. (Cambridge, 1968), I, 458.

nature. It is already well known that the contemporary lawyers' understanding of natural law was closely tied up with the concept of divine law.[38] Both natural law and divine law were thought to be grounded upon the unchanging and eternally valid reason (*ratio*). The point was clearly demonstrated by St German. According to his famous work, *Doctor and student*, the 'law eternal is nothing else than that supreme reason (*summa ratio*) in God for governing things'. Law of nature, which he prefers to call the law of reason, is participation or knowledge of eternal law made available to human beings by virtue of the light of natural reason (*lex rationis nichil aliud est quam perticipatio vel notio legis eterne in creatura rationali ei reuelate per lumen naturale rationis*). Thus understood, law of nature has the essential characteristics of the immutable, God-given law which transcends time and space.[39]

Calvin's case further demonstrates that the proponents of the union with Scotland resorted to this concept of natural law in order to overcome the constraints of the established common law rules regarding allegiance. By asserting that the allegiance and the division between aliens and subjects are the work of natural law, they attempted to achieve what was impossible under the existing framework of the common law, namely, uniting two kingdoms under one allegiance. One may still debate how successful was their attempt for the union. But what is not to be doubted is that they pushed the opinion of their opponents and predecessors (such as Littleton and Fortescue) into an almost complete oblivion and impressed the posterity with the 'rationality' of the division between aliens and subjects. The division is no longer viewed as a product of human law and legal conventions. The legal categories of aliens and subjects have been raised to the rank of conceptual categories grounded upon reason. The division between aliens and subjects, as it was now thought to rest upon reason, came to transcend time and space. Such a 'rational' and 'natural' division can never be completely erased or altered *ex loco nec tempore* because it is written in the heart of men.

This is probably why lawyers and legal historians are still experiencing difficulty in postulating and explaining the beginning of the law of alien status. The fact that some efforts have so

---

[38] Gierke, *Natural law and the theory of society*, vol. I, pp. xxxvi–xli.
[39] *Doctor and student*, 91 Selden Society (1974), pp. 8, 12–15.

far been made to envisage the so-called 'beginning' does not
vitiate our claim. The efforts, as we pointed out, are directed to
the explanation of a *temporary* lack where the division between
aliens and subjects is thought to have been 'obscured' by certain
intervening circumstances. Such an outlook still lies wholly
within the conceptual framework which many of us have know-
ingly or unknowingly inherited from the early modern proponents
of the natural law argument. St German himself conceded that the
law of nature, though it never mutates, could sometimes be
obscured: 'one cause for giving written law . . . is said by holy
men to have been the darkening of the law of reason and not its
changing (*propter legis rationis obfusciationem et non propter eius
mutationem*)'.[40]

Calvin's case itself was never meant to be a forum for historical
investigation into the law of alien status. Legal historians,
however, have accepted most of Edward Coke and Francis Bacon's
interpretation of the medieval texts regarding the treatment of
foreigners as historically accurate. As a result, they have built a
historiographical tradition which is difficult to understand without
a close look at the case. As far as the law of alien status is concerned,
legal historians and the sixteenth- and seventeenth-century
lawyers seem to share two things in common: modernity of
outlook and insensitivity to historical changes of legal terminology.

[40] Ibid., p. 14.

9

CONCLUSION

'All men are either slaves or free men.' This statement had long been the basis, the starting point of all reflections on personal legal status in Europe. The statement, however, conceals an outlook which has become unreachable for people today. It expresses ideas which are so grotesque and disturbing to the modern mind that they have been gently removed from the realm of the thinkable and put away in an obscure corner of our mental world where access is prohibited. In short, the statement contains ideas which are now taboo.

The voluminous studies on slavery[1] accumulated during the last two centuries have, on the whole, failed to dismantle the mechanism of taboo which shields these forbidden ideas. The reason for their failure can be explained as follows. Most studies on slavery start with the assumption that slaves were chattels, or objects which need not and must not be discussed on the same platform as persons.[2] Once slaves are thus removed from the company of persons, slavery can be discussed and understood using the terminology and the categorical divisions familiar to us. First, for example, it is entirely proper to maintain a sharp

---

[1] For a critical historiographical appraisal, see M. Finley, *Ancient slavery and modern ideology* (London, 1980). To cite but a few works, among numerous others, Henri Wallon, *Histoire de l'esclavage dans l'antiquité*, first published in 1847, reprinted with a bibliography by J. C. Dumont (Paris, 1988); Paul Allard, *Les esclaves chrétiens depuis les premiers temps de l'Eglise jusqu'à la fin de la domination romaine en Occident*, 2nd edn (Paris, 1876); Alan Watson, *Roman slave law* (Baltimore, 1987). Keith Bradley, *Slavery and society at Rome* (Cambridge, 1994) has a useful bibliography. There is, of course, a vast amount of literature on slavery in the New World, which cannot properly be discussed in the present work.

[2] For example, Finley, *Ancient slavery and modern ideology*, pp. 67ff.; Alan Watson, 'Thinking property at Rome', 68 *Chicago-Kent Law Review* (1993) 1355–71 at 1355.

distinction between free-men and slaves because the division is to be understood as drawn between persons and things. There is nothing even remotely surprising about denying personal liberty to entities which we classify as chattels. No one with good sense would today doubt that persons must not be treated in the same way as objects. Second, there is no need to commit the sacrilege to the sanctified legal terminology 'person' because it is not necessary to entertain the dreadful possibility that some persons may be totally and openly denied legal liberty which other persons are allowed to enjoy. By extirpating slaves from the company of persons, one can have the comfort of maintaining the modern legal definition of 'person' as the unfailing subject of legal rights and obligations.

Studies of ancient slavery which start with the assumption that slaves were not persons have thus allowed us to discuss slavery without having to rethink and unsettle the semantic basis of the modern legal vocabulary. According to this vocabulary, persons and things are mutually exclusive categories; a thing cannot be the subject of legal rights and obligations; persons, on the other hand, must *all* be the subjects of legal rights and obligations. In other words, these studies are based on the very language which operates as the mechanism for locking away the disturbing features of ancient slavery in a conceptual black hole where our vocabulary, our meanings cannot reach. That a great number of human beings had long been openly and completely denied personal liberty may be disconcerting enough for many people today. But what is even more disturbing about the ancient slavery is that slavery did not at all disturb our remote ancestors. Studies of ancient slavery uncritically using our own language have deprived us of the linguistic means of approaching slavery in the way it was approached by those who approved of the institution. These studies – conducted in a language which accurately reflects the modern man's disapproval of slavery – have reinforced rather than dismantled the mechanism of taboo. While we discuss slavery using our own terms, slavery remains an impenetrable topic. All we can do is to point out the otherness, the inaccessible and inscrutable bizarreness of a remote era. Indeed, many would agree that it is somewhat odd to classify creatures of human form as chattels. But it is a move which can willingly be made by modern students of slavery with condescension, rather than dismay. Surely, the proposition that slaves were chattels can go down well as one of those sweet little idiosyncrasies of the 'ancient civilisation'. You only need to say once at the outset that slaves were – er, well – chattels. You can then discuss slavery without unsettling the vocabulary which is familiar to you.

That slaves were 'persons' – 'persons' in the Roman legal vocabulary did not mean much more than human beings – and that a slave could be described both as a 'person (*persona*)' and as a 'thing (*res*)', we probably need not spend much time in asserting. A century ago, William Buckland published a most emphatic and authoritative article demonstrating these points.[3] What we do need to discuss, however, is how and why the unhistorical proposition that slaves were not persons appeared in the first place. The appearance of this remarkable proposition and its widespread acceptance are the signs of the major shift of outlook on personal status in the European legal development – the topic of this book – and our discussion can perhaps shed some light on this shift of outlook.

The sixteenth-century French jurist Jean Bodin has attracted a great deal of attention because of his thesis about sovereignty.[4] But his works deserve even greater attention as they reveal how the late medieval developments concerning the law of personal status (English sources showing these developments have been discussed in the first half of this book) were finally summarised

---

[3] W. W. Buckland, 'Wardour Street Roman law', 17 *Law Quarterly Review* (1901) 179–92. What provoked this impassioned article was the unanimous view among the nineteenth-century German and French scholars that slaves in Roman law were not persons. See also his *Roman law of slavery* (Cambridge, 1908) pp. 3–4: 'There does not seem to be a single text in the whole Corpus Iuris Civilis, or in the Codex Theodosianus, or in the surviving classical legal literature which denies personality to a slave.'

[4] Jean Bodin, *Les six livres de la republique* (hereafter, *République*), reprinted with editorial corrections by Christiane Frémont, Marie-Dominique Couzinet and Henri Rochais, 6 vols. (Paris, 1986); Jean Bodin, *Method for the easy comprehension of history*, trans. Beatrice Reynolds (New York, 1945). The Latin text and French translation of *Methodus ad facilem historianum cognitionem* can be found in *Oeuvres philosophiques de Jean Bodin*, ed. trans., Pierre Mesnard (Paris, 1951) pp. 101–475 (hereafter, *Methodus*). See also Julian Franklin, *Jean Bodin and the rise of absolutist theory* (Cambridge, 1973); *Jean Bodin: actes du colloque interdisciplinaire d'Angers, 24 au 27 mai, 1984*, 2 vols. (Angers, 1985). For a recent bibliography on Bodin's theory of sovereignty, see Julian Franklin, ed. and trans., *On sovereignty: four chapters from the six books of the commonwealth* (Cambridge, 1992).

and how the earlier legal vocabulary was reinterpreted and rear-
ranged to accommodate the changed outlook. On a number of
occasions, Bodin made it clear that his mission was to replace the
Aristotelian explanations of the State and citizenship with a new
set of explanations.[5] How did Aristotle define citizenship, then?
According to the Greek philosopher, citizens must be defined as
those who are endowed with a certain quality (excellence) which
would allow them to participate in the political (public) life.[6] His
definition of citizenship no doubt enjoyed an unchallenged acceptance throughout the Middle Ages.[7] But the sixteenth-century
jurist Bodin finds it wholly unacceptable because it does not at all
take account of the bond of allegiance linking the prince and his
subjects. In Bodin's mind, this reciprocal bond of obedience and
protection must be the essence of citizenship. He accordingly
proposes as follows:

It must be said that privileges [enjoyed by Aristotelian citizens] do not
make a citizen. It is the acknowledgement and obedience of a free subject
towards his sovereign prince, and the guidance, justice and the defence of
the prince towards the subject which makes the citizen and which is the
essential difference between a citizen and a foreigner.[8]

Bodin, like his contemporaries in England, was assuming that

---

[5] The opening paragraphs of ch. 6 of *Methodus* show that Bodin was determined to
reject Aristotelian explanations: 'Authority, however, should not weigh more
than reason in this discussion, and we thus refute first of all Aristotle's definitions
of citizenship, city, state, sovereignty and public office with the necessary
arguments because they are at the core of the debate' ('Sed ne plus auctoritatis in
disputando, quàm rationum momenta quaerantur, priùs Aristotelis definitiones
de cive, de civitate, de Republica, de summo imperio, de magistratu: quae sunt
hujus disputationis fundamenta, necessariis argumentis refellendae sunt'). *Methodus*, p. 167. The same argument is more elaborately spelled out in *République*, I,
ch. 6.
[6] Aristotle, *The politics and the constitution of Athens*, ed. and trans. Stephen
Everson (Cambridge, 1996) pp. 61–3 (1275a 23, 1275b 19).
[7] Mario Grignaschi, 'La Définition du *Civis* dans la scholastique' in *Gouvernés et
gouvernants*, part 3 (Brussels, 1966) pp. 71–88.
[8] *République*, I, pp. 131 and 141 ('Il faut bien dire que les privileges ne font pas le
citoyen, . . . C'est donc la recongnoissance, et obeïssance du franc suject envers
son Prince souverain, et la tuition, justice, et la defense du prince envers le suject,
qui fait le citoyen; qui est la difference essentielle du bourgeois à l'estranger'). An
earlier stage of Bodin's reflection on citizenship can be found in *Methodus*, p. 169
('Respublica nihil aliud sit, quàm familiarum aut collegiorum sub unum & idem
imperium subjecta multitudo: civis autem qui communi libertate fruitur, ac
imperii tutela'). It seems, therefore, that subjection to the sovereign authority of
the State constitutes the basis of the citizen's liberty and the sovereign's
protection of its citizens.

human beings must first of all be divided into citizens and foreigners and that this division must turn on the political submission (allegiance) to the ruler. Also, like Coke and Bacon who saw the division between subjects and aliens as an eternal and everlasting division grounded upon nature and reason, Bodin was convinced that his understanding of citizenship was of universal and permanent validity transcending time and place.[9] But unlike the English common lawyers of the time, Bodin had to cope with the Roman legal texts where slavery featured prominently. Could his argument (i.e., political subjection must be the decisive criterion of personal status) – if it indeed had the universal validity as he claimed – be reconciled with the status of slaves? Bodin does recognise that because citizenship, as he sees it, depends on obedience and subjection to the sovereign prince, it is necessary to explain why a slave cannot claim citizenship 'even though the slave may be as much subject, or even more subject to [the ruling authority of] the State than his master is'. This is how Bodin came up with the astonishing solution that 'in legal terms, slaves were counted for nothing'.[10] Armed with this proposition – which can claim no textual support from the Roman legal sources[11] – Bodin and succeeding generations of lawyers and historians have managed to ignore the whole corpus of texts which show that, to a great extent, personal legal status was determined quite independently of the question of political subjection.

[9] The 'universalist' approach of Bodin is fully discussed by Julian Franklin, *Jean Bodin and the sixteenth-century revolution in the methodology of law and history* (Westport, Conn., 1977, first published in 1963); Donald Kelley, 'The development and context of Bodin's method' in *Jean Bodin: Verhandlungen der internationalen Bodin Tagung*, ed. H. Denzer (Munich, 1973) pp. 123–50. See also Jean Bodin, *Exposé du droit universel*, trans. Lucien Jerphagnon (Paris, 1985).

[10] *République*, I, pp. 113–14: 'car combien que l'esclave soit autant, ou plus subject de la Republique, que son seigneur, si est-ce que tous les peuples ont toujours passé par commun accord que l'esclave n'est point citoyen, et en termes de droit est conté pour rien'.

[11] In saying that slaves were counted for nothing, Bodin refers to *Digest*, 50. 17. 32 (Ulpian) without quoting the passage. The passage, however, needs to be quoted in full: 'As far as *ius civile* is concerned, slaves are counted for nothing; this, however, is not the case in *ius gentium* for, as far as *ius gentium* is concerned, all men are equal.' Bodin truncated this statement of Ulpian and apparently convinced himself that the first half gave him sufficient ground to say what he did. For an authoritative argument that this passage and other similar passages (*D*. 28. 8. 1 and *D*. 50. 17. 209, for example) cannot be a ground for denying personality to slaves, see Buckland, 'Wardour Street Roman law'.

In fact, Bodin's solution amounts to nothing less than erasing the past. Men's outlook on society and its component individuals (including free-men as well as slaves) had been built around the institution of slavery. Slavery had been the very foundation of the law of personal status. Slaves were one of 'the two great classes of men' known to Roman jurists (*omnes homines aut liberi sunt aut serui*). To say that slaves were counted for nothing is to turn a blind eye to all this history and deny that there ever was such a history. Students of slavery who keep saying that slaves were not persons are doing precisely this. By suggesting that slaves need not and must not be discussed in connection with the law of persons, they have succeeded in destroying both the forum and the topic for the discussion through which the past language of the law of personal status may be recovered. While the language of the past describing its law of persons is thus kept beyond recovery, the present language, the present outlook reigns as the only possible language, the only possible outlook. The ancient law of slavery is described using the modern terminology reflecting the modern outlook.[12]

As far as essentials are concerned, all that needs to be said about the present law of personal status was already said by Coke and Bacon in *Calvin's case*: 'Every man is either an alien born, or a subject born.' This is an outlook which is thoroughly familiar to us. There is, after all, nothing unusual about modern men and women taking for granted the modern outlook on which the modern law of personal status is grounded. In chapters 1 and 8 of this book, I have attempted to explain why historians too might have failed to recognise the modernity of this outlook. We saw how historians studying the beginning of the law of alien status attempted to postulate a period when the division between aliens and subjects was supposedly lacking. The contrived absence of the division is explained by reference to some extra-legal circumstances such as the Norman Conquest and feudalism. The beginning of the law of alien and subject status is then portrayed as an appearance – after a period of absence – of the division between aliens and subjects. It is just as the sun or the moon may appear and disappear. One may study the mechanism of its disappearance

---

[12] For a fuller discussion of the historical change of language and the nature of history writing, see 'Excursus', below.

and reappearance. But such a study will never explain the beginning or the end of the sun or the moon itself.

For the early modern lawyers like Coke and Bacon, the division between aliens and subjects was indeed a 'natural' division, as natural as the sun or the moon. Moreover, just as the overwhelming majority of judges in *Calvin's case* viewed the division between aliens and subjects as a permanent, immutable and inevitable division rooted in the natural law ideology of the time, so did the humanist jurist Bodin believe that his definition of citizenship (grounded on the bond of allegiance) must be 'universally' valid regardless of time and place. Legal historians have apparently inherited this sixteenth-century language. The history of the law of alien status is therefore discussed just as one would discuss the eclipses and reappearances of celestial bodies made in heaven. Perhaps lawyers and historians are not alone in doing this. Until the advances of the physical and mathematical sciences of this century provided a scientific language to discuss the beginning and the end of the universe, scientists too had only the language to talk about the eclipses and reappearances of the heavenly bodies. The beginning and the end of these 'eternal' bodies were shrouded in the mythical language.

While English jurists and historians were content to deploy the explanations of the appearances and disappearances of the law of subject and alien status, Jean Bodin undertook to provide a mythical explanation of the beginning of the 'permanent' categories of aliens and subjects. Bodin did this through his version of the genesis of the State. His tale revolves around the theme of primeval violence and subjugation. In the beginning, according to Bodin, the force and violence provoked wars. These wars resulted in conquest and subjugation. This provided the context in which individual heads of family (reflecting his Roman law training, Bodin's analysis is couched in the Roman legal terminology of *pater familias*) came out of their households and entered into 'political' relationships with one another. This is how the State is formed, according to Bodin. Now, those (heads of family) who submitted and adhered to the commander of the original conquest were the 'loyal subjects'. The natural liberty which they had enjoyed before the creation of the State was diminished to the extent of their obedience to their sovereign commander. The 'others', who did not obey the triumphant commander, were reduced to 'pure servitude'. Bodin explains as follows: 'he who did not want to give up some of his liberty, which is necessary to live under the laws and commands of someone else, lost all of his liberty'.[13] They are the foreigners, the disobedient lot.

According to this story, the relationship of obedience and protection between the ruler and the ruled ought to be primeval. The relationship dates back to the very beginning of the political existence of human beings. This is how Bodin and his followers discovered the primordial importance of sovereignty – the converse image of the *obedience* of all faithful subjects. Bodin was unable to imagine that the genesis of the State could ever be explained otherwise. The fact that for such a long time, so little attention was paid to the notion of sovereignty puzzled Bodin. But instead of doubting the universal and transcendental validity of his thesis, Bodin was rather inclined to explain his predecessors' lack of interest in the concept of sovereignty as a sign of their oversight or academic incompetence. In his celebrated work, *Les six livres de la republique*, Bodin remarked in amazement that 'no jurist or political philosopher has yet defined the concept [of sovereignty] even though it is the chief point, and the one that needs most to be explained, in a treatise on the commonwealth'. He also claimed that 'among a million books that we see in all sciences, there are just three or four books on politics'. And these three or four books were obviously inadequate because, according to him, 'two thousand years or so since Plato and Aristotle had written on this topic, political science was still shrouded in thick veils of darkness'.[14]

At any rate, Bodin's version of the genesis of the State proved to be a great success. There is, however, an important point which must not be overlooked. His version of the genesis makes use of a theme which is familiar to all of us, namely, the theme of a 'fall'. The genesis of the State is portrayed as human beings' fall from

---

[13] *République*, I, pp. 111–12. A similar explanation of the genesis of the State and the ensuing relationship between the ruler and the ruled can be found in Hobbes, *Leviathan*, ed. Richard Tuck (Cambridge, 1996) pp. 120, 121 and 150 ('For in the act of our *Submission*, consisteth both our *Obligation*, and our *Liberty*'). The theme of primeval violence and conquest had already appeared briefly in Bodin's *Methodus*, pp. 191, 382.

[14] *République*, I, ch. 8 (p. 179); the Preface (p. 11). More scathing remarks about the supposed deficiency of the works of his predecessors, including Plato and Aristotle, can be found in his *Methodus*, p. 349.

the pristine condition where everyone had unrestricted natural liberty. In the course of the fall, two great classes of men were created: subjects and aliens. The former had their natural liberty diminished to the extent of their political subjection. The latter had their natural liberty completely removed because of their disobedience to the supreme ruler. The only way the former (the subjects) can once again have a taste of the blissful sweetness of liberty is through faith and obedience to 'our lord the king'. For those who accept this version of the genesis of the State, there is not much one can do to study the history of the law of alien status apart from describing the eclipses and reappearances of the permanent and indelible categories of aliens and subjects. Those who dwell in a universe created by the universalist approach of Bodin have no linguistic means of describing the historicity of their conceptual universe. All they can do is to deploy the mythical language which is itself the axiomatic basis of their conceptual universe.

For our present purpose, we only need to point out that Bodin's version of the birth story allows no role to be played by slaves. Having completely removed the slaves from the scene ('slaves were counted for nothing'), Bodin redefined the meaning of slavery (*servitude*) and liberty. The 'pure servitude' mentioned by Bodin is no longer a private law concept. Unlike the Roman jurist Florentinus who explained that slavery was about the relationship between one private person (a slave) and another (his master), Bodin redefined *pure servitude* so that it is now *collectively* applicable to those who do not owe obedience to the sovereign ruler. They are under *pure servitude* not because they are subjected to a master, but precisely because they do not have the proper master. Nor does liberty mean what it used to mean. Liberty is now inseparably bound with obedience to the proper master. Liberty became an epithet indiscriminately applicable to all the 'loyal and faithful subjects' of the sovereign ruler.[15]

Aristotle, needless to say, had a very different explanation for the origin of the State. His version does not even mention the division between aliens and subjects nor the concept of sovereignty. Slaves, on the other hand, play an indispensable and primordial role in his

---

[15] Hobbes' analysis of liberty is also based on these premises. See *Leviathan*, ch. 21, 'Of the liberty of subjects'.

story. Aristotle's explanation of the origin of the State is designed
to reconfirm and justify the division between slaves and free-men.
Aristotle did this by placing slavery at the very beginning of the
State.[16] Bodin did the same thing with the division between aliens
and citizens. Bodin's birth story of the State is presented as an
explanation of how the division between aliens and citizens was first
created. Just like any other creation myths, however, it cannot
explain the origin of what it purports to explain. Conversely, the
implicit assumptions about the division between aliens and citizens
commonly held by Bodin and his contemporaries can explain why
the origin of that division was portrayed in such a way and why
Bodin's portrayal has enjoyed such a great success.

This brings us back to the question we posed at the outset:
'How do we explain the *beginning* of the law of alien status?' The
least we can say is that the beginning of the law of alien status
cannot be explained by a contrived 'appearance' of the category of
aliens. In order to talk about the appearance, one has to postulate a
period of 'absence'. No amount of imagination, however, will
allow us to envisage a society or a situation where human beings
were incapable of distinguishing 'we' from 'they'. Rather, the
beginning must be studied by investigating the historical changes
in the *relative* importance of various legal divisions of persons.
After all, the division between aliens and subjects is only one out
of numerous *divisiones personarum*. When this particular division
was accorded the supreme, overriding importance, the law of alien
status can be said to have begun. The study of the beginning of
the law of alien status, therefore, inevitably involves a study of the
demise of the world where the division between free-men and
slaves was the supreme division (*summa divisio*) reigning above all
other *divisiones personarum*. Viewed from this standpoint, it
should be obvious that the law of *alien* status cannot be studied
without simultaneously investigating the changes in the way
subject status is conceptualised. When the lack of political submis-

---

[16] Aristotle's analysis of slavery has the effect of conferring a transcendental
significance on the division between free-men and slaves (by describing it as
having existed from the beginning). Slavery thus becomes an unassailable
institution within the Aristotelian system. The remarkable achievement of
M. Finley is to see through this argument structure. Finley instead gives a
convincing explanation of the emergence of slavery and demonstrates that
'slavery was a late and relatively infrequent form of involuntary labour'. Finley,
Ancient slavery and modern ideology, pp. 77–86.

sion began to be perceived as making all the difference in one's legal status, a crucial move was made to set up the stage where people of all sorts, kinds, sexes and status could start a long fight to obtain an equal package of legal treatments with no other ammunition than their political submission. What we need to study if we are to understand the beginning of the law of alien and subject status is then the emergence of a 'new' outlook, a new argument structure that personal legal status must turn on obedience and allegiance to the ruling authority of the State. Whether this outlook can be labelled as 'Christian' is perhaps a trivial question. What is not trivial and therefore is worth stating is that the immense prestige and the general approval enjoyed by certain argument patterns of medieval Christian ecclesiology and soteriology (e.g., it is through faith and obedience that one can truly 'belong' to the mystic body of church; the membership of the mystic body of church holds the key to salvation and perfection of one's being; those who obtain perfection through faithful obedience to our lord the king can claim liberty as a matter of grace) greatly contributed to the triumph of the new outlook by providing it with the vital rhetorical momentum to undermine the firm grip of the old outlook.

As far as English sources are concerned, we can conclude that the pivotal achievement of introducing the question of political subjection into the arena of private law discussion was made in the middle of the fourteenth century as revealed by the statute *De natis ultra mare* (1351). The statute was not about personal status as such. It simply dealt with a particular private law right (the heir's position to claim the inheritance) without making any suggestion as to the legal status of the persons involved. But the vocabulary it adopted (*ligeance*) provided a truly remarkable means of expressing the 'futuristic' vision, as it then was, that political subjection should have far-reaching private law consequences, while maintaining a façade of continuity with the past where birthplace did have a private law consequence due to the rules of inquest. This is how allegiance became the basis of the modern law of personal status. The rise of the so-called *ius soli* – an anomaly which was unthinkable in the ancient laws of personal status – can only be understood when one remembers the double meaning of *ligeance* which allowed the question of political subjection to be discussed under the guise of birthplace.

The modest aim of this book has been to advance an argument that the history of the English law of *alien* status cannot be explained by a few worn-out conjectures about the impact of the loss of Normandy. The book therefore has dealt with only one half of the great potential of *ligeance* as the cornerstone of the modern law of personal status. Now, the other half of the story remains to be told, which will be about the law of *subject* status (citizenship). The questions of liberty and equality will then have to be dealt with more explicitly than it was proper for us to do in this book. If, meanwhile, some of the readers see in our foregoing discussions many more topics which may be profitably explored not only to study the history of the law of alien and subject status, but also to deepen the understanding of our present and future world, then the aim of this book can perhaps be said to have been fully achieved.

EXCURSUS

On several occasions during our discussion, I have suggested that
a revolutionary legal change is accompanied by a semantic change
of legal terminology. The underlying assumption is that language,
legal or non-legal, undergoes historical changes. An obvious point
which needs to be reiterated in this connection is that both lawyers
and historians deal with texts composed in the past. Both of them
purport to interpret those texts to uncover their true meaning.
What is the difference, then? The problem presents itself with
some urgency to legal historians who need to explain that what
they are doing is somehow different from what lawyers are doing –
often with the same texts. Maitland, of course, has already noticed
this. He saw that the problem was important enough to be chosen
as a topic of his inaugural lecture as the Downing Professor of
English Laws in the University of Cambridge in 1888. With his
characteristic lucidity, he offered an insightful distinction between
'two different logics, the logic of authority, and the logic of
evidence'. He then went on to explain as follows:

What the lawyer wants is authority and the newer the better; what the
historian wants is evidence and the older the better . . . That process by
which old principles and old phrases are charged with a new content, is
from the lawyer's point of view an evolution of the true intent and
meaning of the old law; from the historian's point of view, it is almost of
necessity a process of perversion and misunderstanding . . . The lawyer
must be orthodox otherwise he is no lawyer; an orthodox history seems to
me a contradiction in terms.[1]

More than a century has passed since. In the meantime, a great
deal of effort has been made by historians and lawyers to clarify
the nature of their respective interpretative activities. It is there-

[1] 'Why the history of English law is not written' in *The collected papers of F. W.
Maitland*, ed. H. A. L. Fisher, 3 vols. (Cambridge, 1911) I, p. 491.

fore not entirely superfluous to attempt to summarise their achievements and explain once again the difference between judicial and historical interpretations of texts.

A few preliminary remarks are in order. We begin by observing that a 'text' is a set of connected words. By 'words', I mean verbal signs – visual or audible – of communication. Since language is an ambiguous means of communication, words require interpretation. For our discussion, I define 'interpretation' as an activity whose aim is to clarify meanings of words. I refrain from offering a definition of 'meaning'. I simply use it to indicate 'that which is communicated' by words. The meaning of a word cannot be discussed unless a system of meanings (i.e., a semantic structure) is postulated. Communication which relies on a system of signs (of which language is an example) is possible 'only by virtue of the fact that . . . signs are all part of a system of signs'.[2] To 'clarify' the meaning of a word is to propose a meaning which is intended to enhance the overall coherence of this semantic structure.

Another point which needs to be made at the outset is that every speech community has only a limited range of texts to draw upon. This phenomenon can be explained on both diachronic and synchronic scales. At any given time, for example, there are several speech communities (theologians, lawyers, mathematicians, engineers, etc.), each drawing upon a distinctive range of texts. In this case, systematic attempts are often made to delimit the range of texts which can be legitimately exploited by members of the speech community. Canonisation, for instance, serves this purpose in theological discourse. Codification in civil law countries is also aimed at delimiting the range of texts which can properly be used in legal discourse. However, the systematic delimitation of texts is accomplished mostly by professional training. An adequately trained common lawyer, for example, should know the range of texts which it is permissible to draw upon in legal argument. Also, if we focus on a particular speech community and observe it diachronically, we may see that the range of texts which are communicated or communicable within

---

[2] '[Communication of meaning] is possible only by virtue of the fact that verbal signs are all part of a system of signs. [I]t is this system which makes meaning possible, since the signs of any code are only defined by other signs.' Eugene A. Nida and Johannes P. Louw, *Lexical semantics of the Greek New Testament* (Atlanta, 1992) p. 4.

the speech community changes over time. New texts are constantly composed and replace old ones to some extent.[3]

Whether or not a proposed meaning of a word contributes to the coherence of a semantic structure, will be judged only within the range of texts thus delimited. 'Coherence' of a systematic structure is not conceivable unless the scope of the system is delineated in the first place. Lawyers, for instance, have a semantic structure for their professional discourse which does not interfere with the one observed in colloquial discourse. Colloquial interpretation of a text, therefore, does not have immediate relevance to legal interpretation of the same text. Similarly, an interpretation of a text which creates least inconsistency within the semantic structure of a sixteenth-century speech community may well create an unacceptable level of inconsistency for a thirteenth-century speech community.

Consider, for example, a text, 'aliens cannot claim inheritance in England'. In the sixteenth-century legal vocabulary, it is better to interpret 'aliens' as 'persons who were born out of the king's allegiance'. Such a rendering will contribute to the overall semantic coherence of the sixteenth-century legal vocabulary where the word 'alien' was invariably used in connection with subjection, allegiance, legal protection, kingdom, liberty, equality, etc. But the same interpretation will create an unacceptable level of inconsistency in the thirteenth-century legal vocabulary. If, however, 'alien' is rendered as a 'person who was born out of England', it will enhance the semantic coherence of the thirteenth-century legal vocabulary, where the term was closely associated with trial, jury, cognisance, king's writ, bastardy, inheritance, proof, etc. But, of course, such a rendering will be damaging to the semantic coherence of the sixteenth-century legal vocabulary. One can also understand, for example, that in the sixteenth century, 'God' was depicted as *summa ratio*'; and 'reason' was portrayed as 'the most precious gift of God' to human beings. These meanings would certainly be detrimental to the semantic coherence of the eighteenth-century philosophical discourse where 'God' was attacked in the name of 'reason' and 'humanity' (as opposed to 'divinity').

---

[3] Texts are either visible or audible; in the latter case, it is perhaps better to say that the new 'modes of speech' replace the old ones to some extent.

One of the aims of language learning is to enable one to judge which of the various proposed meanings of a word – in a particular text – is more conducive to the overall coherence of a given semantic structure. This is how communication is usually possible among adequately trained users of a language. Contested cases, however, will arise. A speech community often has a formally established mechanism of determining which of the proposed meanings will create least inconsistency of meanings. Judges and influential jurists, for example, are called upon when the ambiguity of legal vocabulary in a particular text cannot be resolved between the parties. Ecclesiastical hierarchy and theologians carry out the same function. In the case of historical interpretation, established historians do the same job.

Unlike judges or the ecclesiastical hierarchy, however, established historians do not have at their disposal an institutionalised means of coercing their judgement. Why? Because historical interpretation of a text is not immediately concerned with distribution of resources. Religion and law, on the other hand, involve distribution of resources, spiritual or material. Law is responsible for distribution of material resources among members of society. To a large extent, successful law enforcement depends on human beings' acquiescence to the power of words, hence, the importance of the interpretation of legal texts (although the ultimate source of the power of words may probably reside in violence). Also, just as much as our spiritual needs and aspirations are defined and expressed in words, so much will the attainment of spiritual liberation depend on words and their meanings. Exegesis, therefore, is vitally important in many religious dogmas because whether or not one will be given spiritual reward often depends on interpretation of canonised texts. In short, legal and religious texts are instrumental to the distribution of material and spiritual resources. Resource distribution, however, will inevitably require coercion. For material resources, their limited availability explains the need for coercive distribution. For spiritual resource, coercion is required to uphold a distribution pattern where a certain group of people shall remain deprived of spiritual reward. Without such a distribution pattern, spiritual reward would become valueless because the inexhaustible nature of spiritual resource would lead to a situation where everyone can have an unlimited enjoyment of spiritual resources. Accordingly, priests and judges (priests of the law[4]) have the means of coercing their decision.

Allocation of resources is a matter of *praxis* here and now. A legal text is not a set of gnomic statements embodying eternal values. Rather, it is a 'utilisation manual' according to which the institutionalised power is to be mobilised here and now. The commands included in a legal text – regardless of its date of composition – need to be intelligible to the participants of the law-enforcement mechanism. This means that legal texts and the commands contained therein are invariably interpreted according to the present semantic structure shared by those currently involved in law enforcement. No doubt, texts which were composed in the past may well be discussed by lawyers. For that matter, moreover, *all* recorded texts are – strictly speaking – texts which were composed at some point in the past. But lawyers and judges refer to them because those texts can provide the discursive contents which can be profitably exploited to strengthen the persuasive power of their present legal argument, which is invariably about how the present case should be decided *now*.

Unfortunately, this point is not always fully appreciated. The constitutional jurisprudence of the United States, for example, is heavily burdened by allusions to the 'intentions of the "founding-fathers"'. In a similar vein, lawyers have made claims about the supposed relevance of the 'legislative intention'.[5] But, why do they do this? Are they really interested in knowing the social, economic and ideological circumstances of the late eighteenth-century North America? Do they really want simply to know how a particular clause of a statute was intended to be understood at the time and under the circumstances it was composed, and stop there, rejoicing in the historical accuracy of their interpretation? The only reason they recite the so-called 'legislative intention' is because such a recital is thought to add some weight to their present legal argument. The sole concern of lawyers is to offer a

---

[4] Cf. *D.* 1. 1. 1 ('cuius merito nos [jurists] sacerdotes appellet').

[5] Francis Bennion, *Statutory interpretation*, 2nd edn (London, 1992) p. 345 ('The sole object in statutory interpretation is to arrive at the legislative intention'). Note, however, that Bennion defines 'legislative intention' as 'what the legislator is taken to have intended'. See Ibid. This is how Bennion can recognise that 'on arrival in the present, they [i.e., statutes composed in the past] deploy their native endowments under conditions originally unguessed at' (p. 618).

persuasive argument that the allocation of resources under dispute must be carried out according to their interpretation of the text, rather than their opponent's. All they say is that their client should win the present case. Lord Reid's following remark explains this point most elegantly:

We often say that we are looking for the intention of Parliament, but that is not quite accurate. We are seeking the meaning of the words which Parliament used. We are seeking not what Parliament meant but the true meaning of what they said.[6]

The preoccupation with the so-called 'founding-fathers' intention' or with the 'legislative intention' has a curious feature. The gist of the argument is that since a particular text was intended to have such and such a meaning, the same meaning – as *was* originally intended, or as *is taken to have been* intended – must also be assigned to the text now. What the parties strive for is to ascertain the *present* meaning of the text. The supposed 'original' meaning is invoked merely to add weight to the party's current assertion as to the present meaning of the text. The emphatic argument that we must 'go back' to the original intention of the legislator is therefore disguising the transcendental conception of law which recognises no historical change of law. If it is to be acknowledged that law does change over time and according to the changed circumstances, then what is the point of talking about the intention of the legislators, who operated at a different time and under different circumstances? No wonder Edward Coke – who believed in the transcendental validity of the common law – claimed that the court's duty was to interpret an act 'according to the intent of them that made it'.[7] Coke could make such a claim because he did not recognise that common law could ever change. According to him, law – understood as *optima regula* – can never change; it can only be 'found' or 'hidden'.

Historical interpretation of a text, on the other hand, does not aim to resolve the question of resource distribution here and now.

---

[6] *Black-Clawson International Ltd.* v. *Papierwerke Waldhof Aschaffenburg AG* [1975] AC 591, 613. Quoted from Rupert Cross, *Statutory interpretation*, 2nd edn (London, 1987) p. 25.

[7] *The Fourth part of the Institutes of the laws of England* (London, 1797) IV, p. 330. Blackstone repeats the same view. He argues that the courts are bound 'to interpret statutes according to the true intent of the legislature'. *Commentaries on the laws of England*, 4 vols. (Oxford, 1765–9) III, p. 222.

The aim of historians, when they interpret a text, is to clarify the meanings of a text according to the semantic structure of a certain epoch in the past. We have already suggested that semantic structures change over time. Semantic changes open up new possibilities of interconnecting old words. Morphology of vocabulary usually survives semantic changes. This is why old terminology is continually used; but in constantly different ways. When we say 'new' texts replace old ones, we are in fact referring mainly to the changing ways of putting the words together. The range of available 'texts' – defined as 'sets of *connected* words' – undergoes constant change. Words themselves seldom change.

For the purpose of a historical interpretation of a text, it is therefore necessary to reconstruct the semantic structure of an epoque in the past. In order to do so, one must first of all establish the range of texts which were available to the contemporaries of the period which one proposes to study. This is because the contemporaries' system of meanings (semantic structure) is valid only within the range of texts available to them. As the range of available texts changes, so does the pattern of semantic coherence change. No doubt, historians will consult texts which were composed earlier than the period of their study. This is inevitable because, at any given time, a certain amount of anterior texts would survive; and they form part of the *corpus* of texts upon which the contemporaries' semantic structure is constructed. Also, historians will consult texts which were composed later than the period they proposed to examine (knowing that they were composed later). This is simply because the posterior texts – because of, say, their chronological proximity to the period being studied – might throw some light on the semantic structure of the period in question. Whether historians consult anterior texts or posterior texts, their aim is always the same. That is, to ascertain the meaning of a text which will – in the opinion of the historian – create least inconsistency within the semantic structure postulated as having been prevalent during the period under investigation.

It has often been suggested that the meaning of a text must be ascertained in light of the historical context in which it was composed. It is a cliché which is familiar to all of us, historians as well as non-historians. But, what is context? Is there *any* context (social, military, cultural, economic, etc.) which is knowable without having to rely on some textual sources? Of course, if a person is presented with a bill after having a meal in a restaurant, for example, he will understand the bill (a text) in light of the fact that he has finished a meal. In this case, the usefulness of the notion of context, as distinct from the text, is obvious. The person's understanding of the circumstances accompanying the composition of the text is non-linguistic and immediate. Food does not talk. But, can a historian hope to be in a comparable situation? The least we can say is that a historian is not a story-teller who recounts his own personal, first-hand experience of an event.

If, however, the person of our example keeps the bill, and later explains the situation to his friends and shows them the bill, his friends are in a situation somewhat comparable to that of a historian. Now, which is the text and which is the context? Both the bill and the accompanying explanation are in the form of words, the only difference being that the former is written and the latter is spoken. His friends have no means of understanding the so-called 'context' other than by textual means. Can they under-stand any of the texts offered to them – spoken or written – without having to 'interpret' them? By distinguishing a text from its historical context, and implicitly suggesting that the context is somehow not of textual nature, one commits the cognitive fallacy of confounding the reality with the means of knowing it. How do we know, for example, the so-called 'social context' of a thir-teenth-century English town, unless we rely on an interpretation of some texts? In fact, the distinction between a text and its historical context shows a crude resemblance with a type of laboratory experiment technique. There, measurement of a vari-able is conducted in an artificial environment where all other variables are controlled. Historical interpretation of a text cannot be done in this way. It is, as it were, a multi-variate analysis where not a single variable can be controlled.

We must reject the notion of 'historical context' because it is prone to epistemological errors. For a historian, the only sensible distinction – if one insists on having one – is between 'a text' and 'other texts'. In short, the precise meaning of a historical text can only be ascertained in relation to other texts which were simulta-neously available to the speech community of the period under investigation. Any reference to 'historical context' – if the term is employed to mean something other than texts – is misleading as well as unnecessary.[8]

To some extent, this point has already been recognised. Professor Skinner, for instance, points out certain inadequacies of the contextual approach, and characterises his approach as 'intertextual'.[9] However, he does not seem to be entirely consistent in rejecting the notion of context. Instead, he still stresses the supposed importance of 'the context and occasion of utterances'.[10] Moreover, he appears to suggest a distinction between the 'social context' and the 'wider linguistic context'.[11] In other words, he does not question the propriety of using the notion of 'context' as such. This is precisely the point to which I object. For example, he reaffirms Collingwood's argument in the following terms: '[U]nderstanding any proposition requires us to identify the question to which the proposition may be regarded as an answer'.[12] But how do we 'identify' the question? Is it a process which is somewhat different from the process of 'understanding' the proposition? Can we somehow get a free ride straight to the stage where the question is already 'identified' so that we do not have to go through the process of interpretation and understanding? Or, is it possible to introduce a time sequence so that the question is first identified before one embarks on an understanding of the proposition?[13] Ultimately, is it possible to 'identify' the question without 'understanding' the proposition? No proposition is born with labels such as 'proposition' or 'question'. All we have

---

[8] I have sometimes used the term 'context' in this book. However, that was to avoid a lengthy explanation of the process through which we arrived at our proposed interpretation of the given text. What I meant by 'context' is in fact the co-textual determinants within a given text, or the broader textual environment in which the given text is located. See Keith Allan, *Linguistic meaning*, 2 vols. (London, 1986) I, pp. 36–54 for a definition of 'context'.

[9] 'Meaning and understanding in the history of ideas', 8 *History and Theory* (1969) 3–53 at 47; 'A reply to my critics' in *Meaning and context, Quentin Skinner and his critics*, ed. James Tully (Oxford, 1988) p. 232, respectively.

[10] 'A reply to my critics', p. 274.

[11] 'Meaning and understanding', 47, 49.

[12] 'A reply to my critics', p. 274.

[13] Professor Skinner argues that '[t]o recover that context in any particular case, we may have to engage in . . . historical research' ('A reply to my critics', p. 275). Probably, he is assuming that this 'historical research' is to be conducted either prior to, or separately from, the research of the 'particular case' to be investigated (so that the particular case can *then* be interpreted once the context has been recovered as a result of the said 'historical research').

are propositions; and every proposition poses the same kinds of interpretative problems *all at the same time*. As far as I can see, there is no difference between 'understanding' of a proposition and 'identifying' of a question. In both cases, what we have is a proposition that needs 'interpretation'.

It has also been suggested that in order to understand the meaning of a statement, the circumstances under which it was issued must be recovered; for, otherwise, we may not know the intention of the agent (the issuer of the statement). It has been strenuously put forward that '[w]e need to find a means of recovering what the agent may have been *doing* in saying what was said, and hence of understanding what the agent may have meant by issuing an utterance'.[14] This approach, of course, is grounded upon the assumption that 'words are also deeds'. According to Professor Skinner, 'Austin's analysis of speech-acts provides us with a convenient way of making a point of fundamental importance about the understanding of utterances, and hence interpretation of texts.'[15] It is not my aim to examine whether the assumption that '[s]peech is also action' is in itself philosophically defensible. I simply wish to point out certain difficulties which might ensue when this assumption is applied to historical interpretation of a text.

Consider, for example, a text from Justinian's *Digest* 1. 5. 3, 'all men are either free-men or slaves (*omnes homines aut liberi sunt aut serui*)'. It may be a legitimate aim for a historian to interpret the meaning of the text. We may agree that in order to do that, it is necessary to recover what the 'agent', who issued the statement in the East Roman Empire in the sixth century, may have been *doing* in issuing the statement. We may – following Professor Skinner, who accepts Austin's terminology – suppose that the 'illocutionary force of the utterance' must be fully analysed before the meaning of the statement can be understood.

However, who was the 'agent' responsible for the issuance of the text of *D.* 1. 5. 3? The text itself was a sixth-century restatement of a second-century text of the Roman jurist Gaius. Who knows, Gaius himself might have copied it from yet another anterior author. Of course, copying of a statement does not destroy or replace the original statement. To re-issue a statement

---

[14] 'A reply to my critics', p. 260.   [15] Ibid.

is merely to compose yet another statement which has to be interpreted on its own. Consider, therefore, the text of *D*. 1. 5. 3 as an 'original' statement issued in the sixth century. Still, we may ask who the 'agent' was. Was it Justinian, who gave the final approval for the text of the *Digest*? Was it Tribonian, who was responsible for general editing work? Was it the individual jurists, who were involved in the compilation of the *Digest*? Was it all, some or none of the foregoing? How are we to assess the degree of involvement and the relative importance of these individuals' 'intentions'? If one wishes to rely on the notions of the 'agent' of a text and the 'intention' of the agent, one must be prepared to meet the following remarks of Sir Rupert Cross:

Only human beings can really have intentions, purposes or objects . . . The words [such as Parliamentary intention, legislative intention, etc.] are used by close analogy to the intentions of a single legislator. The analogy is more remote when the 'intention of Parliament' is used as a synonym for what the average member of Parliament of a particular epoch would have meant by certain words or expected as the consequences of a statutory provision . . . The analogy with the human mind emphasises a certain coherence and consistency. Consistency and coherence are values which guide judicial interpretation of the law, and the metaphor of a single legislative will or intention gives expression to this ideal. The expression is thus not so much a description as a linguistic convenience.[16]

His remarks are focused on the 'intention of Parliament'. But they are equally applicable to any text which cannot be proved to have been the result of sole authorship.

Austin's proposition 'speech is also action' may hold true if, and only if, one observes the speech *while it is being uttered*. The moment the speech is completed, however, it ceases to be action and, provided that its contents have somehow been recorded or registered, it begins a new life as a text. In other words, speech may be an action, but a text is not an action: it is the remnant of an action. This is why I believe that the 'speech-act' theory (which entails the concept of the 'agent' of an action) creates more problems than it can solve if it is invoked in interpreting a text. Recorded words must be distinguished from an action. An action is a singular event. It is possible, and indeed necessary, to postulate the 'agent' of an action. Being a singular event, an action need not, and cannot, be examined separately from its agent and

---

[16] Cross, *Statutory interpretation*, p. 26.

the circumstances under which it was carried out. Once the action is removed from its agent and the circumstances, it loses its singularity, and it is no longer an action. Words, while they are being composed and issued, have the characteristics of a deed. But once they are completed and registered in memory or recorded in physical devices, words cease to be an action; they become 'traces' of an action.

Traces can remain. They can exist as a topic of analysis over a period of time. An action, however, cannot be said to exist as soon as it is completed. Between the present moment of analysis and the past moment of its singular occurrence, the action cannot be said to continue its existence as an object of analysis. Therefore, each time an action is analysed, one must always go back to the original circumstances of its occurrence. In this case, the investigator would have no choice but to examine the 'intention' of the 'agent' and various other factors which are necessary to reconstruct the singularity of the event. But, a text can be said to exist even after the moment of its initial issuance. Furthermore, as soon as the issuance is completed, the agent or the circumstances of utterance quickly lose significance. From then on, it is the singularity of reception, rather than the singularity of issuance, which determines the meaning of a text.[17] The 'agent' and the 'intention' of the agent – as they are merely some of the factors contributing to the singularity of the issuance – need not necessarily be taken into account because they no longer conclusively determine the meaning of the text.

In my view, the model which is grounded upon the 'speech-act' analysis is somewhat inadequate to bring out the characteristics of the historical interpretation, which is not so much about utterances currently being issued as about the remnant of utterances issued earlier. One may perhaps understand 'issuing' in a broad sense so that each time a text is communicated to a user, it is being issued anew by an 'imaginary' agent which the user might

---

[17] The 'historical' interpretation is no doubt a 'modern' approach to texts. Before historicism became fashionable, texts had been received and interpreted with very different aims and concerns. The meanings reached thereby may be different from those arrived at through a 'historical' interpretation of the same text. The 'unhistorical' meanings of a text, however, must not be brushed aside as 'wrong' meanings. Ultimately, historicism itself is no more than one particular way of *receiving* a text.

postulate. This will provide a means of explaining that a text is reusable over a long period of time in many different ways. This will also enable one to claim that a text is no different from utterance of a speech; therefore, if historians want to ascertain the meaning of a text, they must always investigate the 'original' circumstances of utterance, or, to use Professor Skinner's phrase, 'what the agent might have been doing in issuing the statement'. But I doubt whether such an explanation – let us ignore the violence it does to the conventional usage of the term 'issue' – can resolve the problem which I shall now discuss.

Whenever a text is communicated to a user, the user interprets the text. In this sense, a historian is also a 'user' of a text. Historians who embark on an interpretation of a text will often find that they are not the only users of the text. A text can, in theory, have an infinite number of users before it reaches a historian. Moreover, no historian can claim to be the last user of the text. All users interpret the text. Now, my question is: what distinguishes a historian's interpretation of a text from all other users' interpretation of the same text? Especially, how is historical interpretation to be distinguished from legal interpretation? As we saw, some lawyers claim that their aim is to understand the 'true intent of the legislature'.

To say that historians deal with 'old' texts does not explain any features peculiar to historical interpretation of a text. Since *all* recorded texts are *past* texts – no matter how brief is the time which has lapsed since the text was issued – *all* interpreters deal with 'old' texts. As we saw, however, 'issuing' may be understood in such a way as to allow no time lag between issuance and interpretation of a text. In that case, *all* texts would be *present* texts.

Professor Skinner, on the other hand, offers the following explanation which stresses the methodological uniqueness of historical interpretation:

[T]he appropriate methodology for the history of ideas must be concerned, first of all, to delineate the whole range of communications which could have been conventionally performed on the given occasion by the utterance of the given utterance, and, next, to trace the relations between the given utterance and this wider linguistic context as a means of decoding the actual intention of the given writer.[18]

---

[18] 'Meaning and understanding', p. 49.

If, however, one explains that decoding of the 'actual intention of the given writer' is the aim of historical interpretation, it would be somewhat difficult to maintain a distinction between historical interpretation and the legal interpretation of those who claim that their mission is to 'arrive at the legislative intention'. This is not to suggest that Professor Skinner does not, or will not, recognise the difference between legal, theological or literary interpretation of texts on the one hand, and historical interpretation of texts on the other.[19] The point I am making is simply that if one insists on having an issuer/interpreter (or agent/historian) model, one is likely to experience some difficulty in explaining the characteristic features of historical interpretation which distinguish it from other types of text interpretation activities.

In my view, the only 'agent' worth postulating is the interpreter himself. The only 'intention' worth mentioning is the interpreter's intention to understand the texts which he investigates. The business, therefore, is between the interpreter – a historian, a lawyer, a theologian, a literary critic, etc. – and the texts. The composer of a text, whether dead or alive, can never interfere with this business and *dictate*[20] to the interpreter how he should interpret his (the composer's) text. This point can be illustrated by what my readers may do with this very text of mine. Those who read the text which I now compose will form a view as to what I intend to mean by this text (or what I intend to achieve by issuing this text). But their attribution of my intention is a business of their own, about which I cannot do anything authoritative. If I should say or write something to correct my interpreters and clarify what I really meant to say, I should simply have composed yet another text. Both my former and latter texts would then be in the hands of my interpreters, who may make another attempt at attributing an intention to me in light of the added information. In other words, each time an author issues a text, the text is wholly and irrevocably removed from the author

---

[19] Rather, he has certainly recognised that the distinctive feature of historical interpretation must be sought in its contribution to illuminating the change of language. See 'Meaning and understanding', p. 50 ('The understanding of statements uttered in the past clearly raises special issues and might yield special insights, especially about the conditions under which languages change').

[20] A living author can, of course, *influence* the interpretation of his texts. But his interpreters are no less *influential* in this matter.

and falls into the hands of its interpreters. As soon as a text is communicated to its interpreters, the author loses the authority as to the meaning of that text. If the author wishes fully to retain his authority over the meaning of his text, there is only one possible way of doing it: not to communicate the text. As far as communicated texts are concerned, the question is not what senses the supposed 'agent (author)' must have made, would have made, or is deemed to have made. The question is what senses can the interpreter make of the texts.

Discarding the concepts of 'agent' as well as its 'intention' and focusing instead on the text and its reception do not necessarily lead, as some post-modernist authors would appear to claim, to the 'vastly open field of indeterminate and indeterminable interpretations' where each interpreter can claim an unencumbered right to play an endless game.[21] As each speech community draws upon a *limited* range of texts at any given time, the possibility of interpreting a text located in a given speech community is also limited. The so-called limitless play of meanings must remain an improbable hypothetical possibility which is conceivable only when *all* texts available to human species are aggregated over an indefinite period of time. In reality, a text situated in a particular moment in history carries a limited range of possible meanings. Whether or not a particular historian's interpretation of the text is an optimum solution can, and can only, be determined by the good judgement of the professional body of historians. Whether they like it or not, they are the ultimate arbiters. There is, after all, no agency over and above the present body of established historians which retains a superior authority to determine the ultimate truth of a historian's interpretation of text.

An interpreter can, of course, choose to remain silent. All we can say is that we are not concerned with such an interpreter. We only deal with those interpreters who choose to communicate their understanding. Communication cannot succeed unless the

---

[21] See, for example, Jacques Derrida, 'La structure, le signe et le jeu' in his *L'écriture et la différence* (Paris, 1967) p. 411 ('L'absence de signifié transcendantal étend à l'infini le champ et le jeu de la signification'); p. 427 ('Dans le hasard absolu, l'affirmation se livre aussi à l'indétermination *génétique*, à l'aventure *séminale* de la trace').

participants share the same semantic structure.[22] In this respect, lawyers, theologians, literary critics and historians all rely on the present semantic structure to communicate their understanding of texts. This, however, is where the unique feature of historical interpretation comes to the fore. What distinguishes history writing from other text interpretation activities is that the history writer relies on the semantic structure of the present in order to talk about a semantic structure of the past. Lawyers, even when they claim to investigate the intention of the legislator, remain entirely within the semantic structure of the present. The 'original' intention of the legislator is discussed, understood and communicated among lawyers and judges who need not postulate any semantic structure other than the present one. The uniqueness of historical interpretation must be found in the intention of the historians themselves. In other words, historians have the two-fold intention: i) to ascertain the meaning of a text which will create the least conflict with a postulated semantic structure of the past; and ii) to communicate such an interpretation to his colleagues, or to the general public, using the semantic structure of the present. The interesting thing about language is that it allows a means of talking about itself – its past, present, and future self.

[22] Skinner, 'Meaning and understanding', p. 24 ('If there is to be any prospect that the observer will successfully communicate his understanding within his own culture, it is . . . inescapable that he should apply his own familiar criteria of classification and discrimination').

BIBLIOGRAPHY

NOTE

A brief chapter on 'Aliens' in Pollock and Maitland, *The history of English law*, which first appeared in 1895 (vol. I, pp. 441–50) forms the basis of modern British historians' understanding of the history of the English law of alien status. Sir Maurice Powicke's monumental work on the loss of Normandy (1913) discusses the circumstances surrounding the seizure of *terrae Normannorum* in great detail. But Powicke does not doubt Maitland's thesis that 'the king's claims to seize the lands of aliens is an exaggerated generalisation of his claim to seize the lands of his French enemies' (p. 423). A relatively longer chapter entitled 'subjects and aliens' in Holdsworth, *A history of English law*, vol. IX (first published in 1926, pp. 72–104) does not contain much original argument as far as the origin of the law of alien status is concerned. He repeats Maitland's claim that the English law of alien status began with the loss of Normandy. Holdsworth adds, unhelpfully, a further confusion that the doctrine of allegiance 'has its roots in the feudal idea of a personal duty of fealty to the lord from whom land is held' (p. 72). This confusion, of course, dates from some of the sixteenth-century authors (see our discussion in chapter 7). The confusion lingered on into the twentieth century. The second half of John Salmond's somewhat jurisprudential speculation on 'Citizenship and allegiance' – appearing in the *Law Quarterly Review* in 1901 and 1902 – revolves around the conviction that 'the modern law of citizenship has its immediate source in feudalism'. Salmond's attempt to trace the origin of the modern law of citizenship was done without any reference to Maitland's work: understandably so, because Maitland was of opinion that 'feudalism is opposed to tribalism and even to nationalism: we become a lord's subjects by doing homage to him, and this done, the nationality . . . and the place of our birth are insignificant'. Clive Parry's *British nationality law and the history of naturalisation* (Milan, 1954) offers some discussion of materials antedating the statute *De natis ultra mare* (1351) and a great deal of discussion on the letters patent issued to foreigners in the fourteenth and fifteenth centuries. His argument is, on the whole, judicial rather than historical. He assumes Maitland's explanation of the origin of the law of alien status as unquestionable and proceeds

228

to argue that the mid-fourteenth-century letters patent granting the liberties of a city (London, usually) must be viewed as the forerunners of the letters of denization (see our discussion in chapter 2). There are a number of works of varying quality dealing with nationality from the viewpoint of immigration law and international law. They sometimes contain a chapter on the history of nationality law which simply reproduces the works of Maitland and Holdsworth in a summarised format. A useful bibliography for this type of work can be found in Ann Dummett and Andrew Nicol, *Subjects, citizens, aliens and others: nationality and immigration law* (London, 1990). On the history of the Scottish law of alien status, see A. C. Evans, 'Nationality law in pre-union Scotland', 28 *Juridical Review*, n.s. (1983) 36–50. On the history of the law of alien status in the Irish context, see G. J. Hand, 'Aspects of alien status in medieval English law' in Dafydd Jenkins (ed.) *Legal history studies, 1972* (Cardiff, 1975) pp. 129–35.

MANUSCRIPT SOURCES

BL Hargrave MS 379, fos. 202–6 (Liber primus, Johaniis Page, De personis)
BL Harleian MS 555, fos. 11r–47v (Anthony Brown's treatise)
BL Harleian MS 849, fos. 1–18 (Plowden's treatise, 1567)
BL Harleian MS 4627, fos. 10r-26v ('Allegations against the Surmised Title . . .')

Cambridge University Library, MS Gg. iii. 34, fos. 107–17 (an answer to 'Allegations against . . .')
Cambridge University Library, MSS Mm. 6. 70. f. 1–30; Add. 9212 ('Certaine errours uppon the statute. . .')

Public Record Office, King's Remembrancer, Memoranda rolls, 18 m. 12d
Public Record Office, Charter rolls, 14 Henry III, part 2, m. 1; 21 Henry III, m. 6; 37 Henry III, m. 21
Public Record Office, Close rolls, 17 Edward III, part 2, m. 29v
Public Record Office, Patent rolls, 17 Edward II, part 2, m. 5; 9 Edward III, part 2, m. 4; 17 Edward III, part 2, m. 32v; 25 Edward III, part 1, m. 27; 50 Edward III, part 1, m. 5

Borthwick Institute, York, Reg. 10, fo. 255v
Cumbria County Record Office, Carlisle, DRC/1/1, fo. 240
Cambridge University Library, G/1/1 (Ely diocesan records), fo. 89v

PRINTED SOURCES

Selden Society publications

Beverley town documents (1900)
Borough customs, 2 vols. (1904, 1906)

Doctor and student (1974)
Early thirteenth-century registers of writs (1970)
The eyre of Kent, 6–7 Edward II, 1313–1314, vols. I and III (1909, 1913)
The eyre of London, 14 Edward II, 1321, 2 vols. (1968–9)
The eyre of Northamptonshire, 1329–1330, 2 vols. (1981–2)
Fleta, vols. II and III (1955, 1972)
Hale's prerogative of the king (1975)
Leet jurisdiction in the city of Norwich during the thirteenth and fourteenth centuries (1891)
The mirror of justices (1893)
Novae Narrationes (1963)
Reports from the lost notebooks of Sir James Dyer, 2 vols. (1993–4)
Royal writs in England from the Conquest to Glanvill (1958–9)
Select cases before the King s Council, 1243–1482 (1918)
Select cases concerning the law merchant, 1270–1638, vol. I (1908)
Select cases in the court of King's Bench under Edward I, vols. I and III (1936, 1939)
Select passages from the works of Bracton and Azo (1894)
Select pleas in manorial and other seignorial courts, vol. I (1888)
Year Books of 1–2 Edward II, 1307–1309 (1903)
Year Books of 3 Edward II, 1309–1310 (1905)
Year Books of 3–4 Edward II, 1309–1311 (1907)
Year Books of 4 Edward II, 1310–1311 (1911)
Year Books of 9 Edward II, 1313–1316 (1928)

Rolls series

Annales Monastici, 5 vols,. ed. H. R. Luard (1864–9) vol. III
Cartulary of the Abbey of Ramsey, 3 vols., ed. W. H. Hart and A. L. Ponsonby (1884–93)
Chronicles of the reigns of Edward I and Edward II, 2 vols., ed. W. Stubbs (1882–3) vol. I (*Annales Londonienses*)
Chronicon Abbatiae Rameseiensis, ed. W. D. Macray (1886)
Cotton, Bartholomew, *Historia Anglicana*, ed. H. R. Luard (1859)
Grosseteste, Robert, *Epistolae*, ed. H. R. Luard (1861)
Munimenta Gildhallae Londoniensis: liber albus, liber custumarum, et liber Horn, 3 vols., ed. H. T. Riley (London, 1859–62) vol. I (*Liber albus*)
Paris, Matthew, *Chronica majora*, 7 vols., ed. H. R. Luard (1872–83)
Year Books of 11–20 Edward III, ed. A. J. Horwood and L. O. Pike (1883–1911)

Records Commission

Foedera, conventiones, litterae, et cujuscunque generis acta publica . . ., ed. T. Rymer, 4 vols. (1816–69)
Placita de Quo Warranto, ed. W. Illingworth (1818)
Rotuli de oblatis et finibus in Turri Londiniensi asservati . . ., ed. T. D. Hardy (1835)

Rotuli Normanniae in Turri Londiniensi asservati . . . ed. T. D. Hardy
     (1835)
Statutes of the realm, 9 vols. (1816–28)

Public Record Office

Calendar of charter rolls
Calendar of close rolls
*Calendar of entries in the papal registers relating to Great Britain and
     Ireland*, Papal letters
Calendar of fine rolls
Calendar of inquisitions miscellaneous
Calendar of patent rolls
Close rolls 1242–1247
Curia regis rolls
Patent rolls of Henry III

Early printed statute-books (in chronological order)

The earliest extant abridgement of statutes (printed in *c.* 1481). *Short-title
     catalogue of English books 1475–1640* (STC) No. 9513
Nova statuta, printed by W. de Machlinia (*c.* 1482)
Abbreuiamentum statutorum . . ., printed by R. Pynson (London, 1499).
     STC No. 9514
John Rastell's statute-books, British Library classmark B. E. 11/1 (1519);
     C. 65. aa. 13 (1527)
Abbreuiamentum statutorum . . ., printed by R. Pynson (1521). STC No.
     9516
Le breggement de touts les estatuts . . . printed by R. Pynson (London,
     1528). STC No. 9517
*Magnum abbreuiamentum statutorum Anglie usqz ad annum xv H. viii
     inclusiue*, printed by J. Rastell (London, 1528)
The great boke of statutes, printed by R. Redman, T. Berthelet and
     J. Rastell (London, *c.* 1533)
*The greate abbrydgement of all the statutes of Englande untyll the xxx yere of
     the reygne of our moste drad souerayne lorde kynge Henry the eyght* . . .,
     printed by W. Rastell (London, *c.* 1538)
Abridgement of statutes, printed by R. Redman (London, 1539). STC No.
     9542
The great charter called in latyn Magna Carta with divers olde statutes,
     printed by R. Redman (London, *c.* 1540s)
A collection of all the statutes . . ., printed by W. Rastell (London, 1557,
     1559)

Other printed sources

Andolf, Sven (ed.) *Les péages des foires de Chalon-sur-Saône* (Göteborg,
     1971)

Aristotle, *The politics and the constitution of Athens*, ed. and trans. Stephen Everson (Cambridge, 1996)

d'Aungerville of Bury, Richard, *Fragments of his register and other documents*, ed. G. W. Kitchin, 119 Surtee society (1910)

Ballard, Adolphus (ed.) *British borough charters, 1042–1216* (Cambridge, 1913)

Bateson, Mary, 'A London municipal collection of the reign of John', 17 *English Historical Review* (1902) 495–502, 711–18

Beaumanoir, Philippe de, *Coutumes de Veauvaisis*, ed. Amédée Salmon, 2 vols. (Paris, 1899–1900)

Bracton on the laws and customs of England, 4 vols., trans. S. Thorne (Cambridge, Mass., 1968–77)

Britton, 2 vols., ed. and trans. F. M. Nichols (Oxford, 1865)

Brook, R., *Graunde Abridgement* (London, 1573)

Calendar of letter-books preserved . . . at the Guildhall, Letter Book E, c. 1314–1337, ed. R. R. Sharpe (London, 1903)

Cobbett, W., et al. (eds.) *Complete collection of state trials*, vol. II (London, 1809)

Coke, Sir Edward, *The first part of the Institutes of the laws of England; or a commentary upon Littleton* (Coke on Littleton) 18th edn, 2 vols. (London, 1823)

Dictionarium Linguae Latinae et Anglicanae, ed. Thomas Thomas (Cambridge, 1587)

Dictionary of medieval Latin from British sources, fasc. III (London, 1986)

The Digest of Justinian, Latin text edited by T. Mommsen and P. Krueger, English translation supervised by A. Watson, 4 vols. (Philadelphia, 1985)

Downer, L. J. (ed.) *Leges Henrici primi* (Oxford, 1972)

Fitzherbert, Anthony, *Diversite de courtz et lour iurisdictions et alia necessaria et utilia*, printed by R. Redman (London, 1523)

    Graunde Abridgement (London, c. 1514–16)

    [The new] *Natura brevium* (London, 1730)

Fortescue, Sir John, *De laudibus legum Anglie*, ed. and trans. S. B. Chrimes (Cambridge, 1942)

Gordon, W. M., and O. F. Robinson (trans.) *The Institutes of Gaius*, from the Latin text of E. Seckel and B. Kuebler (Ithaca, N.Y., 1988)

Hall, G. D. G. (ed.) *The treatise on the laws and customs of the realm of England commonly called Glanvill*, reprinted with a guide to further reading by M. T. Clanchy (Oxford, 1993)

Hansisches Urkundenbuch, ed. K. Höhlbaum (Halle, 1876–)

Harington, John, *A tract on the succession to the crown* (written in 1602) ed. Clements Markham (London, 1880)

Historia Dunelmensis . . ., ed. J. Raine (London, 1839)

Holmes, Thomas S. (ed.) *The register of Ralph of Shrewsbury, bishop of Bath and Wells, 1329–1363*, 2 vols. (London, 1896)

The Jacobean union: six tracts of 1604, ed. B. Galloway and B. Levack (Edinburgh, 1985)

King James VI and I, *Political writings*, ed. Johann P. Sommerville (Cambridge, 1994)

Le livre des assises et pleas del Corone (London, 1679)

Leslie, J., *A defence of the honor of Mary* . . . (London, 1569)

Lewis, Frank, Pedes finium; *or fines relating to the county of Surrey* (Guildford, 1894)

Li livres de jostice et de plet, ed. P. N. Rapetti (Paris, 1850)

Liebermann, Felix (ed.) *Die Gesetze der Angelsachsen*, vol. I (Halle, 1903)

Littleton, T., *Tenures*, printed by R. Pynson (London, *c.* 1510)

Littleton's Tenures in English, trans. E. Wambaugh (Washington, D.C., 1903)

Mittellateinisches Wörterbuch, vol. I fasc. 3 (Munich, 1960)

Monumenta Germaniae Historica, LL. Capitularia, vol. II

Nevill, Ralph, 'Surrey feet of fines', 13 *Surrey Archaeological Collection* (1897), pp. 139–40

The Old tenures, c. 1515, and the Old natura brevium, c. 1518, reprinted with an introduction by M. S. Arnold (London, 1974)

Ordonnances des roys de France de la troisième race . . ., vol. III (1355–64), ed. D.-F. Secousse (Paris, 1732)

Paris, John of, *On royal and papal power*, trans. J. A. Watt (Toronto, 1971)

Plowden, E. *Les Comentaries ou les reportes de dyvers cases* (London, 1571)

Rastell, John, *The exposicions of the termys of the law of england and the nature of the writt . . . gaderyd and brevely compylyd for yong men very necessarye* (*c.* 1525–7)

Tabula libri magni abbreviamenti librorum legum Anglorum (1517)

Regesta pontificum Romanorum, 2 vols., ed. A. Potthast (Berlin, 1874)

Revised medieval Latin word-list from British and Irish sources, ed. R. E. Latham (London, 1965)

Riley, Henry T. (trans.) *Liber albus, the whitebook of the city of London* (London, 1861)

Rolle, Henry, *Abridgment des plusieurs cases*, 2 vols. (London, 1668)

Rotuli Parliamentorum, 6 vols. (London, 1767–77)

Stones, E. L. G., *Anglo-Scottish relations 1174–1328*, 2nd edn (Oxford, 1970)

Storey, R. L. (ed.) *The register of John Kirkby, bishop of Carlisle, 1332–1352 and the register of John Ross, bishop of Carlisle, 1325–1332*, 2 vols.,(Woodbridge, 1993, 1995)

Tanner, J. R. (ed.) *Constitutional documents of the reign of James I, 1603–1625* (Cambridge, 1930)

Thesaurus Linguae Latinae, vol. I (Leipzig, 1903)

Thorpe, Benjamin (ed.), *Ancient laws and institutes of England*, vol. I (London, 1840)

Year Books of certain regnal years of Edward III and Edward IV (London, 1679–80, the so-called Maynard's edition)

Year Books of Richard II (published by Ames Foundation)

234   *Bibliography*

SECONDARY MATERIALS

Allan, Keith, *Linguistic meaning*, 2 vols. (London, 1986)
Allard, Paul, *Les Esclaves chrétiens depuis les premiers temps de l'Eglise jusqu'à la fin de la domination romaine en Occident*, 2nd edn (Paris, 1876)
Allmand, Christopher, *The Hundred Years War, England and France at war, c. 1300 – c. 1450* (Cambridge, 1989)
Arkoun, Mohammed, *L'Islam*, 2nd edn (Paris, 1992)
Axton, Marie, 'The influence of Edmund Plowden's succession treatise', 37 *Huntington Library Quarterly* (1974) 209–26
Baker, John H., *An introduction to English legal history*, 3rd edn (London, 1990)
    'Records, reports and the origins of case-law in England' in his (ed.) *Judicial records, law reports, and the growth of case law* (Berlin, 1989) pp. 15–46
Ballard, A. and James Tait (eds.) *British borough charters, 1216–1307* (Cambridge, 1923)
Barbey, Jean, *Etre roi: le roi et son gouvernement en France de Clovis à Louis XVI* (Paris, 1992)
Barraclough, Geoffrey, *Papal provisions* (Oxford, 1935)
Barrell, A. D. M., 'The effect of papal provisions on Yorkshire parishes, 1342–1370', 28 *Northern History* (1992) 92–109
    'The ordinance of provisors of 1343', 64 *Historical Research* (1991) 264–77
Bateson, Mary, 'Aske's answer regarding the illegitimacy of Lady Mary', 5 *English Historical Review* (1890) 562–4
Bean, J. M. W., *The decline of English feudalism 1215–1540* (Manchester, 1968)
Beardwood, Alice, *Alien merchants in England 1350–1377: their legal and economic position* (Cambridge, Mass., 1931)
    'Mercantile antecedents of the English naturalization laws', 16 *Medievalia et Humanistica* (1964) 64–76
Bennion, Francis, *Statutory interpretation*, 2nd edn (London, 1992)
Blackstone, William, *Commentaries on the laws of England*, 4 vols. (Oxford, 1765–9)
Bloch, Marc, 'Liberté et servitude personnelle au moyen âge, particulièrement en France: contribution à une étude des classes', in his *Mélanges historiques*, vol. I (Paris, 1963) pp. 286–355
    'Pour une histoire comparée des sociétés européennes', 46 *Revue de Synthèse Historique* (1925) 15–50
Bodin, Jean, *Exposé du droit universel*, trans. Lucien Jerphagnon (Paris, 1985)
    Method for the easy comprehension of history, trans. Beatrice Reynolds (New York, 1945)
    Les Six livres de la republique, reprinted with editorial corrections by Christiane Frémont, Marie-Dominique Couzinet and Henri Rochais, 6 vols. (Paris, 1986)
    Jean Bodin: actes du colloque interdisciplinaire d'Angers, 24 au 27 mai, 1984, 2 vols. (Angers, 1985)

Boizet, Jacques, *Les Lettres de naturalité sous l'ancien régime* (Paris, 1943)

Boulet-Sautel, M., 'L'Aubain dans la France coutumière du moyen âge' in *L'Etranger*, part 2, (Brussels, 1958) pp. 65–100

Bournazel, Eric and Jean-Pierre Poly, *La mutation féodale*, 1st edn (Paris, 1980)

Bradley, Keith, *Slavery and society at Rome* (Cambridge, 1994)

Bradshaw, Brendan and John Morrill (eds.) *The British Problem, 1534–1707: State formation in the Atlantic Archipelago* (Basingstoke, 1996)

Brodhurst, Spencer, 'The merchants of the staple', 17 *Law Quarterly Review* (1901) 56–76

Brooke, Christopher, et al., *London, 800–1216: the shaping of a city* (London, 1975)

Brown, A. L., *The early history of the clerkship of the Council* (Glasgow, 1969)

The governance of late medieval England (London, 1989)

Buckland, W. W., *The Roman law of slavery* (Cambridge, 1908)

'Wardour Street Roman law', 17 *Law Quarterly Review* (1901) 179–92

Bury, J. B., *History of the later Roman Empire from Arcadius to Irene* (London, 1889)

Caenegem, R. C. van, *The birth of the English common law*, 2nd edn (Cambridge, 1988)

Caillet, Louis, *La Papauté d'Avignon et l'église de France – la politique bénéficiale du pape Jean XXII en France, 1316–1334* (Paris, 1975)

Carpenter, D. A., 'King Henry III's "statute" against aliens, July 1263', 107 *English Historical Review* (1992) 925–43

Chaplais, Pierre, 'La souveraineté du roi de France et le pouvoir législatif en Guyenne au début du XIVe siècle', *Le Moyen Age*, 4th series (1963) 449–69

Cheyette, F., 'Kings, courts, cures, and sinecures: the statute of provisors and the common law', 19 *Traditio* (1963) 295–349

Clerke, William, *The triall of Bastardie . . .* (London, 1594)

Coleman, Janet, 'Medieval discussions of property: *Ratio* and *Dominium* according to John of Paris and Marsilius of Padua', 4 *History of Political Thought* (1983) 209–28

'Property and poverty' in *The Cambridge history of medieval political thought, c. 350 – c. 1450*, ed. J. H. Burns (Cambridge, 1987) pp. 604–48

Congar, Yves, ' "Ecclesia" et "populus (fidelis)" dans l'ecclésiologie de S. Thomas' in *St Thomas Aquinas 1274–1974*, ed. Armand Maurer (Toronto, 1974) pp. 159–73

Constable, Marianne, *The law of the other: the half-alien jury and changing conceptions of citizenship, law and knowledge* (Chicago, 1994)

Craecker-Dussart, Cr. de, 'L'Evolution du sauf-conduit dans les principautés de la Basse-Lotharingie du VIIIe au XIVe siècle', 80 *Le Moyen Age* (1974) 185–243

Cross, Rupert, *Statutory interpretation*, 2nd edn (London, 1987)

Deeley, Ann, 'Papal provisions and royal rights of patronage in the early fourteenth century', 43 *English Historical Review* (1928) 505

Denton, Jeffrey H., *Robert Winchelsey and the Crown 1294–1313* (Cambridge, 1980)

Derrida, Jacques, *L'Ecriture et la différence* (Paris, 1967)

Devisscher, F., *Nouvelles études de droit romain public et privé* (Milan, 1949)

Dickinson, J. C., *The later Middle Ages: from the Norman Conquest to the eve of the Reformation – an ecclesiastical history of England* (London, 1979)

Doehaerd, Renée, 'Féodalité et commerce: remarques sur le conduit des marchands, XIe – XIIIe siècles' in *La Noblesse au moyen âge, XIe–XVe siècles*, ed. Philippe Contamine (Paris, 1976) pp. 203–17

Dollinger, Philippe, *La Hanse, XIIe–XVIIe siècles* (Paris, 1964)

Drake, Francis, *Eboracum: or the history and antiquities of the city of York* (London, 1736)

Duby, George, *Guillaume le Maréchal* (Paris, 1984)

Ehrhardt, Arnold, 'Das Corpus Christi und die Korporationen im spät-römischen Recht', 70, 71 *Zeitschrift der Savigny-Stiftung für Rechtsgeschichte* (1953, 1954) 299–347; 25–40

Eliachevitch, Basile, *La Personnalité juridique en droit privé romain* (Paris, 1942)

Elliott, John, 'National and comparative history', an inaugural lecture in Oxford University, 10 May 1991

Enever, F. A., *History of the law of distress* (London, 1931)

Favier, Jean, *De l'or et des épices: naissance de l'homme d'affaires au moyen âge* (Paris, 1987)

Finley, M., *Ancient slavery and modern ideology* (London, 1980)

Fisher, H. A. L. (ed.) *The collected papers of F. W. Maitland*, vol. I (Cambridge, 1911)

Flahiff, G. B., 'The writ of prohibition to Court Christian in the thirteenth century', 6, 7 *Medieval Studies* (1944, 1945) 261–313; 229–90

Fogle, French and Louis Knafla (eds.) *Patronage in late Renaissance England, papers read at a Clark Library Seminar, 14 May 1977* (Los Angeles, 1983)

Franklin, Julian, *Jean Bodin and the rise of absolutist theory* (Cambridge, 1973)

  Jean Bodin and the sixteenth-century revolution in the methodology of law and history (Westport, Conn., 1977, first published in 1963)

Franklin, Julian, ed. and trans., *On sovereignty: four chapters from the six books of the commonwealth* (Cambridge, 1992)

Frederickson, G. M., 'Comparative history' in *The past before us*, ed. M. Kammen (Ithaca, 1980) pp. 457–73

Le Fonctionnement administratif de la papauté d'Avignon: aux origines de l'état moderne (Paris, 1990)

Galloway, Bruce, *The union of England and Scotland, 1603–1608* (Edinburgh, 1986)

Ganshof, François-L., 'L'Etranger dans la monarchie Franque' in *L'Etranger*, part 2 (Brussels, 1958) pp. 5–36

Qu'est-ce que la féodalité? 5th edn (Paris, 1982)

Ganzer, K., *Papsttum und Bistumsbesetzungen im der Zeit von Gregor IX. bis Bonifaz VIII.: ein Beitrag zur päpstlichen Reservationen* (Cologne, 1968)

Garnett, George, '"Franci et Angli": the legal distinctions between peoples after the Conquest', in *Anglo-Norman studies*, ed. R. Allen Brown, vol. VIII (Woodbridge, 1986) pp. 109–37

Gaudemet, Jean, *La Collation par le roi de France des bénéfices vacants en régale, dès origines à la fin du XIVe siècle* (Paris, 1935)

Le Gouvernement de l'église à l'époque classique, vol. II, *Le gouvernement local* (Paris, 1979)

'Un point de rencontre entre les pouvoirs politiques et l'église: le choix des évêques' in *Etat et Eglise dans la genèse de l'état moderne*, ed. J.-P. Genet and B. Vincent (Madrid, 1986) pp. 279–93

'Régale' in *Dictionnaire de droit canonique*, vol. VII (Paris, 1960) cols. 494–532, cols. 514–19

Genet, J.-P. (ed.) *L'Etat moderne: genèse – bilans et perspectives* (Paris, 1990)

Genet, J.-P. and B. Vincent (eds.) *Etat et Eglise dans la genèse de l'état moderne* (Madrid, 1986)

Gierke, Otto von, *Natural law and the theory of society, 1500 to 1800*, trans. E. Barker, 2 vols. (Cambridge, 1934)

Giordanengo, Gérard, 'Etat et droit féodal en France (XIIe–XIVe siècles)' in *L'Etat moderne: le droit, l'espace et les formes de l'état*, ed. N. Coulet and J.-P. Genet (Paris, 1990) pp. 61–83

Given-Wilson, Chris, *The English nobility in the Middle Ages: the fourteenth-century political community* (London, 1987)

Given-Wilson, Chris and Alice Curteis, *The royal bastards of medieval England* (London, 1984)

Gouron, André and A. Rigaudière (eds.) *Renaissance du pouvoir législatif et genèse de l'état* (Montpellier, 1988)

Graham, Rose, 'Four alien priories in Monmouthshire', 35 *Journal of British Archaeological Association* (1929) 102–21

'The papal schism of 1378 and the English province of the order of Cluny' in her (ed.) *English ecclesiastical studies* (London, 1929) pp. 46–61

Gras, Norman, *The early English customs system* (Cambridge, Mass., 1918)

Gray, J. W., 'The *Ius praesentandi* in England from the Constitutions of Clarendon to Bracton', 67 *English Historical Review* (1952) 481–509

Griffiths, Ralph A., 'The English realm and dominions and the king's subjects in the later Middle Ages' in *Aspects of late medieval government and society*, ed. J. G. Rowe (Toronto, 1986) pp. 83–105

Grignaschi, Mario, 'La Définition du *Civis* dans la scholastique' in *Gouvernés et gouvernants*, part 3 (Brussels, 1966) pp. 71–88

Gross, Charles, *The gild merchant: a contribution to British municipal history*, 2 vols. (Oxford, 1890)

Grossi, Paolo (ed.) *Storia sociale e dimensione giuridica* (Milan, 1986)

Guillemain, Bernard, *La Politique bénéficiale du pape Benoît XII, 1334–1342* (Paris, 1952)

Güterbock, Carl, *Henricus de Bracton und sein Verhältniss zum Römischen Rechte* (Berlin, 1862)

Guterman, Simeon L., *The principle of the personality of law in the Germanic kingdoms of western Europe from the fifth to the eleventh century* (New York, 1988)

Haller, J., *Papsttum und Kirchenreform*, vol. I (Berlin, 1903)

Hand, G. J., 'Aspects of alien status in medieval English law' in *Legal history studies, 1972*, ed. Dafydd Jenkins (Cardiff, 1975) pp. 129–35

Harbin, George, *The hereditary right of the crown of England asserted* (London, 1713)

Harouel, J. L., J. Barbey, E. Bournazel et al., *Histoire des institutions: de l'époque franque à la Révolution*, 2nd edn (Paris, 1989)

Harvey, Margaret, 'The benefice as property: an aspect of Anglo-Papal relations during the pontificate of Martin V, 1417–1431', in *The church and wealth*, ed. W. J. Sheils and Diana Wood (Oxford, 1987) pp. 161–73

Hazeltine, H. D., et al. (eds.) *Maitland – selected essays* (Cambridge, 1936)

Heath, Peter, *Church and realm, 1272–1461: conflict and collaboration in an age of crises* (London, 1988)

Helmholz, Richard H., 'Bastardy litigation in medieval England' in his *Canon law and the law of England* (London, 1987) pp. 187–210

Highfield, J. R. L., 'The relations between the Church and the English crown from the death of Archbishop Stratford to the opening of the Great Schism, 1349–1378', Oxford Univ. D.Phil. thesis, 1951

Hilton, Rodney H., *English and French towns in feudal society – a comparative study* (Cambridge, 1992)

Hobbes, *Leviathan*, ed. Richard Tuck (Cambridge, 1996)

Hohenberg, Paul, et al., *The making of urban Europe, 1000–1950* (Cambridge, Mass., 1985)

Holdsworth, W. S., *A history of English law*, vol. IX (London, 1926)

Hourlier, J., *L'Age classique, 1140–1378: les Religieux* (Paris, 1973)

Howell, M., 'Abbatial vacancies and the divided mensa in medieval England', 33 *Journal of Ecclesiastical History* (1982) 181–7

Regalian right in medieval England (London 1962)

Huvelin, P., *Essai historique sur le droit des marchés et des foires* (Paris, 1897)

Jacob, E. F., 'On the promotion of English university clerks during the later Middle Ages', *Journal of Ecclesiastical History* (1950) 172–86

Jacques, François, ed., *Les Cités de l'occident Romain* (Paris, 1992)

Jacques, François and John Scheid, *Rome et l'intégration de l'empire, 44 av. J. C. – 260 ap. J. C.*, vol. I, *Les Structures de l'empire Romain* (Paris, 1990)

Jeulin, Paul, 'L'Hommage de la Bretagne . . .', 41 *Annales de Bretagne* (1934) 380–473

Kantorowicz, Ernst, *The king's two bodies: a study in mediaeval political theology* (Princeton, N.J., 1957)

'*Pro patria mori* in medieval political thought', 56 *American Historical Review* (1950–1) 472–92

Kantorowicz, H., *Bractonian problems* (Glasgow, 1941)

Kelley, Donald, 'The development and context of Bodin's method' in *Jean Bodin: Verhandlungen der internationalen Bodin Tagung*, ed. H. Denzer (Munich, 1973) pp. 123–50

Kim, Keechang, 'Etre fidèle au roi: XIIe–XIVe siècles', 293 *Revue Historique* (1995) 225–50

Kiralfy, Albert, 'Law and right in English legal history', 6 *Journal of Legal History* (1985) 49–61

Knafla, Louis, *Law and politics in Jacobean England* (Cambridge, 1977)

Knowles, D., *The monastic order in England 940–1216*, 2nd edn (Cambridge, 1966)

The religious orders in England, vol. II (Cambridge, 1955)

Labande, Edmond René, 'De quelques Italians établis en Languedoc sous Charles V' in *Mélanges d'histoire du moyen âge: dédiés à la mémoire de Louis Halphen* (Paris, 1951) pp. 359–64

Laprat, R., 'Incapacité bénéficiale des aubains' in *Dictionnaire de droit canonique*, ed. A. Villien et al. (Paris, 1924–65) vol. I, cols. 1332–80

Le Goff, Jacques (ed.) *L'Etat et les pouvoirs, histoire de la France*, vol. II (Paris, 1989)

Marchands et banquiers du moyen âge (Paris, 1972)

Le Patourel, J. H., *The medieval administration of the Channel Islands, 1199–1399* (London, 1937)

Lefebvre-Teillard, Anne, '*Ius sanguinis*: l'émergence d'un principe (éléments d'histoire de la nationalité française)', 82 *Revue Critique de Droit International Privé* (1993) 223–50

Levack, Brian, *The formation of the British State: England, Scotland and the Union, 1603–1707* (Oxford, 1987)

Levine, Mortimer, *The early Elizabethan succession question, 1558–1568* (Stanford, Calif., 1966)

Lipson, E., *The economic history of England*, vol. I, *The Middle Ages*, 9th edn (London, 1947)

Lloyd, Terence H., *Alien merchants in England in the high Middle Ages* (Brighton, 1982)

England and the German Hanse, 1157–1611: a study of their trade and commercial diplomacy (Cambridge, 1991)

Lonis, Raoul, *La Cité dans le monde grec: structure, fonctionnement, contradiction* (Paris, 1994)

Lonis, Raoul (ed), *L'Etranger dans le monde grec*, 2 vols. (Nancy, 1988, 1992)

Lopez, R. S., *The commercial revolution of the Middle Ages, 950–1350* (New Jersey, 1971)

Luchaire, Achille, *Les Communes françaises à l'époque des Capétiens directs* (Paris, 1911)

Maitland, F. W., 'Corporation sole' in *Maitland – selected essays*, ed. H. D. Hazeltine, et al. (Cambridge, 1936) pp. 73–103

Roman canon law in the Church of England (London, 1898)

'Why the history of English law is not written' in *The collected papers of F. W. Maitland*, ed. H. A. L. Fisher 3 vols. (Cambridge, 1911) I, pp. 480–97

Maitland, F. W. and M. Bateson (eds.) *The charters of the borough of Cambridge* (Cambridge, 1901)

Martin, Thomas, '*Nemo potest exuere patriam*: indelibility of allegiance and the American revolution', 35 *American Journal of Legal History* (1991) 205–18

Mason, E., '*Pro statu et incolumnitate regni mei*: royal monastic patronage 1066–1154' in *Religion and national identity*, ed. S. Mews (Oxford, 1982) pp. 99–117

Matthew, Donald, *The Norman monasteries and their English possessions* (Oxford, 1962)

Mews, Stuart (ed.) *Religion and national identity* (Oxford, 1982)

Milsom, S. F. C., *Historical foundations of the common law*, 2nd edn (Toronto, 1981)

Mirot, Léon, *La Colonie lucquoise à Paris du XIIIe siècle au XVe siècle*, (Paris, 1927)

Mollat, G., 'L'Application du droit de régale spirituelle en France du XIIe au XIVe siècles', 25 *Revue d'Histoire Ecclésiastique* (1929) 425–46, 645–76

'Bénéfices ecclésiastiques en occident' in *Dictionnnaire de droit canonique*, ed. A. Villein et al. (Paris, 1924–65) II, cols. 406–49

La Collation des bénéfices ecclésiastiques sous les papes à Avignon, 1305–1378 (Paris, 1921)

Moore, E. W., *The fairs of medieval England: an introductory study* (Toronto, 1985)

Morgan, Marjorie M., *The English lands of the abbey of Bec* (Oxford, 1946)

'The suppression of the alien priories', 26 *History*, new series (1941) 204–12

Morris, Colin, *The papal monarchy, the western Church from 1050 to 1250* (Oxford, 1989)

Mossé, Claude, *Le Citoyen dans la Grèce antique* (Paris, 1993)

Nevill, Cynthia, 'Border law in late medieval England', 9 *Journal of Legal History* (1988) 335–56

New, Chester, *History of the alien priories in England to the confiscation of Henry V* (Chicago, 1916)

Nicolet, Claude, *Le Métier de citoyen dans la Rome républicaine*, 2nd edn (Paris, 1976)

Nida, Eugene A. and Johannes P. Louw, *Lexical semantics of the Greek New Testament* (Atlanta, 1992)

Onclin, W., 'Le Statut des étrangers dans la doctrine canonique médiévale' in *L'Etranger*, part 2, (Brussels, 1958) pp. 37–64

Origo, Iris, 'The domestic enemy: the eastern slaves in Tuscany in the fourteenth and fifteenth centuries', 30 *Speculum* (1955) 321–66

Ourliac, Paul and Jean-Louis Gazzaniga, *Histoire du droit privé français – de l'an mil au Code civil* (Paris, 1985)

Page, William (ed.) *Letters of denization and acts of naturalization for aliens in England, 1509–1603* (Lymington, 1893)

Pantin, W. A., *The English church in the fourteenth century* (Cambridge, 1955)

Parry, Clive, *British nationality law and the history of naturalization* (Milan, 1954)

Peck, G. T., 'John Hales and the Puritans during the Marian exile', 10 *Church History* (1941) 159–77

Pennington, Kenneth, *Pope and bishops, the papal monarchy in the twelfth and thirteenth centuries* (Pennsylvania, 1984)

Petit-Dutaillis, C., *Les Communes françaises: caractères et évolution des origines au XVIIIe siècle* (Paris, 1947)

Philipsborn, Alexander, 'Der Begriff der Juristischen Person im römischen Recht', 71 *Zeitschrift der Savigny-Stiftung für Rechtsgeschichte*, Rom. Abt. (1954) 41–70

Phillips, William D. Jr, *Slavery from Roman times to the early transatlantic trade* (Minneapolis, 1985)

Piergiovanni, Vito, 'La "peregrinatio bona" dei mercanti medievali: a proposito di un commento di Baldo degli Ubaldi a X. I. 34,' 105 *Zeitschrift der Savigny-Stiftung für Rechtsgeschichte*, Kan. Abt. (1988) 348–56

Pirenne, Henri, *Les Villes et les institutions urbaines*, 2 vols., 2nd edn (Paris, 1939)

Piton, C., *Les Lombards en France et à Paris*, 2 vols. (Paris, 1893)

Pocock, J. G. A., 'Two kingdoms and three histories? Political thought in British context' in *Scots and Britons, Scottish political thought and the union of 1603*, ed. Roger Mason (Cambridge, 1994) pp. 293–312

Pollock, F. and F. W. Maitland, *The history of English law before the time of Edward I*, 2nd edn, reissued with an introduction by S. F. C. Milsom, 2 vols. (Cambridge, 1968)

Post, Gaines, 'Two notes on nationalism in the Middle Ages', 9 *Traditio* (1953) 281–320

Poudret, Jean-François and Danielle Anex-Cabanis, 'L'Individu face au pouvoir seigneurial d'après chartes de franchises de suisse romande au moyen âge' in *L'Individu face au pouvoir*, 5 vols., vol. III, *Europe occidentale XIIe–XVIIIe siècles* (Brussels, 1989) pp. 175–228

Powicke, F. M., *The loss of Normandy, 1189–1204* (Manchester, 1913)

Prestwich, M., *English politics in the thirteenth century* (London, 1990)

Price, Polly, 'Natural law and birthright citizenship in *Calvin's case* (1608)', 9 *Yale Journal of Law and the Humanities* (1997) 73–145

Rebuffi, Petri, *Praxis beneficiorum absolutissima acquirendi, conservandique illa, ac amittendi, modos continens* (Lyons, 1570)

Renouard, Yves, *Les Hommes d'affaires Italiens du moyen âge* (Paris, 1968)

Reventlow, Henning Graf and Yair Hoffman, *Justice and righteousness: biblical themes and their influence* (Sheffield, 1991)

Richardson, H. G., 'Azo, Drogheda, and Bracton', 59 *English Historical Review* (1944) 22–47

Ridgeway, H. W., 'Foreign favourites and Henry III's problems of patronage', 104 *English Historical Review* (1989) 590–610

Rubin, Miri, *Corpus Christi: Eucharist in the late medieval culture* (Cambridge, 1993)

Ruddock, Alwyn, *Italian merchants and shipping in Southampton, 1270–1600* (Southampton, 1951)

Runciman, Steven, *The Byzantine theocracy* (Cambridge, 1977)

Sack, A. N., 'Conflicts of laws in the history of the English law' in *Law, a century of progress, 1835–1935*, ed. A. Reppy, 3 vols. (New York, 1937) III, pp. 342–454

Sagnac, Philippe, *La Législation civile de la Révolution française, 1789–1804: essai d'histoire sociale* (Paris, 1898)

Salmond, John, 'Citizenship and allegiance', 17, 18 *Law Quarterly Review* (1901, 1902) 270–82; 49–63

Sayers, Jane, *Papal government and England, during the pontificate of Honorius III, 1216–1227* (Cambridge, 1984)

Schulz, F., 'Bracton on kingship', 60 *English Historical Review* (1945) 136–76

Schulze, Reiner, 'European legal history – a new field of research in Germany', 13 *Journal of Legal History* (1992) 270–95

Sewell, W. H., 'Marc Bloch and the logic of comparative history', 6 *History and theory* (1967) 208–18

Shaw, William A. (ed.) *Letters of denization and acts of naturalization for aliens in England and Ireland 1603–1700* (Lymington, 1911)

Sherman, Gordon E., 'Emancipation and citizenship' in 15 *Yale Law Journal* (1905–6) 263–83

Sherwin-White, A. N., *The Roman citizenship* (Oxford, 1965)

Sieghart, Paul, *The international law of human rights* (Oxford, 1983)

Simpson, A. W. B., *An introduction to the history of the land law* (Oxford, 1961)

Skali, Faouzi, *La Voie Soufie* (Paris, 1985)

Skinner, Quentin, 'Meaning and understanding in the history of ideas', 8 *History and Theory* (1969) 3–53

Smith, A. L., *Church and State in the Middle Ages* (Oxford, 1913)

Sommerville, Johann, *Politics and ideology in England, 1603–1640* (London, 1986)

Stein, Peter G., 'Donellus and the origin of the modern civil law', in *Mélange Felix Wubbe* (Fribourg, Switzerland, 1993) pp. 439–52

Stein, Peter G. and John Shand, *Legal values in Western society* (Edinburgh, 1974)

Stenton, F., *The first century of English feudalism 1066–1166* (Oxford, 1961)

Stubbs, W., *The constitutional history of England*, 3 vols., vol. II, 3rd edn (Oxford, 1887)

Swanson, R. N., *Church and society in late medieval England* (Oxford, 1989)

'Universities, graduates, and benefices in later medieval England', 106 *Past and Present* (1985) 28–61

Syme, Ronald, 'Liberty in Classical Antiquity' in *Aspects of American liberty – philosophical, historical and political*, ed. American Philosophical Society (Philadelphia, 1977) pp. 8–15

Thayer, James, *A preliminary treatise on evidence at the common law* (London, 1898)

Thompson, Benjamin, 'The statute of Carlisle, 1307 and the alien priories', 41 *Journal of Ecclesiastical History* (1990) 543–83

Thompson, P., *The history and antiquities of Boston* (Boston, 1856)

Thrupp, Sylvia, *The merchant class of medieval London, 1300–1500* (Chicago, 1948)

Timbal, Pierre-Clément, 'Les Lèttres de marque dans le droit de la France médiévale' in *L'Etranger*, part 2, (Brussels, 1958) pp. 108–38

'La Vie juridique des personnes morales ecclésiastiques en France aux XIIIe et XIVe siècles' in *Etudes d'histoire du droit canonique dédiées à Gabriel Le Bras* (Paris, 1965) pp. 1425–45

Tully, James (ed.) *Meaning and context, Quentin Skinner and his critics* (Oxford, 1988)

Ullmann, Walter, 'The development of the medieval idea of sovereignty', 64 *English Historical Review* (1949) 1–33

Verlinden, Charles, *L'Esclavage dans L'Europe médiévale*, 2 vols. (Bruges, 1955)

Villers, Robert, *Rome et le droit privé* (Paris, 1977)

Viollet, Paul, *Précis de l'histoire du droit civil français* (Paris, 1905)

Wahnich, Sophie, *L'Impossible citoyen, l'étranger dans le discours de la Révolution française* (Paris, 1997)

Wallace, Willard M., 'Sir Edwin Sandys and the first Parliament of James I', PhD thesis, Univ. of Pennsylvania (1940)

Wallon, Henri, *Histoire de l'esclavage dans l'antiquité*, first published in 1847, reprinted with a bibliography by J. C. Dumont (Paris, 1988)

Watson, Alan, *The making of the Civil Law* (Cambridge, Mass., 1981)

'Morality, slavery and the jurists in the later Roman Republic', 42 *Tulane Law Review* (1967–8) 289–303

Roman slave law (Baltimore, 1987)

'Thinking property at Rome' 68 *Chicago-Kent Law Review* (1993) 1355–71

Watson, William, *The clergy-man's law, or the complete incumbent* (London, 1701)

Whitehead, D., *The ideology of the Athenian Metic* (Cambridge, 1977)

Wormald, Jenny, 'The creation of Britain: multiple kingdoms or core and colonies?', 2 *Royal Historical Society Transactions*, 6th series, (1992) 175–94

'James VI and I: two kings or one ?', 68 *History* (1983) 187–209

Wright, J. R., *The Church and the English crown, 1305–1334* (Toronto, 1980)

INDEX